SPIN-OFF CHURCHES

HOW ONE CHURCH SUCCESSFULLY PLANTS ANOTHER

SPIN-OFF CHURCHES

RODNEY HARRISON | TOM CHEYNEY | DON OVERSTREET

FOREWORD BY ELMER TOWNS | AFTERWORD BY ED STETZER

Nashville, Tennessee

978-0-8054-4685-2

Published by B&H Publishing Group
Nashville, Tennessee

Dewey Decimal Classification: 254.1
Subject Heading: CHURCH DEVELOPMENT, NEW\CHURCH PLANTING\
CHURCH GROWTH

1 2 3 4 5 6 7 8 9 10 11 12 • 16 15 14 13 12 11 10 09 08
VP

Contents

Thank you to my wonderful family,
especially my wife Julie!
What would I do without you!?
Thank you also to the nine students
who reviewed and critiqued the material
for Spin-off Churches.
This book is dedicated to you.

Rodney Harrison

To Cheryl!
My best friend, life companion,
and one who challenges me every day
to be the best I can be for my Lord.
As a church planter's wife,
you have been courageous to go
even when the path seemed unclear
and yet the hand of God was certain.

Tom Cheyney

Foreword

This is a necessary book written by Thomas Cheyney, Rodney Harrison, and Don Overstreet, for it covers some areas of church-planting never before covered, it tells workable principles that church planters need, and it will make church planters face issues they must face.

This is a well-researched book that brings authority and credibility to the table. It's not a church-planter writing a "How-I-did-it" book, nor is it a self-disillusioned expert writing, "Here's-how-to-do-it." Look beyond this book to the research that makes it believable.

When I wrote *The 10 Largest Sunday Schools*,[1] I discovered four of the pastors of the largest churches in America had planted and grown their church. That pricked my curiosity about church planting. I wanted to study more about church planting but didn't know how to go about it.

Then I cofounded Liberty University with Jerry Falwell (who planted Thomas Road Baptist Church). The second chapel of the university was preached by Danny Smith, a young man from Falwell's church who began a prosperous church in Richmond, Virginia. He preached by telling the story of how he planted Open Door Baptist Church; at that time attendance was about 1,000.

Half way through his sermon, a bolt of lightning hit me—an idea—I grabbed some paper and copied his sermon furiously. Then I took him out to lunch and wrote the first half of his sermon. That sermon became a chapter in a church planting book.[2]

---

[1] Elmer Towns, *The Ten Largest Sunday Schools* (Grand Rapids: Baker Book House, 1969). The church planters were Jerry Falwell, Harold Hemiger, John Rawlings, and Dallas Billington.

[2] Elmer L. Towns, *Getting a Church Started in the Face of Insurmountable Odds with Limited Resources, in Unlikely Circumstances* (Nashville: Impact Books, 1975). The title suggests these churches were planted by entrepreneurial pastors, who did it by themselves, in an area that was new and/or hostile to them. The title suggests only one type of church planting.

Since I was in charge of chapel, I invited successful church planters to come preach, to tell the story of getting their church started. These sermons produced two obvious results. First, they helped me write a book on church planting, and second, they gave a vision to our new students to go plant a church.

The chapel speakers were friends of Jerry Falwell, and most of them did it the way Jerry did it. When our students graduated, they went out and did it the way Jerry did. Later, I taught the course on church planting at Liberty, and I taught our students to do it the way Jerry did it.[3]

That method worked for most, but it didn't work for all. Jerry's way worked for a while, and as time changed culture, one day I realized Jerry's way didn't work the way it once did.

Spin-off Churches doesn't give just one way to plant churches. There are many different ways to do it. Why? Because people change, culture changes, tradition changes, worship styles change, and evangelistic methods change. But I'm still a fundamentalist; theology never changes because God never changes; and the Bible is still the same – without alteration – it's the basis of planting churches. Today I teach:

> Methods are many,
>> Principles are few.
> Methods may change,
>> But principles never do.

I stopped teaching our courses on church planting about six years ago. Now younger professors at Liberty, who graduated from Liberty and planted a church different from the way Jerry did it, are using updated methods to old fashion passion: and they are doing it better and greater.

When I quit teaching the course on church planting, I had broadened my syllabus to at least 12 different ways to plant a church. I've discovered a few more different new ways in a book I wrote last year, *11 Innovations in the Local Church.*[4]

During the 70s and 80s there were only two places that a broad spectrum of denominational people could go to learn church planting. The first I've mentioned, Liberty University and Jerry Falwell, but many were not fundamentalist and couldn't do it the way Jerry did it. The second was a one-week seminar taught by Dr. C. Peter Wagner of Fuller Theological Seminary, usually during October of each year.

---

[3] Elmer L. Towns, *Getting a Church Started Manual* (Lynchburg, VA: Liberty University, 1982). I wrote a work text for classes on church planting. The secret of this book was chapter 13, "84 Steps to Plant a Church."

[4] Elmer Towns, Ed Stetzer, and Warren Bird, *11 Innovations in the Local Church* (Ventura, CA: Regal Books, 2007). This book suggests church planting by four methods: The Organic House Church, the Multisite Church, the City-Reaching Church, and Cyber-Enhanced Churches. Technically, all the various methods in this book lead to church planting.

Today the impetus is coming from many sources, i.e., seminaries, denominations, mega churches, and interdenominational agencies. Praise God that church planting is growing as a movement. Why?

- New churches win more to Christ than most old churches.
- New churches revitalize their people more than most old churches.
- New churches take bigger steps of faith than most old churches.
- New churches reach new communities, win new believers, and instigate revival in old churches.

Church planting is not a denominational priority; any church can plant a new one. Church planting is not the outgrowth of a particular theology. All groups can do it, whether Presbyterian, Baptist, Pentecostal, Mennonite, Community, or other. Church planting is not a strategy of mega churches; all sizes of churches can plant a new church.

Praise God for this new resource volume on church planting.

Dr. Elmer L. Towns
Dean, School of Religion
Cofounder and Vice President, Liberty University
Distinguished Professor of Systematic Theology

Introduction

I am a Starbucks person in an ordinary coffee world here in Kansas City. In fact, the working title for this book was originally *Starbucks Churches in a Folgers World*. You see, Midwestern Baptist Theological Seminary is just a few miles from the headquarters for Folgers Coffee Company in downtown Kansas City, Missouri.

Folgers traces its roots to 1850, just a few years after the start of the Southern Baptist Convention. It is a famous company with a proud heritage. However, each morning, my colleagues and I enjoy a cup (or two) of Starbucks, not Folgers. In the evenings, it is not uncommon to find us stopping off at Starbucks for a frappacino or hot chai. Many of my friends, coworkers, and students drink Starbucks. Each time I drive by the Folgers plant, I wonder why this once-thriving coffee company has been all but overshadowed by Starbucks among those of my generation and younger. Several reasons come to mind.

First, Folgers is only available in the grocery store. Sure, grocery stores are accessible, but if I am craving a cup of Folgers's Classic Blend coffee, I have to go to the store, buy a 39-ounce container, and brew it at home. When I grocery shop, my focus is upon bread, milk, meat, and eggs and not a cup of coffee. Somehow, I just cannot get into the coffee mood in a grocery store. However, if I did, Starbucks has operations inside each of my favorite grocery stores!

Second, Folgers lacks variety. Sure, an easy-open plastic container (39 oz) has finally replaced the decades-old red three-pound can, but the coffee is the same. Even the new varieties offered under the Folgers label taste somewhat the same. Seriously, Folgers French Roast tastes almost exactly like their Classic Blend! The same can be said of their new Gourmet Supreme and Breakfast Blend. I know because an older colleague in the office brews these blends. Pizzazz is not a word that comes to mind when I think of Folgers in my cup.

Third, the mental images conjured up by Folgers coffee are few. Some relish the "reliability" of the brand and taste. But the images are often of a quite morning, reading the paper, and not interacting with a greater community. It is

1

not that Folgers coffee is bad. It is not. For some, coffee is coffee and they like Folgers. However, the only connection point that comes to mind is that my parents and grandparents drank Folgers. No mental images of special moment; no special friends around a table, just a red can sitting on the kitchen counter.

The Starbucks Alternative

Why is Starbucks successful? Following the same line of thought as above, first, Starbucks is readily available in my neighborhood. I can enjoy a cup at the shopping center just down the road from our house. Another store is conveniently located across the street where I work. When the girls want to go shopping at the mall, I can drop them off and enjoy a Starbucks while they shop. My favorite Starbucks even has a drive through for those mornings I really do not want to get out of my car. When I feel like coffee, I know a good cup is only moments away.

Next, Starbucks provides variety. Hot or cold, strong or weak, tall or venti, white or black. Just the right number of choices, without having to resort to a menu. Starbucks's frappacinos are my summer favorite—especially the new "lite" varieties with half the calories. An extra-hot quad shot cappuccino in the morning is an excellent way to start the day. In the evening, a chai tea is a great sipping beverage. You can get it to go in a paper cup with the famous sleeve to keep your hand from burning (it shows they care!) or order it "for here" and enjoy a real ceramic mug—just the right number of choices.

Third, Starbucks conjures up good memories. Gathering around a table with friends, reading a good book while the ladies are shopping, enjoying the aroma therapy of fresh ground coffee—these are all reasons I enjoy going to Starbucks. Dedicated coffee houses offer an environment that ferments ideas, calms the soul, and promotes relationships. No wonder the idea for the original Baptist association came together in an English coffee shop! Come to think of it, I know of several church starts and sponsoring church agreements that were forged over a cup of Starbucks. When my daughter and I were overseas, a Starbucks connected us with good memories of home.

Finally, Starbucks is affordable pleasure. I know $4.00 for a cup of coffee is crazy. But, for most of us, $4.00 is doable. It's not like buying a new car or major appliance. Moreover, on those frequent days I find myself "financially challenged," I can order a tall Coffee of the Day, and for under two bucks, enjoy the above benefits.

As one who is a Southern Baptist by conviction and by choice, I see many of the churches in my denomination taking on the flavor of Folgers rather than Starbucks. One might even say that Southern Baptists are the Folgers of evangelical denominations. Like Folgers, we are big—sixteen million strong and growing. We have a proud and rich heritage. Like Folgers, we are accessible—almost 50,000 churches and missions are scattered throughout every state and province. Many communities boast multiple Southern Baptist churches. Our growth, however, has slowed to a trickle. Yes, it is good is that we are still growing when most mainline denominations are in decline, but North America's population growth is far outpacing the denomination's growth, which, like Folgers, has found its market share declining.

It might be that our familiarity works against us. Most young adults know that church is out there. It's just that the traditional church (as they understand it) has been a part of the cultural background for so long that they are turning to what they perceive as new and exciting spiritual expressions. The seemingly exotic nature of New Age and eastern religions is attractive to postmoderns. The "church on every corner" strategy that was a key to our growth during modernism is now working against us in this new post-Christian ethos.

Second, we still lack the right variety. Southern Baptists are a relatively analogous bunch. Eighty percent of our churches are Anglo. Moreover, many of our existing ethnic churches would be impossible to tell apart from the traditional Anglo congregations except for the language spoken. For example, one Hispanic church I recently visited sang four traditional hymns translated from English into Spanish. The overall experience was indistinguishable from the Anglo church I had worshipped in earlier that morning. Accessibility to these churches if often good, but like the red containers of coffee on the grocery store shelf, when the unchurched decide to have a drink, they don't choose our brand of church. When exploring a church-planting strategy, you will be asked to consider the question, "Will the unchurched of this community choose this new church?"

A word of warning is due! Putting a new label on the same old methods or strategy does not change things. Just as Folgers has not successfully distinguished (to me) its new varieties, starting a new church and calling it "postmodern" or "cutting edge" (or some other overused term) when it is but a bastion of traditional methods won't work.

I look at it like this: Folgers is religion and Starbucks is relationship. For some, going to church means waking up from a sound sleep to attend a boring Sunday school lesson and an irrelevant sermon. That is religion. In a series of articles carried in *On Mission* magazine, men and women on the street were asked why they did not attend church. Their answers indicate that church was not a place where lost people—and some who claimed to own a Christian faith—wanted to attend. If you ask most teens and twenty-somethings if they want to go to church, they will say, "Huh?" Ask them to Starbucks and they will say, "Sure!"

Finally, church for many means only "take my money." There is a big difference between giving joyfully and giving under compulsion. Many feel that the offering is a time of "compulsive giving," and they understandably find it an uncomfortable experience. I find myself resisting spending $5 for a three-pound can of Folgers, but I will happily pay $13–15 a pound for Starbucks's Sumatra Whole Bean coffee. For many, going to church does not provide a meaningful experience. If the church experience has failed to manifest the presence of the living Christ, then worship (a word whose stem means "worth") has not occurred. In our ministries, Tom and I have visited hundreds of churches. We would estimate that about half of these did not provide a "worthwhile" worship experience. In one church, I was asked to leave the pew where I was sitting. They should have posted signs:

COME TO THIS CHURCH AT YOUR OWN RISK
DO NOT SIT IN THIS PEW
BEWARE OF DIFFICULT CHURCH MEMBERS

Which brings me to the point of writing this book with Tom Cheyney and Don Overstreet: Next to God, the existing church is the greatest resource for church planting. This has not changed in two thousand years. In America's past, churches planted other churches as an outgrowth of our westward expansion. As communities were established, churches would be there to start new churches in that community. We still need to take the gospel to new communities that are being established. But in the past, this usually did not entail crossing major cultural or linguistic barriers, just miles. In today's twenty-first century, Canadians and Americans are no longer an analogous bunch. One size has probably never fit all when it comes to church, but the need for diversity in approach and execution is greater now than ever. We need Starbucks churches. In the years to come, Starbucks will be overshadowed by the next new thing. The need for relevant churches, however, is unending—or at least they are needed until all the signs of Matthew 24 are fulfilled.

It should not go without saying that the process of church planting is predicated upon much prayer. Unless the planting strategy is based upon a God-given vision, the new church will never get off the ground. A God-given vision, which assumes quality time with God combined with a sound strategy and a supportive team, is the only effective way to reduce the unchurched population through church planting. A healthy mother-church sponsor and adequate support will help to ensure the new church grows to viability. A traditional church can effectively reach those who are not attending their congregation by becoming a spin-off church. It is my hope and prayer that the pages of this book will raise the questions and provide insights to make the spin-off strategy successful.

Last night, Tom and I drove through downtown Kansas City. As we passed the Folgers Coffee Roasting Plant, I breathed deeply. The smell of Folgers is not unlike the smell of Starbucks. Since I love the smell of coffee, I asked Tom to roll down the windows. It was wonderful but unfortunately inaccessible to all who passed by. As you consider sponsoring a new church, please take the necessary steps to ensure that the aroma of Christ is both proclaimed . . . and accessible to your community.

So, take this book on over to your favorite coffee house or tea-room, order a large cup "for here," and enjoy an overstuffed chair as you begin the fascinating journey into the missional world of spin-off churches. Each of us has written part of this book, but to reduce stylistic and other differences, we have agreed to write in the first person as a collective author. We challenge our readers to guess who the individual author is.

Rodney A. Harrison

4

Part 1

Sponsoring Church Fundamentals

You might say, "I'm not called to plant churches."
Yes you are! It's always the will of God to have a people
who worship His Son in the nations. You'll never have
to worry about making God mad if you try to plant
a church. It seems crazy to me that people are under
the delusion they need a special calling to save souls,
to disciple them, and to get together to love Jesus.
Whatever ministry you are with, you must understand
one thing: church planting is not for us, it's for God.
We do it so God will have a people to worship Him!

— Floyd McClung

Chapter 1

Recovering a Practical
Theology of Church Planting

I n the past two decades, church planting has moved from the back alley of vocational options for seminarians to the preferred choice for many top students.
The advantages of church planting from the missional, organizational, and
practical perspective are readily extolled by the advocates of most church planting models. Since the early 1990s, dozens of "how to" church planting books have
been published, but most of them focus on the practical and pragmatic aspects of
becoming a church planter. For many pastors, church planting—or sponsoring a
new church—is not a theological endeavor but rather a useful response to what
is being called a post-Christian or postmodern world. In this chapter we seek to
restore the theology of church planting from the perspective of a practitioner-
turned-professor of church planting.

The seldom-raised question is whether church planting is theological in nature.
An argument against the theological nature of church planting could be made
simply by the absence of ink and hours devoted to church planting in the major
theological texts, professional journals, and theological classrooms. I recently
reviewed the theological and historical texts I used during my own theological
studies in the 1980s. Surprisingly, in the pages of these formative texts, I found
no mention whatever of church planting. Moreover, the sections covering the
apostolic (missionary) office, the Great Commission passages, and the historical
creeds of the early church—subjects near to the heart of most church planters—
seemed bloodless. It was as if the authors were merely conveying the thoughts and
ideas of dead theologians in order to concentrate on their own personal scholar-
ship and passion. In retrospect, such treatment of the missional passages should

not have been unexpected, since very few of these great writers had ever been church planters.

How wonderfully different were the human authors of Holy Scripture. Most were church planting missionaries. Peter, for example—the author of the two New Testament epistles bearing his name—was involved in church planting first among the Jews in Jerusalem and then in the home of the Gentile centurion Cornelius, thus ushering in cross-cultural church planting. Peter was a missionary who had studied under the Chief Apostle, Jesus Christ. His ministry opened the door for church planting to the Gentiles during a time when many new believers in the fledgling church were content to maintain a Jewish ethnocentric membership. Then there was Paul and the countless churches he planted. Paul was a theologian who learned under the tutelage of Gamaliel, and God used his experience, training, and skills to plant and strengthen churches in Antioch, Cyprus, Galatia, Macedonia, Achaia, Asia, Caesarea, Rome, and Spain. Likewise, Luke, Timothy, and John Mark were seasoned missionaries and church planters in their own right. These men were also practical theologians whose words and experiences are now immortalized in the canon of Scripture. They experienced first hand that the only correct response to the Great Commission is "to go," and that the best way of accomplishing this task is by sending out members to evangelize and to plant new churches.

Just because most theological texts ignore the topic of church planting, this does not justify adding a theology of church planting. Some might insist that church planting is not a separate theological discipline and should be viewed as but one of many components of ecclesiology—the theology and study of the church. Such a perspective is emphasized by Stuart Murray in his book *Church Planting: Laying Foundations*. Popular pastor Rick Warren agrees with this perspective as he places church planting and evangelism together under the missional purpose of the church.

The challenge facing both theologian and church practitioner is the proliferation of recent writings on the subject of church planting. In the past two decades, the floodgates of interest in church planting have opened. More than one hundred church planting books have been published during this period. A Google search yielded 266,000 Web sites under the category of "Church Planting," where 137,000 Web sites offer "church planting" resources. Amazon recently offered 306 church planting books.[1] During this same period, evangelical seminaries and divinity schools have gone from offering no church planting courses to providing degrees and concentrations in this discipline through the doctoral level of study. At Midwestern Baptist Theological Seminary, where I serve, a partnership with the North American Mission Board has resulted in three church planting courses at the undergraduate level, ten courses at the masters level, and two at the doctorate level. In many ways, this is the golden age for church planting. Could it be that

---

[1] Amazon.com search for "Church Planting Books," http://www.amazon.com, March 25, 2005.

practitioners have rediscovered what theologians have overlooked, namely that church planting is a worthy theological discipline?

I want to challenge Christian leaders to consider a theology of church planting from two perspectives. First is the perspective of the Great Commission as the theological foundation for church planting. The second perspective is from early church history. For this I will use the Nicene Creed as a reaffirmation of church planting as a proper theological enterprise as understood by the early New Testament church.

The Great Commission and Church Planting

Here is the question at the heart of the theological issue: "Can the Great Commission be fulfilled without the planting of new churches?" The Great Commission, as recorded in Mark 16:15, commands the disciples to evangelize (*kêrussô to euaggelion*) all members of creation (*pas ktisis*). The focus of this commission is arguably more individualistic than the Commission as recorded in Matthew 28:19, which commands the followers of Christ to disciple (*mathê-teuô*) every people group (*panta ta ethnê*). Although at least one author suggests a two-fold calling is contained in the commission—one missionary and the other pastoral,[2] the exhortation translated "go" in Matthew 28, repeated in Mark 16:15 and suggested in John 20:21–23, Acts 1:8, and elsewhere, clearly suggests a sending quality over a staying quality.

Acts 1:8 provides a strategy for the *missio Dei*, but not a model or methodology. Hence, the only "staying quality" surrounding the Great Commission is contained in the words of Jesus before his ascension, when "He commanded them not to leave Jerusalem, but to wait for the Father's promise" (Acts 1:4). Waiting for the Holy Spirit is always a biblically sound but often unheeded principle.

A growing number of church leaders over the last few decades have turned to the church growth movement for ideas or insights to accomplish the Great Commission through means other than "sending" and "going." The idea was to get people into church, bring them to Christ, and equip them to serve. One mark of supposed success was the size of the church. In some ways, these leaders, most of whom were pastors, sought to place the Great Commission into a pastoral framework. The mind-set seemed to be that growing bigger and better churches was a Great Commission activity. When C. Peter Wagner wrote that the "third vital sign or characteristic of growing churches in America is that they are big enough,"[3] heads began to nod in agreement that the solution was bigger churches, not just more churches. Seminary students preparing for the pastorate, along with pastoral practitioners of the 1980s and 1990s, were encouraged to look to gigantic

---

[2] Robert Jamieson, A. R. Fausset, and David Brown, *Commentary Critical and Explanatory on the Whole Bible Commentary* (np, 1871), Matthew 28:20.

[3] Peter Wagner, *Your Church Can Grow* (Ventura, CA: Regal), 84.

church models such as the Lakewood Church, the Willow Creek Church, and the Saddleback Church as examples of kingdom growth. These churches were touted as evidence that the "mega-church" focus among some church growth proponents was the key to Great Commission obedience.

Few were willing to acknowledge publicly that the Church Growth Movement was not reaching its lofty goals or actually realizing any true numerical and cultural impact. To the contrary, during the fifty years of the Church Growth Movement in North America, the church-to-population ratio in the United States fell from seventeen churches for every 10,000 Americans in 1950 to less than eleven churches for every 10,000 Americans in 2000.[4] During the same period, the average attendance in American churches remained unchanged. Apparently the Church Growth Movement did not result in widespread revitalization.

As the unofficial spokesman for the Church Growth Movement since the 1960s, Peter Wagner provided practitioners with a needed "missiological" boost when he wrote, "The single most effective evangelistic methodology under heaven is planting new churches."[5] For many church leaders, this was their first exposure to the concept of church planting. The popularity of Wagner's books exposed many to the apostolic ministry of church planting, and it led others to discover the writings of theologians and practitioners such as Francis DuBose, Aubrey Malphurs, and Elmer Towns. As interest in church planting grew, so did the number of "how to" books on the subject. At the same time, popular theologians (a term I am using to describe pastors whose writings were popular) and dispensationalists were arguing the apostolic role was defunct, and therefore church planting should be relegated to the existing theological groups.

The early church possibly grappled with the issue as well. Perhaps their understanding of the apostolic role was not yet clear. The process by which Matthias was chosen might support this idea, but more telling is the *Diaspora* ("scattering") experienced by the church at Jerusalem. In response to the church's complacency, God created an environment prohibiting the church from taking root in Jerusalem. As the believers were scattered, the Great Commission was once again observed. The providential intervention—by sword or plague—catalyzed believers into action and obedience once again. As they dispersed, they planted churches and were challenged to start new churches and send out emissaries of the gospel. A theology of church planting involves providence and planning, growing and going, prayer and persecution, all resulting in obedience to Christ's Great Commission.

Early Church Planting Theology

The next place to explore a theology of church planting is the early church. The hounding, heresies, and controversies during the first four centuries of the life of

---

[4] Tom Clegg and Tim Bird, *Lost in America* (Loveland, CO: Group Publishing, 2001), 30.

[5] Peter Wagner, *Church Planting for a Greater Harvest* (Ventura, CA: Regal Books, 1990), 21.

the Christian church necessitated several gatherings of church leaders. Arguably, one of the most lasting and influential documents of this period is the Nicene Creed, which came out of the church council held in Nicaea in AD 381. In this affirmation of what was viewed as absolutely essential to the Christian faith, one recovers the theological framework behind church planting.

One, Holy, Catholic and Apostolic Church

A document uncovering unfolding church planting theology during the post-canonical period is the Nicene Creed of 381. Most evangelicals in America seldom return to this watershed theological affirmation, even if they knew about it in the first place. Those who do refer to this creed often recite it with nothing more than "vain repetition." Others, unaware of the meaning of the words, misunderstand the creed, thus overlooking the theological truths implicit in the words. The theology of church planting is found in the affirmation "one, holy, catholic and apostolic church."

As a child growing up, we recited the Nicene Creed each week. I always wondered why a Presbyterian church would avow the Catholic Church. Later I came to understand a correct meaning of the term *catholic*, with a small "c." It means comprehensive or universal. The exalted notion of worship behind the word *holy* also took on greater meaning during my theological studies. Yet the term *apostolic* was never addressed in either church or seminary. Like many, I assumed the term referred to the apostles, or maybe it was a reference to the "apostolic fathers" of the Catholic Church. Like the history of most words, it is difficult to identify a point in time when the drift from the historical understanding of the role of the apostle occurred. Polycarp is described in the second century as an "apostolic and prophetic teacher in our own time, a bishop of the holy Church which is at Smyrna."[6] Polycarp was considered an apostle and received as a missionary and evangelist decades beyond the work of the Twelve. Today, many are returning to an understanding of the missional (church planting) nature of the Nicene Creed. In his book *The Nicene Creed*, A. E. Burns writes, "It is with something more than confidence in Episcopal Orders and discipline that the Church claims the attribute Apostolic. It is with the sense of a Divine mission to mankind . . . 'as My Father hath sent me, even so send I you.'"[7] For Burns, the sending nature of the apostolic church is clear.

Luke Timothy Johnson writes that "the church in every age must be measured by the standard of the apostolic age as witnessed not by the later tradition but by direct appeal to the writings of the New Testament. Placing the contemporary church against the one depicted in the Acts of the Apostles makes clear how much the prophetic witness of the church has been compromised by its many

---

[6] The *Martyrdom of Polycarp*, trans. J. B. Lightfoot. http://www.fordham.edu/halsall/basis/martyr-dom-polycarp-lightfoot.html. Accessed 20 April 2004.

[7] A. E. Burns, *The Nicene Creed* (London: Rivingtons, 1909), 100.

strategies of adaptation and survival over the centuries."[8] Ed Stetzer points out that the pre-Reformation confessions referred to the apostolic church, whereas the Reformation confessions referred to the errors of apostolic succession. "By de-emphasizing the 'apostolic' nature of the church, the Reformers also diminished the apostolic-sending nature of the church. The church that 'reformed' lost touch with the God who sends, and the mission of the church suffered."[9]

In his letter to the Ephesians, Paul identifies God as the giver of special gifts for those to "be sent on a mission" (apostles), to others called to "forth-tell God's will" (prophets), to still others as "bringers of good news" (evangelists), and finally to those who are "shepherds and instructors" (pastors-teachers). These gifts were for preparing and equipping the holy body of Christ. It is important that church leaders understand the difference between the missionary role of every believer and the missionary calling. Just as every member is encouraged to give freely to the work of the Lord, not every member has the gift of giving spoken of in Romans 12:8. The role of each member in the "missionary church" is quite different from the role of the "apostolic missionary."

The apostolic missionary in the North American context is often called a "church planter." But not all church planters are apostolic. Some are shepherds who put together their own "flock" instead of being recognized by an existing flock. Others are prophets who "gather a following" through their preaching and proclamation. Yet others are truly evangelists who win souls, many of whom will maintain an on-going relationship with the evangelist. These can all be called "church planters" in their own right. The focus of ministry for each is inherent to the descriptive office they hold. The same is true of the office of apostle, the one "being sent out on a mission." Apostles by office usually do not work with one church over an extended period. Rather, they are always seeking the Holy Spirit's prompting to move on to places where "Christ has not been named."[10] In the same manner as Paul's on-going relationship with the churches he planted and encouraged, the apostle is likely to be working with many churches at any given moment, but with a heart that is always bent towards reaching all people and nations and fulfilling the Great Commission.

In my own Southern Baptist tradition, church planting is the primary focus of our mission efforts. Peter Wagner wrote, "It is not by accident that Southern Baptists have become the largest Protestant denomination in America. One of their secrets is that they constantly invest substantial resources of personnel and finances in church planting."[11]

Some churches understandably are afraid of the implications of missionality. To spin-off their best givers, sharpest leaders, most willing workers, and most fervent witnesses is a receipt for disaster, that is until one fully accepts God's

---

[8] Ibid., 274.

[9] Ed Stetzer, *Planting New Churches in a Post-Modern Age* (Nashville: Broadman and Holman, 2003), 23.

[10] Rom 15:20.

[11] Peter Wagner, *Church Planting for a Greater Harvest* (Ventura, CA: Regal Books, 1990), 19.

economy. Dale Little writes, "Why bother thinking theologically about church planting? Because the ultimate theological goal of church planting transcends the daily business of church planting. Understanding, clarifying, and consciously embracing this theological goal can empower the church to carry out the myriad of details necessary for sticking with the job of church planting and getting it done." [12]

Much has been written to suggest that the early church experienced a movement of unparalleled church planting due to the presence of the "apostles." Is this true? Michael Green, in his excellent work *Thirty Years That Changed the World*, provides the following reality check when he writes, "I do want to awaken us to what these very *ordinary men and women* [emphasis mine] achieved within a single generation. It could encourage us to make a similar attempt in our own day." [13] For those who nostalgically look to the successes of the missionary journeys in Acts, be reminded of the words of Jesus: "I assure you: The one who believes in Me will also do the works that I do. And he will do even greater works than these, because I am going to the Father" (John 14:12). It is not surprising that during the eighteenth century the Sandy Creek Association went from one to forty-two congregations in seventeen years. Two centuries later the California Southern Baptist Convention grew from one to fifty-six congregations between 1936 and 1942. Today, believers in China are starting hundreds of new churches each week, providing evidence that the apostolic work of the missionaries sent out by the churches continues.

God has always been "apostolic." He appeared to Abram and sent him to a new country. He sent Joseph to Egypt to preserve his people. He sent kings and prophets to return the hearts of his people to himself. Ultimately he sent his son, Jesus, "the apostle and high priest of our confession" (Heb 3:1). As disciples, we are to be "imitators" of God,[14] recognizing the empowerment that comes from God to accomplish the divine will. Although the comparative adjective *meizôn* or *megas* in John 14:12 can be understood as quantitative, that is, the number of works, many see a qualitative character to this passage. Although it is hard to imagine greater miracles than those wrought by Jesus in his earthly ministry, reports of healings, deliverances, and other signs and wonders (miracles) are definitely not uncommon from the mission field. In fact, "signs and wonders" arguably constitute the most commonly used church planting "method" worldwide.[15] The growth of Christianity from the original Twelve, to the 120 to 3,000 at Pentecost, to more

---

[12] Dale W. Little, *Japan Harvest*, vol. 54, no. 1 (Summer 2002): 15.

[13] Michael Green, *Thirty Years That Changed the World* (Grand Rapids: Eerdmans, 2004), 10.

[14] Eph 5:1 and 1 Cor 11:1.

[15] Stories of such miracles occurring in China and Asia were told, but unconfirmed, by International Mission Board missionaries during chapel services at Midwestern Baptist Theological Seminary in 2004. C. Peter Wagner has advocated signs and wonders as a church planting and evangelism method in several of his lectures and writings. His most popular works on this subject include *Signs and Wonders Today* (Altamonte Springs, FL, 1987); *How to Have a Healing Ministry without Making Your Church Sick* (1988) and *The Third Wave of the Holy Spirit: Encountering the Power of Signs and Wonders* (Ann Arbor: Servant Books, 1988). John Wimber, whose books and lectures on "power

than two billion people around the globe who today claim the name of Jesus, supports the quantitative argument. The testimonies of the churches and saints through history support a qualitative fulfillment of this promise as well.

It would be impossible to compile a true quantitative analysis of churches planted in the first century, and sadly the same thing must be said for churches in the twenty-first century. Just as there are no surviving records of the total number of churches planted at the beginning of the Christian movement, no record of church plants in our own age is maintained. Even so, it is not difficult to say that today the number of churches worldwide is well into the millions—evidence of the continued intercessory and church planting work of the One called the Apostle and High Priest of our confession. Just as the ongoing apostolic work of our Lord continues to this day, the work accomplished by the power of the gospel proclaimed through apostles, prophets, evangelists and pastor-teachers is an ongoing activity of the Spirit of God through his chosen human instruments who were sent to equip the saints.

Wrapping It Up

Review the number of times that Jesus said, "Come" as compared to the number of times he "sent" or instructed his followers to "go." Explore the context of the times he said, "Come." Then, do the same for those times he "sent" or said, "Go."

What theological motivation resulted in the establishment of your local church?

evangelism" proved popular with students and church growth devotees, influenced Wagner. See John Wimber, *Power Evangelism* (San Francisco: Harper and Row, 1986).

CHAPTER 2

Sponsoring Churches
through the Ages

Michael Green, in his modern classic, *Thirty Years That Changed the World*, assures readers that church planting will never be out of date.[1] I will add to his observation that sponsoring new churches will never be out of date. Church planting and sponsoring efforts are evident from the first century to our present age and, according to Green, it is undeniable that the early Christians felt founding churches was part of their commission.[2] History and the New Testament agree; supporting church planting efforts was indeed a part of their commission.

Church Planting Following Pentecost

Rome, Judea, Samaria, Galilee, Lydda, Joppa, Caesarea, Cyprus, Pisidian Antioch, Iconium, Lystra, Derbe, Philippi, Thessalonica, Berea, Athens, Corinth, and Ephesus. These places were all identified as church plants during the immediate thirty years after Pentecost. Before the close of the first century, additional scriptural accounts attest to churches established in Thyatira, Smyrna, Sardis, Philadelphia, Pergamos, and Laodicea. It is possible that during this same period churches were established in Africa (Babylon, 1 Peter 5:13) and Western Europe (Spain, Romans 15:24). Unquestionably the missional nature of the believers empowered by the Holy Spirit was one reason the gospel spread quickly through the known world. It is naive and disadvantageous, however, to imagine those first-

---

[1] Michael Green, *Thirty Years That Changed the World: The Book of Acts for Today* (Grand Rapids: Eerdmans, 2004), 141.

[2] Ibid., 142.

century Christians as some kind of "super-Christians." The early church membership consisted of men and women who experienced fears, concerns, and limitations similar to those church members experience today. The church of the first century had little, if any, legal status or support. Denominational backing, per se, was not available. For the most part, the challenges to fulfilling the Great Commission were the same or greater than those faced today. The need for finances and workers has not changed in two thousand years, nor has the problem of human frailty, apathy, pride, and misconduct.

Despite these setbacks, the early church grew. In this chapter, I propose laying the historical foundation for sponsoring new works. My feeling is that the activity of sponsoring churches is a biblical pattern or, more correctly, a biblical principle. Sponsorship of churches is true and correct in every culture, every age, every context. And I believe sponsoring new churches was historically practiced in the free church tradition. Through the ages churches have provided leaders, workers, resources, and finances for new church starts. I will offer examples of this using several pivotal periods in history and then culminating with our current age. These early Christians used the resources available in order to establish and grow the fledgling Christian church. In Acts 2:44–47 we have an example of the church members making sacrifices to ensure that everyone's spiritual as well as physical needs were met, going so far as to distribute possessions according to need. They used the temple courts, which gives us an example of using existing facilities. But they also used homes for their meetings. Through sacrificial giving and meeting in homes, the church experienced phenomenal growth.

When Saul arrived on the scene, he was led to Damascus and introduced to a gathering of disciples. Like many of the churches mentioned in the New Testament, we have no really clear picture of how that church was started. Perhaps like the church at Rome, the church at Damascus was established by those converted on the day of Pentecost. What is clear is that God raised up a leader—Saul of Tarsus, who became the apostle Paul and who wrote the next chapter on church planting and partnerships.

Paul and his missionary teams did not hesitate to ask the local church to provide resources for their missional efforts. At Antioch, Paul was on the ground floor of establishing the first major "sending church" recorded in Scripture. When writing to the church at Rome, he sought to establish a second "sending church" to support efforts into Northern and Western Europe. One of the reasons Paul was able to ask boldly for prayer and support was that his mission and his purpose were clear. He had been called by the Holy Spirit (Acts 13:2), the church commissioned him for the task (13:3), and the Holy Spirit sent him forth.

The Roles of Jerusalem, Antioch, and Rome

A close look at these three sending churches shows the degree to which the early church provided a powerful combination of prayer support, financial support, and personnel. Accountability and encouragement also appear to have flowed freely between the churches and the congregations they supported.

Jerusalem

As the first New Testament church, Jerusalem was poised to be a great sponsoring church. It could be argued that the members failed to fulfill the Acts 1:8 mandate, however, and that it took the Diaspora to get the believers from Jerusalem to obey the mandate to "go" throughout Judea and Samaria and the rest of the world. But the church at Jerusalem provided a good starting point for those new to the concept of a missional movement. It was involved in numerous ways:

- **Provisions**
    - † The church actively sold personal property to provide for the physical needs of local members. The church at Jerusalem consisted of many churches that met in homes, and these Christians provided their homes for church gatherings.
- **Personnel**
    - † Barnabas, Silas, and John Mark each originally came from Jerusalem. Philip, a leader in the church, is famous for his work as an evangelist.
    - † Peter obediently witnessed to the first Gentile convert, resulting in a new church at Caesarea.
- **Accountability**
    - † The first Christian council met in Jerusalem (Acts 15) at around AD 49 and resulted in clear parameters for orthodoxy for the new missionary churches and for those serving as missionaries.
- **Prayer**
    - † From the prayer that preceded Pentecost to the prayers that set the captives free, Jerusalem was a praying church.
- **Credibility**
    - † Being the "first church" had its advantages. In the case of Jerusalem, the historic significance of this city can not be underestimated. The death, burial, resurrection, and ascension took place in Jerusalem. The events of Pentecost took place in Jerusalem. During the first twelve years after Pentecost, the disciples could usually be found in Jerusalem.

Antioch of Syria

Beginning in Acts 11, Antioch began taking center stage. As a major commercial center and the third largest city in the Roman Empire, Antioch was the capitol of Syria. Logistically, being close to main roads and the Mediterranean, the city was ideal for the propagation of the gospel. The church of Antioch is the first church mentioned as being fully integrated (Greek and Hebrew). Antioch furthered the nascent mission movement by sending out people, blessings, money, and much prayer:

- **Personnel**
  - † Barnabas, Saul, and John Mark are three mentioned by name who were sent out, and perhaps Luke as well, since he may have considered Antioch his home. Nearly half the New Testament arises from the Spirit-inspired writings of Paul, Luke, and Mark. As a church willing to send her very best leaders, Antioch was exemplary.

- **Blessing**
  - † The laying on of hands was an act of blessing the church at Antioch used to deploy their first missionaries, an act many churches and denominations continue to practice to this day.

- **Provisions**
  - † The first mission offering ever noted in Scripture originated at Antioch.

- **Spiritual example**
  - † The church at Antioch should be commended for their prayer, fasting, spiritual openness, and worship. Antioch was a very prayerful church,[3] resulting in a deep and mature spiritual formation encouraging the members to send out both missionaries and benevolence.

Rome

Many feel that enlisting the church at Rome to serve as a sponsor for missionary work to Spain and the West was Paul's primary purpose in writing Romans.[4] A significant number of Christian writers believe the church at Rome did in fact support a missionary journey, and Paul went to Spain following his first release from Roman imprisonment. This idea is partially based on Clement of Rome's account that reads:

Paul by his example pointed out the prize of patient endurance. After that he had been seven times in bonds, had been driven into exile, had

---

[3] Ibid., 155, 268.

[4] Robert Mounce, *Romans*, The New American Commentary, vol. 27 (Nashville: Broadman & Holman Publishers, 1995), 26.

been stoned, had preached in the East and in the West, he won the noble renown which was the reward of his faith, having taught righteousness unto the whole world and having reached the farthest bounds of the West.[5]

Eckhard Schnabel, in his massive two-volume *Early Christian Mission*, provides a thorough overview of the question of Paul's mission to Spain.[6] What is clear is Paul's attempt to enlist a sponsoring church. Although he had neither planted nor served at Rome, he requested the church provide him with a place to stay and the requisites for the journey to Spain.

Macedonia

The church at Macedonia was noted for its generosity on multiple occasions. In his letter to the Christians in Rome, Paul commended the Macedonians for their support of the poor in Jerusalem.[7] In his letter to the Corinthians, Paul refers to the Macedonian church twice. First, he commends them for sharing "beyond their ability."[8] Later, he praises the Macedonians (and reprimands the Corinthians) by writing, "When I was present with you and in need, I did not burden anyone, for the brothers who came from Macedonia supplied my needs."

Others

Achaia and Galatia are mentioned for their contributions. The book of Acts and the epistles often give thanks, by name or location, to Christians who provided housing, food, and encouragement to those spreading the gospel. Therefore, having established the scriptural foundation for sponsorship, let us consider these examples in history.

The Free Church Movement

Although the annals of history leave many questions, it is plain that during the first two centuries of Christianity, new churches spread primarily and mainly through missionaries sent out from existing churches. These "church planting missionaries" started churches in Armenia, Ireland, and throughout the Roman Empire. Later, during what is often called the "Dark Ages" (fifth century up to the eleventh century), unscrupulous methods of expansion also flourished. Both Christians and Buddhists would require all inhabitants of conquered lands to "convert" or die. Nations such as England would go back and forth between paganism

---

[5] Clement of Rome, *First Epistle to the Corinthians* 5:5–6a, translated by J. B. Lightfoot.

[6] Eckhard J. Schnabel, *Early Christian Mission: Volume 2, Paul and the Early Church* (Downers Grove, IL: InterVarsity Press, 2004), 1272–1278.

[7] Rom 15:26.

[8] 2 Cor 8:1–5.

and Christianity. Despite these travesties, true Christian missionaries continued to take the gospel to all the world.

The Protestant Reformation brought about reform and renewal in the church, leading to the establishment of the free church movement and to a renewal of the worldwide Christian mission. When Christianity reached the shores of the Americas, the stage was set for missional activities that would rival—or surpass—the growth of the church recorded in the book of Acts.

Sandy Creek Baptist Church

One of the oldest and best known Baptist churches in America is the Sandy Creek Baptist Church in North Carolina. In 1755 sixteen people gathered to form the Sandy Creek Baptist Church, and over the next three years, the congregation sponsored six new churches. By 1758 the total membership of the Sandy Creek congregation and her missions was nine hundred. By 1772 the Sandy Creek congregation had a "family tree" of forty-two churches and missions. This resulted in the formation of the Sandy Creek Association, which is still alive today.

Shubal Stearns, pastor of the original church, applied careful, strategic planning in choosing the physical locations for these new church plants. He observed travel patterns and population growth before choosing a site for a new church.[9] Numerous accounts demonstrate how the Sandy Creek church would regularly send out members to establish daughter churches.

It is hard to argue with the conclusion that early Baptist growth was fostered by a missional mind-set. This pattern was repeated in Charleston and later on during the western migration and Great Awakening.

Wrapping It Up

For future study, explore the answers to the following questions: What is the history behind your church? Your region or association? Your denomination/convention? Has there been a period of significant church planting in your state or province? How many churches were started in your state or province in the past year? What about over the past decade? Which churches stand out as "Antioch" churches?

---

[9] Larry McDonald, *Frontier Thunder: Principles of Evangelism and Church Growth from the Life of Shubal Stearns* (Ph.D. diss., Louisville: Southeastern Baptist Theological Seminary, 2000), 11.

Chapter 3

Answering the Critics:
Why Sponsor New
Churches Anyway?

Many pastors who sponsor new works confess that until the Lord got hold of them, they had the attitude "Why do we need another church in our area or any area for that matter? We've got all the churches we'll ever need already!" A pastor friend and church planter made the following remark after God convinced him about church planting and sponsoring other new works: "How foolish and shortsighted my thoughts were. Like some pastors today, my attitude was narrow-minded and limited to new church plants because I viewed them primarily as the 'competition.' The new church plant was invading my territory. Like the old cowboy gunslinger, I was convinced 'this town's not big enough for the both of us!'"

These were Scott Wilkins's words, and they are a challenge for us who take up the mantel of sponsoring new works for kingdom expansion. Larry Lewis, a man with a deeply missional heart, helped m. realize that God's plan to evangelize the nation and minister to the needs of the people everywhere is through the establishment of loving, caring, witnessing, and ministering new churches.[1] In his book he demonstrates the difference between a mission-minded leader and a missional leader. The pastor and Christian with the missional heart will see beyond one's own church and group to something greater for the kingdom of God. Lewis's enthusiasm for extending God's kingdom became mine, resulting in my own church experiencing increased baptisms and growth.

---

[1] Larry L. Lewis, *The Church Planter's Handbook* (Nashville: Broadman, 1992), 9.

20

If the American church is content ministering to whoever happens to show up each week, she misses her missiological purpose. Aubrey Malphurs warns, "The church must no longer remain comfortably situated behind its walls waiting for the community to come to it; rather it must go to the community." The church cannot expect the unchurched world to show up simply because a building is available and a welcome sign is placed along the street.[2] Today the key evangelistic strategy is and should be the starting of new churches to reach the lost. Some today are planting churches to reach the unchurched, but any serious commitment towards church planting by a sponsoring church must include reaching the lost as its primary focus. The size of one's church is not the critical factor in sponsoring a new work, but, rather, having a heart for the kingdom of God. The Lord will honor you and your church's commitment to becoming a missional church.

> When He (Jesus) saw the multitudes, He was moved with compassion for them, because they were weary and scattered, like sheep having no shepherd. Then He said to His disciples, "The harvest truly *is* plentiful, but the laborers *are* few. Therefore pray the Lord of the harvest to send out laborers into His harvest" (Matt 9:36–38 NKJV).

Answering the Critics

Most pastors critical towards church planting usually offer at least three reasons why it ought to be avoided like the plague. There are three basic oppositions (excuses perhaps) that many preachers and churches have against the planting of new churches.

The primary opposition is "there is not enough money in our church to plant a new work." These pastors and churches readily admit that they will not plant new churches because there are simply not enough monetary resources within the church to fund them. One often finds that the first protest towards church planting has everything to do with financial matters. I am sure that could be the case for a few congregations, but I have come to learn during my pastoral ministry that God has resources I do not even know about within my church and a larger scope of ministry. I have been regularly amazed just how often I intoned it could not be done, and then the Lord showed my people and me just how easy it was if we learned how to walk by faith. I also learned that it was those same pastors who said it was not possible, who later shouted from the rooftops that "all things were possible" when they wanted to raise monies for a new state-of-the-art worship center.

For assistance in developing financial resources, chapter 18 in this book is about raising the money necessary to plant a new church work. Since many different

---

[2] John Ewart, "The Great Commission and Strategic Outreach," in *The Challenge of the Great Commission: Essays on God's Mandate for the Local Church,* ed. Chuck Lawless and Thom S. Rainer (Pinnacle Publishers, 2005), 208.

models are used in church planting today, several different sponsorship methods are available to help any church become a part of planning new church starts. Sometimes a sponsoring church can support a pastor or even an entire pastoral team as they venture out to plant a church. A layperson sensing God's call may come under the umbrella of an established church and pastor to help them do a myriad of different church-planting ministries—for example, planting a church in a multi-housing community, or perhaps in a home. Sponsorship models may or may not involve funding. Churches with a keen Great Commission vision, however, will usually find the financial means to undergird the sponsorship of healthy new congregations.

A second objection is that "there is not enough leadership in our church to plant a new work." Their argument goes, "Parting with present leadership would create a hardship because the church does not have extra leaders to focus on the demands of church planting." I see picture after picture flash through my mind of committed godly people from my church plants and pastorates who stepped up and became great leaders for a new work. They never moved forward in the larger (sponsoring) church, often due to a feeling that they were not prepared enough to lead a group or sing a song. But they felt they could use their gifts in a smaller new work. As the new work grew, they were ready to do the exact things they felt intimidated to do in a larger, more established church environment. Pastors always need to search for the potential leaders who could be apprenticed and developed and moved to a new spiritual setting. Not all methods of church planting require an infusion of people and talent from the sponsoring church. But when one does, the sponsoring pastor almost always finds talented people are replaced by others whose spiritual gifts may have lain dormant. The people of First Baptist Church in Woodstock, Georgia, under the leadership of pastor Johnny Hunt, sent out a part of their congregation to be involved in a new church plant. The Sunday the new church started, they reported attendance at the sending church was at an all time high as God brought new people into their mother church. Thankfully churches like Woodstock step out boldly to plant new churches. Those who claim there are not enough leaders to go around might have a problem with priorities. Are we sometimes more concerned with the growth of our own church over and above growth in the kingdom of God?

The third basic opposition to church planting is that "there are not enough active members in our church to spare anyone going out to plant a new work." They simply cannot provide the people necessary. One church in Corpus Christi started thirty-one missions in three years, and the remarkable thing about this great church is that Calvary Baptist Church—the mother church—has only 332 members.[3] Pastor-leaders must resist the temptation to become primarily caretakers of the already established. Talented and alert laymen within thousands of churches stand ready to devote themselves to the task. David Hesselgrave rightly

---

[3] "Factoids," *Essentials Video* magazine (North American Mission Board, 2003).

reminds us, "All that is lacking is the leadership and organization required for their recruitment and deployment."[4]

In Isaiah 6 we read, "Then I heard the voice of the Lord saying: 'Whom shall I send? who will go for us?" Whom was it that the prophet Isaiah said to send? He answered, "Here am I. Send me." Whom will God send, and what churches will he use to bless the kingdom? Whom will the Lord send to the great unchurched cities of North America? To the thousands of communities and rural areas without an evangelical witness? To the suburban areas where young couples and their families have moved and attend no church. Whom will the Lord send? Maybe he will send your people, your church. Many young adults today have a passion to do something new and fresh in the kingdom of God. It is not surprising that church planting is the most attractive option to many of these future leaders. Historically the most effective means of accomplishing the Great Commission has been through the organization of new congregations.[5]

Answering Opposition to Sponsoring New Churches

Opposition to church planting is hardly ever expressed openly. There are many reasons for this, and one obviously is because of the self-seeking nature of such a position. When it is expressed, pastors who are against the sponsoring and planting of new churches often rehearse now well-known negative arguments towards such a missional perspective. Here are some of the ones used most often.

"Sponsoring a new church will subvert the main church's vision." The claim is that the main church will be drained with such effort as church sponsoring will necessitate. Impairing the main church, injuring the body of Christ, or straining the original now-healthy church—all of these things are heard commonly. In the final analysis, many church leaders simply are fearful that sponsoring a spin-off church will drain their current ministry and injure their chances for further growth. But the vast majority of sending churches discover that church-sponsoring activity actually strengthens the church as they participate in the birth of new houses of God and observe first hand God moving through their congregation.

"Sponsoring a new church is too expensive and overburdens the main church." Yet I have discovered a church can sponsor a new church even when the sponsoring church is still relatively small and the dollars are few. Some time ago a few pastor friends asked if I wanted to help them get a new church started over in a certain area of town, and what the church I led might do. We were very small, but besides praying daily and showing up monthly to knock on doors for the new church, we were able even as a small church to help sponsor the new church plant by providing the sound system for the building. Church planting can begin with

---

[4] David J. Hesselgrave, *Planting Churches Cross-Culturally: A Guide for Home and Foreign Missions* (Grand Rapids: Baker Publishing Group, 1980), 86.

[5] Lyle E. Schaller, *21 Bridges to the 21st Century: The Future of Pastoral Ministry* (Nashville: Abingdon Press, 1994), 144–45.

but a small outlay as part of a larger sponsoring team of churches. Down the road as your church expands, you might have the tremendous blessing of sponsoring the entire new work.

Sponsoring does not mean opulently spending money your church does not have. And it doesn't mean becoming so excessive as to overburden the missional church seeking to be part of kingdom work. It also does not mean a missional church should sponsor a new plant at the cheapest means possible. Thousands of churches today could sponsor a new church without ever feeling a financial or personnel "crunch." Within most of these congregations are mission-minded saints just waiting for an opportunity to be blessed by God through their own giving towards a new church. Numerous diverse sponsorship methods are available to help any church start new churches. Many different models are being used in church planting all over the world today, so there is no reason a sponsoring church can't support a pastor or even an entire pastoral team, or anything else in between. And there is no reason to miss out on the opportunity just because resources seem to appear limited.

"Sponsoring a new church swamps the overloaded staff of the main church." It is easy for leaders of an existing church to feel overwhelmed due to pressing needs surrounding the ministry. Members and clergy alike can often sense a closing in on their work due to high goals and expectations on the part of the congregants. When a pastor feels overtaxed, that sense of being swamped diminishes any objective consideration of sponsoring a new church. Time restraints and a sense of neglecting or overlooking the home church can cause both pastors and people to forget the Great Commission. But a careful reminder of the Great Commission may be what the doctor has ordered because keeping a biblical missional mind-set is always in season.

"It is not the right time or moment to sponsor a new church because God has not yet shown us when, where, and how." Many believe that unless God shows them where and how, they will not sign on to church planting. It's better to keep waiting for a sign. But this approach fails to notice the various people groups that are within their ministry area. Seeing the need might be as simple as agreeing to become an entry-level partner or co-sponsor. Perhaps beginning a new church could be accomplished within an already established church by launching a foreign language service using the mother church's facilities when they are dormant. The gospel is available for every man and woman of every tribe and nation, and sponsoring a church within a church or becoming an entry-level partner is a great way to discover if the right time is now.

"Sponsoring a new church will sabotage our own chance for numerical growth." Sadly the truth is that quite a number of pastors are concerned first and foremost about their own kingdom expansion in the church they lead. Anything that could compromise their own chance for growth is avoided, even if it means fewer people coming into the kingdom of God. Now I know they would not say it that way, but after all I am a Yankee and I usually call it the way it is. Many pastors believe that if something—anything—could soften the impact within their immediate ministry, then it must be avoided. "If it does not bring people into our fellowship then it is undermining the work we are called to accomplish," they say. Or, "If we sponsor a new church, it could short-circuit or handicap any chance we have to ever grow this church." In other words, new church plants are seen as competition. But they should never be seen in this way; rather, they should be seen as a fulfillment of the kingdom of God and a raising of the bar for existing churches. This can be illustrated by looking at Starbucks. Like it or not, Starbucks has changed expectations of how coffee should taste. They've done a great job of raising coffee standards, and their tasters and quality control team taste an average of one thousand cups per day. This has forced McDonalds and Burger King to upgrade their brews,[6] which is good for everyone.

"Sponsoring a new church where one already exists is not the New Testament example." Many leaders of church planting across North America have heard this statement. "Since we already have a church located in this community, we don't need to make room for another! Besides, Mr. Missionary, do you really want to go against the New Testament example of one church for one municipality?" As a former director of missions, I have been asked this question by a number of pastors who objected to having another church in their community. My first thoughts were, "Was your church the first in the community? If not, how did you get started?" When I felt like being somewhat ornery, I wanted to say that church buildings were not around during the New Testament period, so doesn't the idea of a church building go against the New Testament example as well? The point is, I have searched and simply cannot find any scriptural mandate teaching there is to be "one church per community." The squabble of one church in one town is not defendable from Holy Scripture.

"Sponsoring a new church does not spotlight what I have accomplished." Personal magnification is never part of sponsoring new churches. Many pastors, regardless of denominational alignment, believe the sponsoring of new churches will not enrich their appearance in the eyes of other pastors. Put another way, the enriching of one's career is seldom tied to the sponsoring of new works for many preachers. New churches are planted in different places, and this means they are hard to see. When it's not seen, one gets no credit! Church planting usually is not the road taken for a preacher desiring career advancement. Furthermore, a minister's prestige almost always depends on what he does within one local church and not on the multiplication of other churches.

Until our ultimate goal is to please God and not our peers, the church planting movement will be hampered. Our thinking must be polished. In considering church growth, pastors must get beyond simply comparing attendance figures from the previous Sunday. What is required is hard thinking, strategizing, and training opportunities for members to be participating in planting ministries and practicing

---

[6] "Starbucks Aims beyond Lattes," *USA Today* (May 19–21, 2006), section A, page 2.

the mission efforts of evangelism (like starting new churches). A church must not be measured by its seating capacity but by its sending capacity.

So Why Should We Sponsor Churches Anyway?

Some missionaries and mission leaders have an antimissional mentality. The term *missional* denotes missionary activities, and thus a missional church is one on mission in its societal setting and geographic context. Pastors and sometimes even whole denominations develop an antimissional mentality, and when this happens, it hurts the entire body of Christ, not just new church plants and sponsoring churches. In the early 1990s an antimissional virus swept Protestant Evangelicalism. During this period many churches disbanded their traditional mission education programs, such as the Women's Missionary Unions (WMU), Girls in Action, Acteens, and Royal Ambassadors. Movements such as Promise Keepers replaced mission-focused men's ministries like Brotherhood. Ed Stetzer summed up the changing attitude towards missions during this period when he wrote, "As long as they're going overseas to a place where there aren't any similar churches, missions are considered 'acceptable.'"[7] Or, as long as they are on the home front, far removed from the centralized location of the established church. This attitude still keeps us from planting churches and missional enterprises along vast stretches of North America.

Why this attitude? Usually it is due to one or more of the following prevailing ideas.

The Bigger-Is-Better Mentality of the 1990s

We all know that bigger or larger does not always equate with better. In reality the church needs to be everywhere and in all shapes and sizes, mega as well as mini. It should go without saying that all churches have an important place in reaching the world.

Only the Seminary-Trained Need Apply

When people are called by God to the work of church planting, they will receive on-the-job training just when they need it. All that is required is regular people praying for a church planting movement to break out.

---

[7] Ed Stetzer, *Nehemiah Project Professors Course Notes: Introduction to Church Planting* (NAMB, 2003). Used by permission.

One Is the Holiest Number

I believe that limiting a target area to a single church is a dramatic waste of time, unless we are talking about an extremely rural area. Yet many preachers believe there is a need for only one church in any given community.

Peter Wagner said, "Some are reluctant to start new churches for fear of harming those churches that are currently located in the target community. They feel that doing so could create undesirable competition between brothers and sisters in Christ. In more cases than not, a new church in the community tends to raise the religious interest of the people in general, and if handled properly can be a benefit to existing churches. That which blesses the kingdom of God as a whole also blesses the churches that truly are a part of the Kingdom." He went on to cite that in the town of Ewa, Hawaii, a Southern Baptist church was planted. This church plant raised the spiritual level so high in the community that the Roman Catholic Church witnessed a 100% attendance growth, and the local Congregational church saw an attendance increase of 155%.[8] Lyle Schaller similarly observed, "Contrary to conventional wisdom, congregations usually benefit from interdenominational competition. While it is impossible to isolate one factor as being decisive, the presence of two or more congregations with the same denominational affiliation usually results in a higher level of congregational health and vitality than if one congregation has a denominational monopoly in that community."[9] Many types of churches are needed to reach the multitudes for Christ.

Let's Strengthen Those Churches We Already Have

Many pastors will say most of their congregants believe we ought to help churches already in existence instead of spending time, effort, and money planting new churches. Helping somnolent and dying churches is important, of course, but what we need to do is adopt a strategy including both church planting and church strengthening. It is simply true that new churches win more individuals to Christ per attendee than existing churches. Church plants are therefore an inimitable arm of the "gift of evangelism" for the body of Christ. Each mission dollar invested in church planting goes farther for evangelism than dollars devoted to existing church expenditures.[10] We should never stop supporting established churches, but we must put more of a focus on church planting. There needs to be balance, but since there is a tendency to ignore church planting, we need to think more and plan more than we usually do on the process.

---

[8] C. Peter Wagner, *Church Planting for a Greater Harvest* (Ventura, CA: Regal Books, 1990), 40.

[9] Lyle E. Schaller, *Forty-four Questions for Church Planters* (Nashville: Abingdon Press, 1991), 29–30.

[10] Ed Stetzer, *Nehemiah Project Professors Course Notes: Introduction to Church Planting* (North American Mission Board, 2003); used by permission.

North America Is Already Christian

Who would not agree that the United States and Canada have not been reached with the gospel? North America is part of what are being called "post-Christian nations." Perhaps at one time they were nominally Christian, but such definitely is not the case today. There are no absolutes and there is out-and-out moral confusion. Everything is relative. So much so that in 1988 Win Arn reported, "In America we are closing seven more churches per day than we are opening!"[11] In 2003 the North American Mission Board estimated the non-Christian population in North America to be in excess of 228 million.

The fact is that North America is not being reached for Christ. The one-church, one-location mentality is not doing it. Rescuing declining churches is necessary and important, but it is not enough unless there is a corresponding interest in planting new churches. North America is in need of healthy new churches, and happily all over the continent hearts and minds are being opened to the need for planting new churches.

Wrapping It Up

Church members and leaders often ask why the church should start new churches when it appears that a church exists already on every corner. The answer is that there are a theological underpinning, a biblical pattern, and practical benefits that mandate the church attempt to reach every people and cultural group in our community and in communities across the world.

Theological Underpinning

As was pointed out earlier, the God in Scripture is a missionary God. He promised to bless the nations through Abraham and his descendants. He called Jonah to preach repentance in Nineveh. The Son of God gave us the Great Commission. Revelation 5 tells of people from "every tribe and language and people and nation" who were purchased by Jesus Christ for the kingdom of God. Based on a biblical understanding of God as a missionary God and of his Son as the direct path to the Father, we have no option but to be colaborers in God's redemptive purpose for the world.

Biblical Pattern

There is often disparity on how best to accomplish the Great Commission. The book of Acts gives examples of witnessing methods used by the early church, and

---

[11] Win Arn, *The Pastor's Manual for Effective Ministry* (Monrovia, CA: Church Growth, 1988), 16. Fortunately, the renewed emphasis on church planting is helping reverse this statistic. Southern Baptists have gone from planting a church a day in 1988 to more than four a day in 2005.

these methods consisted of mass evangelism, healing, teaching, confrontational witnessing, one-on-one witnessing, persuasive arguments, intellectual debate, and personal testimony. Whereas these techniques are used to spread the Word of God, the book of Acts also reveals the most effective strategy for fulfilling the Great Commission, the approach of the apostle Paul. During his three missionary journeys, Paul traveled the then-known world planting healthy New Testament churches. Although this greatest of missionary church planters used every evangelistic technique possible to fulfill the Great Commission, his deliberate strategy to accomplish that purpose was to plant healthy churches.

Practical Certainty

I have mentioned that some preachers and lay people are hesitant to support church planting because (1) it hurts existing churches by draining financial and personnel assets, (2) it "robs" too many members from other established churches, (3) there is a sufficient amount of churches already existing to do the job of evangelism, (4) it fosters a spirit of rivalry, (5) most church starts are feeble and predestined to fail or stay small, (6) new churches don't have a high opinion of tradition, and (7) it costs too much. These things can all be true if a church plant is ill-conceived, poorly planned, or haphazardly implemented. But church planting can be a great blessing and benefit for kingdom growth, for the spiritual health of the sponsoring church, and certainly for those who need to be introduced to Christ.

1. New churches can bring new focus, purpose, energy, and excitement to the sponsoring congregation. Once members of an existing church see how God can use a new church to reach new people in a new way, they will want to do it again and again!
2. New churches usually cost less to get going than it takes to preserve the programs of an existing church.
3. New churches can focus in new and creative ways on unreached people groups, whether they are defined by ethnicity, language, generation, location, or a subculture affinity. The purpose is to grow by conversion, not by transfer from other churches.
4. New churches commonly baptize more people per capita than do older churches.
5. New churches can shape themselves to reach specific communities and groups. They are not bound by traditional styles and methodologies, and they can change and adapt quickly if needed.
6. New churches do not harm the ministry of existing churches, and in fact most church planters appreciate very much the concepts of heritage and tradition. They also realize, however, that the

challenge of a postmodern anti-Christian culture demands new techniques and approaches.

7.   New churches are needed to get the job done. The regrettable fact is that almost all denominations are declining and the majority of churches are in decline—and this is true despite a general population that is growing at unprecedented rates. New churches are desperately needed just to stay even with population growth.

8.   New churches are fertile ground for calling out and developing new leaders, whether church planters, pastoral staff members, or especially lay leaders.

9.   Finally, when done right, new churches actually encourage cooperation in the kingdom, not rivalry. This is true if all involved understand the purpose of a healthy new church plant.

10.   The authors of this book are passionate and committed to strategic church planting in North America and cooperatively throughout the world. Is your congregation ready to become a church-planting church?

Part 2

Attitudes toward Church Sponsorship

No generation of Christians has been fully obedient to Christ's Great Commission. And yet, no generation of human beings can be reached except by the Christians of that generation. For fifty-nine generations of lost people it is too late. And yet, according to the promise of God, some generation will stand before the Lord and say, "It is finished. The task you have given us to do, we have accomplished."

— Robertson McQuilkin

There are people who, instead of listening to what is being said to them, are already listening to what they are going to say themselves.

—Albert Guinon

Introduction to Part 2

As a part of my (Rodney) doctoral work in 1999, I conducted a survey of 100 church leaders in central California. The study was designed to determine if the need for additional sponsoring church training and resources, such as this book, existed. To my surprise, not a single church leader indicated that they had received at least some preparation or training while in seminary to prepare them or their church to sponsor a new work. Only one pastor in the survey had received training after seminary to equip him for the task of church sponsorship. It was apparent from this sampling that sponsoring church resources—at least in California—were needed.

In 2000, mission leaders from across the United States and Canada were invited to Atlanta to discuss the need for sponsoring church resources. Their comments and observations reinforced what I had observed in California and supported my assumption that many pastors and church leaders in North America are interested in church planting but simply do not know where to start.

In my role as Nehemiah Church Planting Director at Midwestern Baptist Theological Seminary, I developed a survey to determine sponsoring church attitudes among church and denominational leaders. The survey concentrated on five areas: (1) theological assertions relating to church planting and sponsoring; (2) perceived hindrances to sponsoring new churches; (3) important factors related to the sponsoring church; (4) role expectations of the sponsoring church; and (5) current and anticipated missional involvement. The study was made available to readers of the *Church Planting Update* and visitors to the churchplantingvillage.com Web site. This section is based upon 342 survey participants.

In August 2007, the data from the study was provided to the Nehemiah Center at Midwestern Baptist Theological Seminary, broken down into respondent groups, and compiled into tables. The general feeling among participants supports our conviction that church planting is not only biblical; it is essential to fulfilling the Great Commission. Respondents also strongly agreed that churches, through sponsoring new work, should be the primary agents of this Great Commission task.

It should be noted that Tom and I recognize those responding to the survey were either visiting a church planting Web site or subscribed to a Southern Baptist church planting resource. As such, the participants of the survey were already reading and researching church planting material, much as you are now. Therefore, the results of this survey are likely to reflect the attitudes of the readership of this book better than those of church leaders in general. It is our hope that this study will provide a springboard for you to explore and discuss your own sponsorship attitudes as compared to the attitudes and responses of those in the survey. It should also be noted that the following three chapters are based upon responses from the three primary respondent groups: the local church pastor or staff, church planters, and denominational leaders. Tom and I also wish to extend our appreciation to Richie Stanley of the North American Mission Board's research team for his work in compiling the survey results, and to Ed Stetzer, whose previous research is referred to in this section.

Chapter 4

What Pastors Are Saying

S ince a significant number of the readers of this book are church leaders, it was decided to begin this section with the survey responses of pastors. According to the study, pastors strongly agreed with the statements "The Great Commission cannot be fulfilled without starting new churches" and "Sponsoring new churches is biblical." Most significantly, pastors believe it is the local church who carries the primarily responsibility for sponsoring church planting efforts. The following results demonstrate this conviction.

Primary Sponsorship of New Churches Is the Responsibility of the Local Church			
Strongly Agree	**Moderately Agree**	**Moderately Disagree**	**Strongly Disagree**
67%	20.5%	3.4%	4.5%

. . . About Church Planting Responsibility

It is the responsibility of existing churches to spin-off new churches, according to more than 92% of the pastors surveyed. With 67% strongly agreeing and another 20.5% moderately agreeing, the question of "who is responsible" clearly seems to land in the lap of the local church. So far, so good. The next question dealt with how pastors felt about sending what is likely the single most important earthly resource required by a new church—people.

Sending out members to the church plant: The pastors in the study also seemed surprisingly willing to send out faithful members to help start the new work: 46.6% strongly agreed, and another 37.5% moderately agreed, that sending out faithful members to join the new church is one of the roles of the sponsoring church.

Send Out Faithful Members Who Will Join the New Church			
Strongly Agree	**Moderately Agree**	**Moderately Disagree**	**Strongly Disagree**
46.6%	37.5%	9%	3.4%

Providing an umbrella covering for the new church: Pastors also agreed that "the sponsoring church role includes providing an umbrella covering for the new church." On this point 59.1% strongly agreed and 25% moderately agreed. Generally, until a new work constitutes or incorporates, an umbrella covering that includes liability insurance and legal status is provided by the sponsoring church.

Meeting with the church planter: However, when it came time to commit to meeting weekly with a church planter, pastors were somewhat less willing to devote their time, despite studies that show weekly meetings with church planters are significant contributors to the success of church plants.[1] Only 46.6% of pastors (the lowest group in the survey) cited weekly meetings as very important. In fact, the percentage of pastors who felt weekly meetings had little or no importance was three times higher than the percentage of church planters or denominational workers who felt the same.

Importance of Weekly Meetings with the Church Planter					
	Very Important	**Somewhat Important**	**Little Importance**	**Not Needed**	**No Response**
Pastor	46.6%	31.8%	14.8%	3.4%	3.4%
Church Planter	48.8%	41.5%	4.9%	2.4%	2.4%
Denominational	56.7%	36.7%	5%	1.7%	0%

Denominational resources: When asked if a lack of denominational resources would cause "certain death" for the new church, only 6.8% of pastors said yes. A noteworthy percentage (68.2%) felt a lack of denominational resources was not a hindrance or only a minor hindrance for church planting. However, of the groups surveyed, the percentage of pastors who felt a lack of denominational resources would result in certain death was the highest among the respondent groups.

---

[1] Edward J. Stetzer, "An Analysis of the Church Planting Process," Atlanta, North American Mission Board, May 2003.

The Result of a Lack of Denominational Resources for Church Planting					
Group	No Response	Certain Death	Major Hindrance	Minor Hindrance	No Hindrance
Pastor	2.3%	6.8%	22.7%	45.5%	22.7%
Church Planter	7.3%	0%	43.9%	24.4%	24.4%
Denominational	0%	5%	16.7%	55%	23.3%

When it came to the importance of a fully funded church planter, it appears that pastors agreed with church planters that a fully funded ministry is important. It was interesting to note the disparity between pastors and church planters versus those who were denominational leaders.

The Need for a Fully Funded Church Planter (Pastors' Response)				
	Very Important	Somewhat Important	Little Importance	Not Needed
Pastor	48.9%	32.9%	12.5%	2.3%
Church Planter	63.4%	19.5%	9.8%	4.9%
Denominational	23.3%	43.3%	25%	6.7%

Hindrances to Sponsoring

When asked questions relating to those factors that hinder spin-off success, pastors noted the lack of qualified church planters as the major hindrance, taking precedence over financial concerns.

Lack of Qualified Church Planters			
Certain Death	Major Hindrance	Minor Hindrance	No Hindrance
13.6%	47.7%	21.6%	8%

Financial limitations are a concern for pastors. Only 10.2% felt financial limitations are of no hindrance to church planting while 8% saw financial limitations as certain death. The majority (77.2%) felt finances are either a major or minor hindrance. Financial limitation in the sponsoring church was cited as certain death for the new church by 8% of pastors, as a major hindrance by 38.6%, and as a minor hindrance by 38.6%.

Financial Limitations in the Sponsoring Church			
Certain Death	**Major Hindrance**	**Minor Hindrance**	**No Hindrance**
8%	38.6%	38.6%	10.2%

Fear of failure was also a greater concern for pastors than either church planters or denominational leaders. Only 14.8% answered "no hindrance" to the question relating to the fear of failure as a perceived hindrance.

Fear That the New Church Will Fail			
Certain Death	**Major Hindrance**	**Minor Hindrance**	**No Hindrance**
13.6%	35.2%	30.7%	14.8%

What Pastors Are Saying about the Church Planter

One surprise arising from the survey was that pastors felt that a church planter who knows and understands the community is more valuable than one with a proven record for conversion growth. A full 72.7% of pastors viewed "knows and understands the community" as a very important trait. This may suggest that pastors recognize that knowing one's community is a prerequisite for lasting church growth and for developing evangelism methods that result in disciples and not just numbers. Such growth requires a church planter who *engages* rather than *abrases* the community.

A Church Planter Who Knows and Understands the Community			
Little Importance	**Not Needed**	**Somewhat Important**	**Very Important**
3.4%	2.3%	17%	72.7%

A proven ability for conversion growth remains a trait valued by pastors. Only 12.5% felt this characteristic is not needed or of little importance, whereas 48.9% viewed it as very important and another 32.9% as somewhat important. I would note that 64.3% of church planters, when asked the same question, felt that a proven ability for conversation growth is very important.

A Church Planter with a Proven Ability for Conversion Growth			
Little Importance	Not Needed	Somewhat Important	Very Important
11.4%	1.1%	32.9%	48.9%

Pastors are also looking for church planters who have gone through a "Mentor and Basic Training" type of process and who have a proven track record of ministry experience. In our survey, 80.6% rated "proven ministry experience" as very important or somewhat important.

In my work with churches, I have been hearing pastors speak of the importance of church planters having "business and administrative ability." However, this trait was cited as very important by only 27.3% of pastors. Nevertheless, pastors were more likely to rate business and administrative ability as "very important" than either church planters or denominational workers. Conversely, pastors rated the following as "less important" than either church planters or denominational workers:

- seminary training in church planting
- a high church planter assessment score
- a proven ability for conversion growth

Pastors believe that the primary supervision and accountability of a church planter should be the responsibly of the sponsoring church. Only 10.2% disagreed with this statement. Recall, however, that less than half of all pastors surveyed felt weekly supervision or mentoring meetings with the church planter are very important.

Primary Supervision and Accountability for Church Planters Is the Responsibility of the Sponsoring Church			
Strongly Agree	Moderately Agree	Moderately Disagree	Strongly Disagree
60.2%	25%	6.8%	3.4%

Sponsoring 101

Of all respondents, 80.6% indicated the need for sponsoring training is very important, and an additional 14.6% indicated this need is somewhat important. Only 2.1% believed sponsoring church training is not needed.

Importance of Sponsoring Church Training	
Very important	80.6%
Somewhat important	14.6%
Little importance	2.8%
Not needed	2.1%

Until recently, this training was not available. Only in the past few years have training events for sponsoring churches been available. The North American Mission Board began Kingdom Builders in 2005. This sponsoring of church training provides both seminar opportunities and do-it-yourself resources. More information about Kingdom Builders can be found at the end of this chapter. In 1999 and 2000, I led a series of workshops titled "Prenatal Class for Church Leaders." Originally, I was concerned that the materials presented were too "elementary." For example, the first hour was a "review" of the biblical basis for church planting. The second hour focused on the need for new churches in America, and the third hour addressed the historical role of sponsoring churches in the church in America. My misgivings were misplaced, as the workshop evaluations strongly affirmed the benefit of the basics. Phil Neighbors, copastor of Valley Baptist Church in Bakersfield, wrote, "I needed this in seminary. This training is going to change the way our church does missions." Phil was true to his word. Since the conference, Valley Baptist Church has made international and domestic church planting a priority. Currently, this church is primary sponsor to four local new churches and numerous international congregations. Another participant, the pastor of a very small congregation, led his church to become an "entry level" sponsor of a new ethnic church plant. The venture was so successful that it became the first of several missional and church planting endeavors to follow. These and other spin-off activities occurred because pastors participated in sponsoring church training.

Ideally, pastors will attend such training with other church leaders. In the original sponsoring church training conducted in 1999, I required the pastor bring at least one church leader with him for the full conference. In addition to providing company to and from the training, this requirement resulted in at least two people, not just one, being trained. In the evaluations, several pastors noted that the church leader they brought with them had been instrumental in keeping the spin-off vision alive. Several of these lay leaders volunteered to head up the sponsoring church project. Others helped identify strategic opportunities for church planting. One even provided the start-up funds for the new church. In every case, the church leader who accompanied the pastor ended up playing a crucial role. Of the 21 churches equipped in 1999, 19 went on to sponsor or cosponsor a new congregation.

Participating in some type of sponsoring church training will be the starting point for many pastors. If such training is not available in your area, we hope that this book, along with other resources, will provide you with the information and encouragement needed to develop your own sponsoring church training.

Where Pastors Go for Resources

The survey demonstrates that pastors may not know where to go to find sponsoring church resources. When asked, pastors in the study were more likely to go to NAMB (26.1%) or another pastor or church (19.3%).

First Place to Go for Sponsoring Church Resources			
First Resource	**Senior Pastor/ Church Staff Minister**	**Church Planter**	**All Denominational**
No Response		2.4%	
Another Local Church or Pastor	19.3%	17.1%	8.3%
Internet	12.5%	14.6%	8.3%
LifeWay Christian Resources	3.4%	9.8%	1.7%
Local Association	17%	14.6%	31.7%
Non-SBC Sources	4.5%	4.9%	0%
NAMB	26.1%	22%	18.3%
Other	6.8%	7.3%	8.3%
State Convention	10.2%	7.3%	23.3%

For most pastors, denominational sources will be the first place to look for sponsoring resources. Among pastoral respondents, 30% would turn to a national denominational source (NAMB or LifeWay) and 27% would seek a local (state or associational) denominational resource. More than 19% would seek out another pastor or local church, and 12.5% would go to the Internet. Clearly, one of the challenges pastors face is knowing where to turn to find quality sponsoring church resources.

To know where to go you must know what you want. I would challenge pastors and church leaders to ask, "What are we trying to start?" George Barna notes that by the year 2025, 30–35% of those seeking spiritual experience and expression will primarily turn to alternative faith-based communities rather than what we traditionally call the local church.[2] It is my belief that some house churches, such as the one Philemon attended (Phil 2), would fall into Barna's "alternative faith-based community" category. I believe there are changes afoot as to how people (not God) understand "church." Just as having "church" in the name of an incorporated entity does not make it a true church, leaving "church" or the denominational affiliation out of the name the community calls itself does not mean the assembly is not a church. Admittedly, some, if not many, of these "alternative faith-based communities" Barna speaks of will fall outside of the biblical perimeters of orthodoxy. Nevertheless, many will be expressions of faith far closer to biblical orthodoxy than the "average" church of the 20th century that was content to measure success by seating capacity over sending capacity and members over missionaries. So, what type of new church do you desire your church to birth? It is important to know the answer to this question as you look for resources.

Wrapping It Up

The pastors and staff members responding to this survey are saying, "We are going to be involved." When surveyed about their current involvement, 26.5% were already serving as the primary sponsor of a church plant.

Current Church Sponsorship Involvement	
Primary sponsor of a new church	26.5%
Cluster sponsor (jointly with other churches)	19.3%
Supporting sponsor (short term or one-time events)	9.5%
Not sure	11.3%
Not sponsoring a new church	33.1%

When asked about plans for multiplication, the results were promising.

What Is the Likelihood That Your Church Will Sponsor a New or Additional Church in the Next Five Years?	
Definite (plans already in place)	31.1%
Expected	31.8%
Willing to consider	22.5%
Unlikely	14.6%

[2] George Barna, *Revolution* (Ventura, CA: Barna Group, 2005), 49.

As greater numbers of churches engage in sponsoring new works, the number of qualified coaches, mentors, and supervisors should rise. The potential for developing sponsoring church networks for the purpose of fellowship, sharing of ideas, and support for missional church planting will increase. I would challenge pastors to take time to find others who are sponsoring leaders and meet with them to discuss the process and share your ideas and reflect upon the insights you have gained as a spin-off church.

Resources

For Coaching and Mentoring

Rowley, Robert J. "Successfully Coaching Church Planters." Available as a downloadable file from http://www.newchurches.com/mediafiles/coaching-ch-pl-diss-by-bob-rowley.pdf

"The Mentor Guide, North American Mission Board." Available as a downloadable file from http://www.churchplantingvillage.net/atf/cf/{087EF6B4-D6E5-4BBF-BED1-7983D360F394}/2002_Mentor_Guide.doc

For Sponsoring Church Training

To explore hosting or attending a Kingdom Builder seminar: *tcheyney@namb.net or ldobins@namb.net*

To schedule a Prenatal Class for Churches conference: *rharrison@mbts.edu*

For Reading

Barna, George. *Revolution*. Ventura, CA: Barna Group, 2005.

Kingdom Builders. North American Mission Board, 2005. Request a copy through tcheyney@namb.net

Harrison, Rodney. *Seven Steps for Planting New Churches: Partner Edition*. Atlanta: North American Mission Board, 2005. Contact tcheyney@namb.net for a copy.

Chapter 5

What Church Planters
Are Saying

A few years ago, I took part in a church planting study conducted by J. D. Payne on the concerns and perceptions of church planters. Payne surveyed 190 individuals from thirteen denominations and parachurch organizations in North America who were involved in church planting.[1] This study confirmed some things that those in church planting understood experientially or intuitively, such as the personal financial concerns most church planters and families face. Other things came as a surprise, such as the frustration over the lack of sponsoring church involvement. Knowing the critical issues raised by church planters helps sponsors be better equipped to minister to church planters. As a sponsoring church, you and your congregation may have significant influence upon the church planter's life. By taking time to understand the heart of those called to plant new churches, you can be more effective in your own ministry while assisting your church planters to be more effective in theirs. Here are the top five critical issues as determined by Payne's study. I have included J. D. Payne's suggested responses as they appear in his report, as well as a few thoughts of my own.

---

[1] J. D. Payne is the Nehemiah Professor for Church Planting at Southern Baptist Theological Seminary. His research was summarized in a Church Planter Update article titled, "Five Things Church Planters Wished Their Supervisors Knew," available at http://www.churchplantingvillage.net/site/c.iiJTKZPEJpH/ b.2453553/apps/nl/content3.asp?content_id=%7B9309895B-28B6-48F6-B209-440646A7BAE1%7D&notoc=1 accessed February 16, 2008.

Critical Issue #1: "I am very concerned about my personal finances."

Suggested Responses

- Help church planters develop a personal finance plan. If your church has skilled finance people, ask them to volunteer their time to help the church planter budget.
- Help with financial counseling. Many church planters grew up with a "consumer" mentality. Providing solid financial counseling can help them make wise decisions.
- Encourage bivocationalism and tent-making.
- Work with Christian business owners to develop creative employment and ministry opportunities.

My Thoughts

- Our survey showed that planters, more than any other group, felt that a fully funded church planter is very important.

Importance of a Fully Funded Church Planter			
Very Important	**Somewhat Important**	**Little Importance**	**Not Needed**
63.4%	19.5%	9.8%	4.9%

- Consider asking some of your strongest financial contributors if they would feel led to work with and support the new work.
- Invite other churches to become cosponsors of the new work, or develop partnering clusters to ensure adequate funding for the church-planting team.
- Begin a long-term spin-off funding strategy through estate planning that includes a budget for church planter costs.

Critical Issue #2: "I am struggling with the necessary leadership for this church plant to work."

Suggested Responses

- Send your church planter to leadership development conferences.
- Consider purchasing resources for your church planter such as *Raising Leaders for the Harvest*, by Robert Logan and Neil Cole.
- Commission and send people from your church to help in the work.

My Thoughts

- Our study shows that planters agree that the sponsoring church should provide supervision and accountability.

Primary Supervision and Accountability for Church Planters Are the Responsibility of the Sponsoring Church			
Strongly Agree	**Moderately Agree**	**Moderately Disagree**	**Strongly Disagree**
51.2%	39%	4.9%	2.4%

- Church planters are also more open to weekly supervision meetings than their sponsors are.

Importance of Weekly Meetings with the Church Planter				
	Very Important	**Somewhat Important**	**Little Importance**	**Not Needed**
Planters	48.8%	41.5%	4.9%	2.4%
Sponsors	46.6%	31.8%	14.8%	3.4%

- Introduce the planter into your network of lay leaders and business leaders.
- Attend a leadership conference with the planter and his team.
- Ask a godly, effective lay leader to befriend the church planter and serve as a leadership coach.

Critical Issue #3: "I am frustrated that so few established churches are involved in church planting."

Suggested Response

- Prepare and send out missionaries (Acts 13:1–2).
- Give much congregational prayer support.
- Never cease offering encouragement.
- Serve as the "home church" with whom the church planter can identify.
- Provide pastoral mentoring and accountability for the church planter.
- Provide on-going training.
- Provide resources and financial support.
- Provide meeting space.

- Constantly recognize the church planting team before the whole congregation.
- Allow for much flexibility, remembering that missionaries will sometimes do "strange" (non-traditional) things to reach people with the gospel.
- Establish clear expectations for the relationship that exists between the team and the partnering church.
- Recognize the legitimate nature of the team and their work.

My Thoughts

- Planters, sponsors, and denominational leaders are open to "multipartnership" models. Consider encouraging the church planter to develop additional partners for your new church.

The Importance of Multiple Partnering Churches				
	Very Important	**Somewhat Important**	**Little Importance**	**Not Needed**
Church Planters	73.2%	19.5%	2.4%	2.4%
Pastors	47.7%	37.5%	6.8%	3.4%
Denominational	46.7%	41.7%	5%	3.3%

- Provide a "ministry of reality check." As seen in the chapter on sponsoring churches through the ages, only a handful of congregations in the New Testament truly "came up to the plate" as sponsors. However, the churches that have done this through the ages are the ones that have become "Antioch" churches. They have made a tremendous impact, so share with your planter your commitment to be an "Antioch" church.
- Send your very best. The last thing church planters need is high maintenance help.
- Involve the planter in sponsoring decisions, as appropriate.

Critical Issue #4: "Please be patient with me and my work, at least until you understand my ministry context."

Suggested Response

- Hold church planters accountable, but allow for much freedom in the ministry.

- Don't assume that you know what is best, especially if you are not working in the same ministry context; give them the benefit of the doubt.
- Methods must change: Don't assume what worked "yesterday" will work "today."
- Everyone has different gifts: Just because it worked for you, does not mean it will work for others.

My Thoughts

- Don't be surprised to hear something like "this is not working out as I had planned" from your church planter. He may have many concerns, including that the sponsor will pull the plug on the church plant.
- Don't act upon hearsay. If you get word the church planter is doing something "over the edge," get the full story.

Critical Issue #5: "My family is under an incredible amount of stress related to this church planting ministry."

Suggested Responses

- Periodically check with the family to see how they are doing physically, mentally, emotionally, spiritually, and relationally.
- Inquire into the church planter's personal life; learn to ask tough questions about how they are carrying out all their personal responsibilities.
- Be a friend; take the church planter out for coffee, a ball game, or lunch.
- Take the entire family out for a meal.
- Challenge a family (or small group) in your church to "adopt" the church planter's family.
- Encourage godly women in your church to befriend the church planter's wife.

My Thoughts

For many church planters, the fear of failure is a major concern. Recognize this fear early, and actively address the fears that arise.

For Church Planters, the Fear of Failure Is a...		
Major Hindrance	**Minor Hindrance**	**No Hindrance**
46.3%	22%	19.5%

47

We would all like to engage church planters who have proven track records and experience in understanding and engaging the culture. Keep in mind, however, that the perfect church planter is a mythical beast. Wonderful and talented new church planters are out there, but to work with them effectively, the sponsoring team must understand the needs and concerns of the church planting ministry and, ultimately, the task to which it is called.

Chapter 6

What Denominational Leaders Are Saying

om and I have served as pastors, church planters and denominational servants at all levels—association, state, and national. We both heard jok-
ing remarks when transitioning to the denominational positions that we
were "leaving the ministry." Denominational leaders will always have to deal with
those who fail to find objective scriptural support for their work (although I dare
say Paul's ministry was the model for my work at the state convention level).
Still, the survey demonstrates that in the question of whom one is going to call for
sponsoring resources, denominational leaders are the first ones pastors and church
planters are likely to approach.

. . . About Funding

The survey identifies several challenges for denominational leaders. In responding to the survey, these leaders at the denominational level said that a fully funded
church planter is only somewhat important or of little importance, whereas pastors
and church planters were more likely to feel that full funding is very important.

Group	Very Important	Somewhat Important	Little Importance	Not Needed
Pastors	48.9%	32.9%	12.5%	2.3%
Church Planter	63.4%	19.5%	9.8%	4.9%
Denominational	23.3%	43.3%	25%	6.7%

Potential sponsors and church planters put denominational leadership into a win-lose situation. Both believe a lack of denominational funding is a hindrance to their church planting efforts, but neither planters nor pastors want to give up primary supervision or accountability to the denomination. Now the good news here is that on the whole, denominational leaders, more than the other groups, do not want supervision and accountability responsibility.

Lack of Denominational Funding			
	Certain Death	Major Hindrance	Minor Hindrance	No Hindrance
Pastors	6.8%	22.7%	45.5%	22.7%
Church Planters	0%	43.9%	24.4%	24.4%
Denominational	5%	16.7%	55%	23.3%

The Local Church Should Provide Primary Supervision and Accountability			
	Strongly Agree	Moderately Agree	Moderately Disagree	Strongly Disagree
Pastors	60.2%	25%	6.8%	3.4%
Church Planters	51.2%	39%	4.9%	2.4%
Denominational	60%	36.7%	3.3%	0%

So long as denominational leaders emphasize denominational funding, this difference of perspective will continue to exist. With funding comes accountability, and financial accountability goes beyond good discretion. It is a legal and moral imperative. Therefore, it may be best to limit financial funding as much as possible. Despite what most church planters and denominational leaders believe, the connection between funding and attendance does not appear to exist. Ed Stetzer has shown that financial support is not a primary factor in the success of a church start. He writes, "Greater funding does not automatically lead to a higher mean attendance."[1] Notwithstanding, most church planters surveyed by Stetzer believed that increased funding would result in increased attendance in their situation. If that were true, the following graph, copied from Stetzer's report, would show a steady left-to-right incline. One would expect that greater annual funding from the

---

[1] *An Analysis of the Church Planting Process and Other Selected Factors on the Attendance of SBC Church Plants.* Ed Stetzer (Alpharetta, GA: North American Mission Board), 2003, 22. http://www.newchurches.com/public/resources/research/docs/Summary%20of%20the%20study.pdf Accessed December 11, 2005.

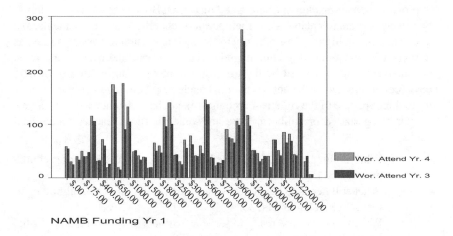

NAMB Funding Yr 1

denomination (the yearly support ranged from 0–$22,500 among those researched) should automatically lead to larger churches. Instead, the results demonstrate little or no relationship between funding and worship attendance.

Denominational leaders were less likely than others to view the financial limitations of the sponsoring church as a major hindrance to church planting. The implication is that they might encourage a church to forge ahead with sponsoring a new work without adequate financial preparation.

Sponsoring Church Financial Limitations			
	Certain Death	**Major Hindrance**	**Minor Hindrance**	**No Hindrance**
Pastors	8%	38.6%	38.6%	8%
Church Planter	2.4%	29.3%	43.9%	22%
Denominational	1.7%	28.3%	50%	18.3%

. . . About Equipping

Our study demonstrates that denominational leaders are in the best position to provide sponsoring church training. In fact, 56.7% of pastors and 53.7% of planters identified a denominational or associational entity as their first stop for sponsoring church resources.

Denominational leaders with church planting assignments must know the available resources when the call for help comes. These leaders are in the right position to provide sponsoring church training and materials. Boot camp or basic training-type events for church planters and their partners, church planter assessments, and help enlisting multiple sponsors/partners for each new church were also rated as important in our sponsoring church study. These services and training are often best delivered and promoted by the local denominational entity. In areas where resources are limited or the denominational leader serves as a generalist, the ability to direct people to the right resource may make the difference between a new church being started or stillborn. Here are some questions for denominational leaders:

- What training events need scheduling for potential sponsoring church pastors and leaders?
- What still needs to happen in order to enlist and prepare qualified mentors for church planters?
- Which churches are ready to serve as partners or sponsors, and at what level of commitment are they prepared to do so?
- Which pastors need to be contacted about potential sponsoring church involvement?
- What is needed to create a "sponsoring church planting friendly" environment?

The answers to these questions may determine the ongoing success of the denominational church planting objectives.

The importance of the supervisor having a weekly meeting with the church planter was noted by 56.7% of denominational respondents as very important. Among pastors and planters, the numbers are about 10% less. These numbers suggest that leaders are taking to heart research that shows weekly meetings with church planters can have a significant impact on the viability of the plant, whereas monthly or quarterly meetings with the planter did not make much of a difference.[2] Some advocate weekly meetings for the first few quarter, biweekly the second quarter, and monthly during the remainder of the relationship.[3]

One challenge not being adequately addressed is supervisor, coach, and mentor development. Many church planters simply do not have anyone qualified to assist in these areas. This is surprising considering the number of successful churches planted in the past decade. Each of these churches should be able to provide at least one coach or mentoring leader, but many "successful" church planters are too busy to provide the time and effort mentoring takes. One step towards the solution will be to ensure pastors and planters recognize that success means they have a successor. Another step is to take part in mentoring and coaching training that is readily available.

Questions that should be asked by both denominational leaders and pastors who are or will be sponsoring new churches are:

---

[2] Ibid, 4.
[3] Steve Onge and Tim Roehl, *Coaching Missional Leaders* (2004, handbook), A.2:1.

- Who am I mentoring?
- Can I measure my success by who I have equipped as a successor?
- Do I need to participate in mentor or coaching training?
- Do I value mentoring/coaching enough to devote time each week to the task?

. . . About the Church Planter

Recently I assessed two potential church planters who did not fit the traditional profile of a church planter. Both men had over twenty years of pastoral experience, both were pastors of successful churches, and both had successfully weathered the ups and downs of ministry. These candidates challenged the stereotype of the church planter in terms of average age and ethnicity. One was Hispanic and desired to plant a multicultural church; the other was over 50 and desired to start a bivocational new work. The point is that the "average" church planter is in reality limited to one's preconceived image. Although some may imagine church planting as a young man's task, lead church planters can be retirees beginning a "second career" or recent immigrants—just as often as they will be twenty-somethings right out of seminary. What is important, at least to 88.3% of denominational leaders surveyed, is that the planter knows and understands the community.

Every church planter needs financial support, ministry workers, and mentors. It is easy to understand how new plants require financial support and workers—I seldom come across a church that does not desire more of these two resources. But the need for mentors is something many do not consider. Over the past few years I have attended several church planting conferences sponsored by nondenominational groups, evangelical denominations outside of my own faith tradition, and my own denomination's North American Mission Board. Many of these conferences have involved hundreds of church planters, pastors, and missional leaders. One topic continuing to rise above the smoke and clouds of methodology in all of these conferences is the need for coaches and mentors. Later in this book, Tom will be sharing insights on the topic of supervision and coaching.

Mentors can ask the relevant questions ensuring church planters are getting to know and understand the community. In my denomination, mentors are invited to be a part of the basic training or "boot camp" for church planters. To encourage participation and understanding of this important role, a separate day-long mentor-training component was developed for prospective mentors. However, while I have trained 320 persons in "Basic Training for Church Planters," only eleven during this time frame participated in the mentor training and only one in five church planting teams had a mentor, despite our request that every team bring one. The church planting goal of "mentor secured" is highlighted in this training[4]; however,

---

[4] *Basic Training for Church Planters* (North American Mission Board: Alpharetta, GA), 2005, 1-04

the selection of a mentor is generally left to the church planter and therefore left undone. Denominational leaders need to work with pastors and successful church planters to raise up a generation willing to strike blows for the kingdom by serving as mentors and coaches. A generation willing to ponder these kinds of questions:

- Have we enlisted a mentor, supervisor, or coach?
- Have we discussed supervision/mentoring with the sponsoring church?
- Are we willing to be accountable to others?
- Who on the team will be participating in "boot camp" or a similar event?
- Have we invited the team's supervisor or coach to this training?

. . . About Multiple Sponsors

The vast majority (amounting to more than 80%) of pastors, church planters, and denominational respondents agree that it is either somewhat important or very important that multiple sponsors work together to help plant a church. Ironically, whereas 73.2% of church planters identified multiple sponsors as "very important," only 46.7% of denominational leaders and 47.7% of pastors marked it so. For church planters, having more sponsors equates to more prayers and resources. But to pastors and denominational leaders, having more sponsors leads to greater potential for communication breakdowns and misunderstandings.

One of the most effective examples of multiple sponsors was the 5-1-5 plan used by the Home Mission Board (SBC) in the 1980s. Rick Warren's Saddleback Church was one of the 5-1-5 church plants, where five partners worked together to start one church with a five-year commitment. Many have no idea that Rick was supported by a network of partner churches. Many who attempted to emulate Saddleback's style and strategy just did not have the strong support base Warren had. For Saddleback, it did not take five years for the church to "go it alone," but the case of multiple partners obviously is strong and should be considered when the culture, context, and need indicate a single sponsor is not enough.

Wrapping It Up

The role of the denomination in church planting has changed, at least for many denominations. Not too long ago, fully funded denominational church planters (called "Church Planting Apprentices") were sent out for two years with the task of starting a new church. Although some were successful, a majority of those I observed spent the last six months of their appointment seeking pastorates or other jobs to fall back on when the funding ran out.

Today, denominational leaders are primarily supporting the local church in their efforts to become successful spin-off churches. Many of these denominational leaders have been pastors or church planters, and most of them are in touch with the heart and mind-set of the local church leader. Nevertheless, the pastor needs to take the lead in providing oversight, finances, and supervision for the new church. To put these roles back upon the denomination is a step away from the New Testament ideal and creates a model ultimately nonreproducible. In the hands of the local church, however, we can radically impact our world through church planting.

Part 3

Finding the Church Planting Model That Fits

Jesus commissioned us to go and make disciples of all nations. Many Christians around the world have the growing conviction that discipling the nations will only be achieved by having a church—the shopping window of God—in walking distance of every person on the globe. The church must again become the place where people can literally see the Body of Christ, where his glory is revealed in the most practical of all terms— hands-on, down-to-earth, right-next-door, unable to overlook or ignore, living every day among us.

— *Wolfgang Simson*

Chapter 7

Becoming a Sending Church

"So Jesus said to them again, 'Peace be with you; as the Father has sent me, so send I you.'"
—John 20:21 NIV

"Beloved, you are acting faithfully in whatever you accomplish for the brethren, and especially when they are strangers; and they bear witness to your love before the church; and you will do well to send them on their way in a manner worthy of God. For they went out for the sake of the Name, accepting nothing from the Gentiles. Therefore we ought to support such men, that we may be fellow-workers with the truth."
—3 John 5–8 NASB

The healthy church today exists by mission just as fire exists by burning. A mission-less church becomes a faithless church. Leighton Ford has said that "God is raising up a new army of Kingdom volunteers in our day. Across every continent are emerging 'World Christians'—young women and men with world horizons, committed to 'Exodus' lifestyles, possessed by the gospel of discipling the nations to Jesus Christ the Lord."[1] Just as the postmodern age is coming into adulthood, the mission field is facing its biggest challenge and brightest possibility of reaching unreached people worldwide. Right in the midst of this challenge, we see that the local New Testament church is still the key to fulfilling the Great Commission, and that there are two ways it can be accomplished. One is by the existing church growing larger, and the other is the birth of new churches.

---

[1] Leighton Ford, *Perspectives on the World Christian Movement* (Pasadena: William Carey Library, 1999), xi.

The purpose of this chapter is to provide assistance to those churches desiring to become true "sending" churches through the planting of healthy reproducing churches. Dawson Trotman is correct that "fulfilling the Great Commission is the ability of the maturing church to be able to reproduce in healthy fashion." [2]

The Nine Who Have Your Back

I encountered a man who worked at the local armory just a few miles up the road from the congregation I pastored. He served as a weekend supply sergeant once a month while working a fulltime job during the week. Over lunch one day he explained to me the power of the United States Army, the preparedness, and what we as Americans do or do not do to prepare our military forces for war. He reminded me that when the United States goes to war, every fighting soldier has nine others behind him, supporting and supplying exactly what is needed to be successful. He told me about a line of communication and supports that is second to no other nation's fighting force. I have never forgotten his comments that day regarding the nine who have your back.

As I have said before, no generation of Christians has been fully obedient to Christ's Great Commission, and no generation of human beings can be reached except by the Christians of that generation. According to the promise of God, some generation will stand before the Lord and say, "It is finished. The task you have given us to do, we have accomplished." [3] The call of God on a church sender's life is equally as vital as the call on the one who does the church planting. As we go out in church planting ministry, let us remember that individuals and churches have our backs. They are absolutely essential in the lines of communication and support for those planters and planting teams. Any individual and any church can get involved in the Great Commission as a sender or sending church! Those who go could never proceed were it not for the senders providing opportunity and support. That is why I love our denomination's method of sending missionaries and planting churches all over the world. I love churches and pastors who realize they can be a growing local church while staying active in the mission's efforts through church planting, which is so vital to reach our world with the gospel.

Mission-minded churches truly bear the label "sending church." What is a sending church, and how can one become that? Tim Steller has said that "there are only two ways for us to respond to the truth about the supremacy of God in missions. We must either go out for the sake of His name, or we must send and support such people who do, and do so in a manner worthy of God." [4] Sending churches are either those who actively go out in missions as an active part of the

---

[2] Pastor's Update Listening Guide: Nurturing a Heart for Birthing New Ministry, Featuring John Vaughan, Tape 5027, vol. 50.

[3] Robert McQuilkin, *The Great Omission: A Biblical Basis for World Evangelism* (Grand Rapids: Baker Book House, 1986), 82.

[4] John Piper, *Let the Nations Be Glad* (Grand Rapids: Baker Academic, 2004), 235.

churches' missions strategy, or those who, also as part of their growth strategy, send out church planters and mission teams to launch new churches. Sending churches have as part of their DNA the call to plant new churches locally as well as globally.

The Church Planting Group of the North American Mission Board reports the following conversion growth statistics for new churches:

- Churches zero to three years in existence average ten converts per year per one hundred members.
- Churches three to fifteen years in existence average five converts per year per one hundred members.
- Churches fifteen plus years in existence average one and a half converts per year per one hundred members.[5]

This seems clearly to affirm the need for churches to be planted, and through the planting of reproducing churches we will reach a diverse world with the gospel.

What Does the Term "Spin-off Church" Imply?

A "spin-off church" can mean different things to different organizations, and it is probably even different for each sending church. For some, a spin-off church will involve the sponsoring church providing the greater part of the prayer, planning, personnel, and proceeds for the church plant. For others, especially those who are testing the water as "entry-level" partners, the process of spinning-off a church with one or two of these resources is a worthy starting point.

What Kind of Churches Can Become Spin-off Churches?

All kinds! Many think only large churches could successfully spin-off a church. But experience has shown that even a church of 100 or fewer people can rally behind a church plant sufficiently to provide not only the emotional and spiritual support needed but in fact most of the financial needs as well. Of course, larger churches can muster even more resources for these needs.

What Are Some of the Requirements for a Sponsoring Church to Spin off a Church Plant?

A sponsoring church must be committed to the cause of discipleship and evangelism, committed enough to be involved solidly in the oversight of their church

---

[5] Richard H. Harris, "Developing a 2020 Vision," Vice President's Address to State Directors of Missions and State Director of Evangelism in Houston, Texas (July 28, 1998).

plant and church planting team. Note that this does not imply the church must have excelled in every facet of evangelism, but rather that they are anxious to see a bigger picture and participate in a more substantial way than simply writing checks. Sending churches need to be involved in at least three areas: growth, love, and trust. If the sending church lays a strong foundation in these three areas, it is likely that every other detail will fall into place.

What Is Meant by Providing "Growth" for the Church Planter?

Each sending church should be providing "growth messages" to its church planters on at least a monthly basis. These messages can go farther than merely written communication. For example, inviting the prospective church planter to spend three months with the senior minister and staff at the sending church can send a definite and encouraging signal to a planter that this effort is put together by a team. Also, it communicates a desire for a true spiritual partnership by showing the sending church taking appropriate responsibility. Furthermore, church planters will sense the shepherding hand of the mother congregation serving as the sponsoring entity.

Study the first eight verses of 3 John and notice that by the time the apostle John wrote this—somewhere around AD 80–95—he was in his latter days of ministry. He was thankful and happy that at this stage of life he could look back and see how young Gaius, one of his ministers, had sent others out for the cause of Christ's name. Now it was reported back to the Elder just how wonderfully pastor Gaius had supported those traveling missionary efforts. John reminds us of the high privilege of working together to build the Christian movement. We should be excited when we hear of a new church being started. Are we willing to send others out to influence the world in the cause of Christ?

How Should We Respond?

This text in 3 John gives us a clear pattern for our sending out laborers into the fields. John declares we are to send them on their way in a manner worthy of God. Young Gaius was encouraged by John the apostle to be a sender. Becoming a sending church always begins with that first effort of becoming missional. When you search the New Testament for the phrase "to send on one's way," you will find nine uses of the phrase, and each time it occurs in a missionary sending context.[6]

Sending individuals out to plant healthy New Testament-style churches is the first way a church can become a sending church. When John wrote to his young pastor and colleague Gaius that "you will do well to send them [Christian missionaries]

---

[6] For further study of the Greek word *propempô* look in Acts 15:3, Rom 15:24; 1 Cor 16:6,11; 2 Cor 1:16; and Titus 3:15.

on their journey in a manner worthy of God," the apostle elevated the idea of church planting and church growth as high as possible. John was a tremendous model for Gaius, for Gaius not only opened his home but also his heart and finances to his guests as they began their journey. This included providing money and food as well as the washing and mending of clothes (cp. 1 Cor 16:6 and Titus 3:13). Our faith must be proved by our works (Jas 2:14–16), and our love must be expressed by deeds, not just words (1 John 3:16–18). There are many common excuses for not becoming mission-sending churches, and here are some of them:

- "If God wants us to do this, he or someone will tell us!"
- "God does not need our church to be a part of this! If he wants it done he can do it without us."
- "We are too young a church to begin mission sending."
- "We are not big enough yet to sponsor a new church."
- "There is no interest in our church for this."
- "We cannot fund a missionary at this time."
- "There is not enough time to do all we are doing and take on a new project."
- "We just can't send out our best leaders, because if we did so, our church would fail!"

None of these excuses begin to stand the test of Scripture. Remember, Moses had similar excuses in Exodus 3–4 for not going out as he was told, and God answered each one of those objections. His hand clearly displayed the majestic power behind those who send and those who go. Like Moses' excuses, ours shrink into the shadow of the Word of God. Remember the one who is boldly doing the work of God is sustained by faithful sending churches that stand tall in the difficult times as the adversary opposes advancement.

What Is the Motivation to Be a Spin-off Church?

It Honors God

We honor God when we practice church planting ministry. Sending out individuals and families to launch a new church is not only worthy of God, it is also befitting that we should seek such activity. A pastor or sponsoring congregation is never more godlike than when sacrificing to serve others. Since church planters are sent out as representatives of the Lord God, it is an act of service to assist them.

It Is a Witness to the Lost in This World

Another motivation for becoming a sending church is that the church's support of God's planter servant is a witness to the lost (3 John 7). When you look again at the passage in 3 John, it is apparent that many wandering teachers in the apostle's day were sharing their needs. While it is clear that God's workmen warrant assistance, the standard in the New Testament is that this support comes from God's people through God's churches. This act is a beginning point in reaching the world for Christ.

Obedience to the Lord

In 3 John 8 the apostle states, "We therefore ought to receive such." The ministry of support is not only an opportunity; it is also an obligation in our obedience to the Lord.

We Become Fellow Helpers and Joint Workers

The apostle John then gives another motivation for becoming a sending church by saying "we might become fellow helpers to the truth" (3 John 8). Young Gaius not only received the truth and walked in the truth, but he was also a coworker with the apostle John who helped to further the truth. John taught the young preacher the blessings of an open heart and a giving spirit towards promoting the truth.

The young preacher was admonished by the apostle to be a sender, and Gaius carried out his assignment diligently by making sure no missionary was lacking. For any church desiring to plant churches and become a sending church, it must be remembered that we plant churches and sponsor new works for the sake of God's name—not ours. And the name of God is at stake in how we treat our missionaries because the Lord is glorified when churches support these planters and ministers substantially through prayers, money, time, and assistance. For a sending church there are a number of practical ways one can accomplish this. The Lord on high is obviously not exceedingly excited when planters and missionaries are merely names on the back wall of the church. The same is true when we add their names to a line item in our church budget that no one knows about. Rather, sending churches keep planters and new plants before God's people so they can undergird them in all sorts of ways to advance the ministry. Sending is a great calling for the local church and the pastor leader of that growing church. The calling to become a sending church is a high one, so it should never be taken lightly, and it should never be dismissed as a job for someone else. Sending missionaries and church planters in a manner worthy of the Lord our God is a call to missional excellence. It is direct participation in the purpose of God.

I learned early as a church planter and member of a sponsoring church that there is a world of difference between a local church having missionaries and a truly missional church training and sending missionaries. Sending churches are intimately engaged in the cause of church planting, and they bring with this a heartfelt, Christ-centered passion for the lost and the advancement of the kingdom. Gaius learned from John how important it was for those who are spiritually healthy to remain obedient to the Word by sharing what they have for the further-ance of the truth. Not everyone is a John or even a Gaius, but all Christians share the same challenge in reaching the world for Christ.

The Challenge for Sending Churches

Today there is an enormous global challenge for all churches interested in send-ing missionaries out for new church plants. Our world is growing faster than the population of our churches. We see that:

- Nearly 360,000 people are born each day on planet Earth.
- Nearly 160,000 die each day all around the world.
- More than 100,000 souls accept Christ every day worldwide.
- Almost 1,000 new churches are born every week within Protestant Evangelicalism.

Of course the current effort for kingdom expansion is commendable in every way. This past year alone the North American Mission Board, along with its part-nering conventions within our denomination, started a record-setting 1,790 new churches. These efforts are encouraging, but the task is still unfinished, and there lies before us a great challenge in reaching North America. Whereas in 1988 there was one church for every 4,000 residents in any given community, by the end of the twentieth century this number declined to one church for every 6,500 resi-dents.[7] To gain the ratio of a century ago, more than 22,500 new congregations would be required right now.

For the last several decades Southern Baptists planted three new churches a day. Currently we have reached the level of 4.7 new church plants on a daily basis. That is an amazing total that probably only the real missionary can even under-stand. Here is how it breaks out: In 1966 we began a push towards church planting that culminated in a bold mission thrust towards the sponsoring of new churches. We slowly rose for the next twenty years to the point where we were planting an average of three churches a day by the end of 1996. Thirty years of continual growth, and yet we seemed to plateau around the 1,300 mark for most of the last third of the thirty-year span. Now we have moved that figure from 3 church starts per day to just short of 4.7 churches started each day for God's glory—in seven years. This is a significant net gain of 200 new churches from last year alone. A gain of 400 vibrant churches from the yearly 1,300 mark for most of the 1990s really is incredible. God is at work and using sending churches as part of this great missional effort. And yet almost every state of the union needs new churches in order to reach its continually growing population.

---

[7] Richard H. Harris, Address to State Directors of Missions and State Directors of Evangelism; Houston, Texas; July 28, 1998.

A Word of Caution

When I was in high school I won a prestigious award in athletics and went forward to receive a rather large trophy. As I walked off the stage, personally patting myself on the back and gazing at the trophy, I slipped off the front of the stage. I fell about three feet and watched my magnificent prize come crashing to the ground—and smash into pieces. I was so busy congratulating myself that I missed the significance of my achievement. I was asked if I wanted them to replace it. I thought about it and replied that I did not. I just took the pieces home and placed them in a drawer so I could be reminded of the achievement and of the need to keep all things in perspective.

Perhaps it is time for a little perspective on the sponsoring and planting of new churches. Maybe you haven't seen a new plant lately. It might not be as obvious in one area of the country as it is in another, but generally we have replaced missional zeal with the practice of organizational birth control. How do I know this? Because most churches across our convention are childless. Recent research found that only 3% of our Southern Baptist churches ever sponsored or planted a new church. Most of our SBC churches, and this is true of churches across all denominations, do not have a philosophy of ministry that promotes birthing new congregations.

How many small groups or Bible study classes in your church are childless? How many in your present congregation are unaware of their roots? Most churches across the land are not even familiar with how their own church was planted. A recent study by John Vaughn revealed that fewer than 1% of groups surveyed have plans to give birth.[8] No doubt the lack of a church birthing strategy and missionary mentality is unintentional. But we need to be intentional about church planting because birthing takes real sacrifice.

The Benefits of Birthing New Churches and Becoming a Sending Church

At least thirteen things (the "lucky thirteen") happen within sponsoring churches when those churches become actively involved in planting new churches:

1. Sponsoring keeps the church fresh and alive to its mission and vision and challenges the church's faith.
2. Sponsoring reminds the church of the challenge to pray for the lost.
3. Sponsoring enables the church to welcome other people into the kingdom that it would not otherwise have assimilated.
4. Sponsoring creates a climate open to birthing a variety of need-meeting groups within the sending church.
5. Sponsoring provides evangelistic vitality and activity.
6. Sponsoring encourages the discovery and development of new and latent leaders.

---

[8] *Nurturing a Heart for Birthing New Ministry Featuring John Vaughan,* Pastor's Update Listening Guide, vol. 50, tape 5027.

7. Sponsoring encourages coaching, mentoring, and apprenticeship in ministry while providing a renewed understanding of how we are all part of a team effort.
8. Sponsoring provides an occasion for church members to get to know missionaries personally.
9. Sponsoring builds on the past and insures the future.
10. Sponsoring minimizes the tendency toward a self-centered ministry.
11. Sponsoring provides an education in missions and serves as a stimulus for young people's dedication to Christian service.
12. Sponsoring provides a visible proof that God is still working through people and that some are responding to his commission to go out and evangelize.
13. Sponsoring provides a new opportunity for personal involvement in missions.

The Exemplary Missional Sending Church

The first five chapters of the book of Acts focus largely on the church as a group and what corporate life was like for the early Christian community. Leaders such as Peter and John figure significantly in these early pages. Beginning with chapter six, however, certain people—certain ordinary people in the sense they were not well-known leaders—begin to be featured in Luke's account. Their lives epitomize the type of people we can discover active within the sending church.

Think about the remarkable deacon Stephen, who was ordained simply to serve behind the scenes, doing everyday tasks and assisting others in ministry. Yet according to Acts 6:8, Stephen was full of faith and power, with the working of signs and wonders. He preached the Word with such fire and authority, and he became the first Christian martyr actually to suffer for the Christian cause in the New Testament. Stephen was not a vocational minister, and he probably was not a church planter, but he was definitely the sort of believer one would find in any sending church. Philip was another outstanding yet "ordinary" believer and church deacon. The book of Acts shows Philip either at home sharing his faith one-on-one or preaching the Messiah to large crowds in such places as Samaria.

Consider Ananias, the courageous helper of the newly converted apostle Paul. Ananias was a man of prayer who heard the voice of God and listened in great detail. Despite his understandable fear of Saul, Ananias obeyed the Holy Spirit, prophesied to Paul, laid his hands on him, and miraculously healed him. Ananias was not a missionary; he was just an ordinary believer whom God used in an amazing way.

The New Testament is chock full of missionary sending people. Many individuals did missionary-like functions but were never specifically called missionaries. Likewise, members of sending churches today assist their church in sending out missionary church planters. Even our Lord himself appointed seventy people to go out and begin missionary work. Sending Christians and planting Christians are all part of the local body of Christ. During the first few decades of the church, perhaps thousands were like Stephen and Philip, flowing with God supernaturally in their everyday lives. This is the kind of power God still wants pervading his sending church in the present day.

Exceptional Features of the Missional Sending Church

What are the common distinguishing patterns of Christians and churches active in sending out people to start new churches? The Bible richly describes the remarkable lives and activities of the Christians in the early church, and we can draw upon those exciting days to find the secrets to their power. Ten features from the Scriptures characterize sending-out people and churches.

One: They Are Highly Relational

An amazing quality of believers in the early church is seen in chapters one, two, four, and five of the book of Acts. Despite their varying racial, economic, and cultural differences, new Christians in the developing early church were in "one accord," remaining virtually unanimous in everything they did. They went from ministry to the Lord to ministry to each other, and they did not allow their differences to divide them. This shows they were highly relational for they produced a type of harmony that cannot be achieved by selfish people. Only those who make relationship with others a priority can access the resources required to live in harmony amid diversity. The sending church participant will also be relational, and both the sending and receiving components will make a priority of connecting with each other.

Two: They Are Energetic

The early church radiated an enthusiastic happiness and fervor for what God was doing in their midst. They were cheerful people, full of vibrant joy as they received the Word, lived and ate together, and preached the good news (Acts 2:41; 11:23; 13:48). When God's leading comes upon his followers, the fruit of joy ought to be evident. It is no secret that the world in our day eagerly awaits people like this. As the Spirit is poured out upon us in these last days, we must become vibrant in all that we do for Jesus. Sending-church participants are energetic and full of life and testimony.

Three: They Are Reverent

Had the early Christians been casual or flippant about their faith, as Christians sometimes are these days, the church would not have accomplished what it did. Instead, they possessed a clear-headed awe and respect for God and his missionaries. We are told that a holy "fear came upon every soul" (Acts 2:43; 5:5,11,13). What would happen if that same holy fear, that same intense awareness of God's awesomeness, came upon us today? I am sure it would move us as it moved them, to take our faith—and the hour we live in—seriously. This same reverence and fear must be present in us as we live for God at this decisive point in history.

Four: They Are Focused

"They continued steadfastly." This is a phrase that describes the early Christians' continual focus upon the kingdom of God (Acts 2:42; 7:55; 14:9). Despite the obvious great excitement of the hour and the lack of formal organizational expertise in the church, these new believers were not distracted by the things that often weigh down God's people today. Like an army, they had a singleness of vision and sense of mission to accomplish great things. If we are to remain a missional sending people, this kind of focus must be found in us, for we are commanded, "Be steadfast, immovable, always excelling in the Lord's work, knowing that your labor is not in vain" (1 Cor 15:58).

Five: They Are Unselfish

The early church was instructed to take care of the needy among them (Acts 2:44; 4:32–35). What must their attitudes have been like to generate and sustain this kind of commitment to one another? They were an unselfish people, willing to share what was theirs with those who lacked, free from the kind of selfishness that keeps people focused only on themselves. They sensitively shared their resources and demonstrated the great virtue of love. In doing so, they became a true pattern for us.

Six: They Are Positive

The second chapter of Acts reveals they were "praising God," a simple clue to their joyful optimism. Why weren't they worried, fearful, and pessimistic? Because they were aware they had a great God and an exciting future. Even in trying circumstances they praised God and gave glory to the Lord. This was one of their greatest qualities, and it should be one of ours as well. Sending or sponsoring church participants display this attitude in direct proportion to their optimism about Christian truth and world evangelism. Without it, we cannot truly be missional.

Seven: They Are Magnetic

The believers in the early church were magnetic people who possessed extraordinary power to attract others. Just as Jesus won the favor of the general public (Luke 2:52; Acts 2:41), these Christians engaged and were accepted by society. They never allowed the gospel message to become bad news; it remained good news—an attractive message. It was only the professional religious groups that hated the new believers. Think about it! What would happen if the sending church today reproduced this same quality of magnetism? No doubt our friends, neighbors, and acquaintances would be powerfully drawn to the Christ in us, instead of feeling that our message is irrelevant to their lives.

Eight: They Are Radiant

When one consults various texts in Acts, such as 2:4; 4:31; 6:3,5; 7:55; 9:17; 11:24; and 13:52, one can see the dynamic life of the Holy Spirit in these men and women who comprised the early Christian community. Believers depicted in Acts were filled with God's Spirit through times of prayer, fasting, and waiting on God to call. Holy Spirit visitation was the center of their activity. They understood and experienced times of refreshing (3:19), and walked with a radiant grace upon their lives (4:33). Without this same radiance present in us, we can never hope to be anything similar to a real missionary-sending church. In our own day we must rediscover the place of prayer in the church so we can try walking as the believers in Acts did, radiating the life of God wherever we go.

Nine: They Are Courageous

Though often overlooked, the fact is that boldly preaching the Word of God reveals a more prominent manifestation of a walk with God (Acts 4:13,29,31; 9:27–29; 13:46; 14:3; 18:26; 19:8; 28:31). When we read about these believers, we are reading about people who were outspoken, unreserved, and crystal clear in communicating with the world. The quality of bold courage is just as essential today for the missional proclamation of truth, to say nothing of the fact it is a solid indication of a right relationship with God. The Bible declares that "the wicked flee when no one is pursuing them, but the righteous are as bold as a lion" (Prov 28:1).

Ten: They Are Progressive

It is striking that the early church quickly broke with the standard religious convention of the day. For example, the temple was the center of activity for Jewish people, and yet the disciples quickly adapted to the use of private homes as meeting places for worship and fellowship. This shows an openness in the Christian community to new ways of doing things. Creative thinking guided their activity.

When they were free from prevailing religious methods, they were effective and grew at an astonishing rate. Today, I am happy to say, we in the church are beginning to show these same signs of innovation and practical thinking. Fresh, God-directed methods of evangelism, outreach, education, and discipleship, as well as inspiring approaches to domestic and world missions, will continue to breathe spiritual life into our ministries.

The Vast and Open Sea

The number one priority of the sending church is to be a sending church! A group of Christians cannot be a scriptural church unless and until it supports missions and does missions. One of the very first things any church can do to become a sending or sponsoring church is to take on and support a church planter.

Our seminaries and divinity schools need to emphasize to pastors-in-training the desperate need to plant churches. That isn't as easy to do early on in the ministry as supporting our world missionary causes, but it ought to be a definite goal and we should pray and plan for this from the very beginning.

The second responsibility of the sending church is to train church planters. We now have two types of planters who usually do church planting. One has been trained elsewhere. They know what they are doing, and they know what they want to accomplish. We need to assist these planters as much as we can, giving them much moral support and encouragement, as well as financial help.

The other type of church planter we have trained ourselves. They come to pastors asking questions about goal planning, and they bounce ideas around and ask for counsel. We are responsible for assessing and encouraging the gifts of these people, and we are responsible for preparing them for a church planting ministry if that is where they are headed. We better know what to tell them.

Third, the sending church is responsible for providing exposure for its church planters by keeping their names always before the congregation in much prayer. They are a "big deal," and we need to make a big deal about them for who they are and what they are doing for God's work on behalf of our church. Pastors should take them to ministerial meetings, introduce them to church staff and guest preachers, and make other pastors aware of their nascent church planting ministry. They are our colleagues in ministry, and they need to be treated as such. Whenever a missionary or guest is invited to speak in church, try arranging for them also to speak at the church plants.

The fourth responsibility is financial. Yes, money is needed for ministry, period. But it is probably best to emphasize that God always provides what is needed for finances, and not the sending church.

Antoine de Saint-Exupery once wrote that "if you want to build a ship, don't drum up the men to gather wood, divide the work, and give orders. Instead, teach them to yearn for the vast and endless sea." We must begin to teach our church members to yearn for the endless sea of the building of God's kingdom. And we need to teach them what it means to be a missional people and a missional church that is life-giving, Christ-glorifying, image-bearing, and multiplying.[9]

Wrapping It Up

A New Company of Spin-off Churches Is Coming!

Christians in "sending churches" are equally as important as the men and women who "are sent." But the senders should be doing a lot more for the sent, more than planning a going away fellowship, patting the church planter on the back, and saying goodbye. Here are five areas of support that most healthy churches could do in sponsoring a church plant.

Be an Anchor at Home

It is amazing how knowing there are individuals and a whole church saying "we are here for you" can make a big difference. When the hard times come, the sponsoring church and its members serve as an anchor for encouragement, advice, and direction.

Dotting the "I's" and Crossing the "Ts"

The fundamental thing a sending church says in sponsoring church plants is that they are willing and able to help in any way they can. This means helping with all the various organizational matters that come up so church planters and teams can do the work of the ministry.

Moolah, Means and Money

When it comes to finances for the mission church, a penny sent is a penny well spent.

Forget the Apples, Pray Instead

"An apple a day keeps the doctor away!" But when it comes to spiritual warfare, a better phrase for sponsoring a new church is "forget the apples and pray instead." Prayers each day will help keep the devil away. In supporting the new

---

[9] Jamye Miller, interview with Milfred Minatrea, June 7, 2002, and quoted in Milfred Minatrea, *Shaped by God's Heart: The Passion and Practices of Missional Churches* (San Francisco: Jossey-Bass, 2004), 8.

church planter and planting team, the prayers of the sponsoring church avail very much.

Repetition Reduces Resistance

"Say my name; say my name" are lyrics to a popular Christian song. Remember that on a regular basis the leaders of the sponsoring church need to say the church planter's name—and the names of his team members—in front of the sending congregation. Members should be encouraged to contact the planter, to be an encouragement, and to keep in close communication. People in every church would love to shoulder this task and make it their special ministry. All that is keeping them from volunteering in this way is that they are not informed of the great need and tremendous opportunity to bless these church planting missionaries by saying hello!

As a sending church, it is vital to develop a high level of support for church plants in every area. The higher the support, the lower the chances churches will become demotivated and sidelined from the cause of evangelization and kingdom expansion.

Have you heard about the new types of people cropping up in our churches? They are called "tater people." Some of them never seem motivated to participate in anything. They are content watching while others do the work. These people are called "spec taters." Others never do anything to help, but they are gifted at finding fault with the way others do things. They are called "comment taters." Some are very bossy and like to tell others what to do, but they don't want to soil their own hands. These are the "Dick taters." Other church people are always looking to cause problems by asking others to agree with them and oppose those who don't. It is too hot or too cold, too sour or too sweet. They are called "agie taters." Then there are those who say they will help, but somehow they just never get around to actually doing what they promised to do. They are "hezzie taters." Some people can put up a front and pretend to be someone they are not. They are "Emma taters." And thankfully there are those who love others and do what they say they will do. They are always prepared to stop whatever they are doing and lend a helping hand. They bring real sunshine into the lives of others. They are called "sweet taters," and they are the ones advancing the kingdom.

How do we build and advance the kingdom of our God? How do we participate in seeing the kingdom come here on Earth as it is in heaven? Do we have a responsibility to work for the kingdom, or can we just sit back and watch it happen? What kind of "tater people" are we? In his book, *Why Prayers Are Unanswered*, John Lavender retells a story about Norman Vincent Peale.

When Peale was a boy, he found a big, black cigar, slipped into an alley, and lit up. It didn't taste good, but it made him feel very grown up . . . until he saw his father coming. Quickly he put the cigar behind his back and tried to be casual. Desperate to divert his father's attention, Norman pointed to billboard advertising the circus. "Can I go, Dad? Please, let's go when it comes to town."

His father's reply taught Norman a lesson he never forgot. "Son," he answered quietly but firmly, "never make a petition while at the same time trying to hide a smoldering disobedience."

This is a great truth, because only when we take personal ownership of the kingdom can the kingdom be built. Do we take personal ownership? Will we take ownership of the kingdom of our Lord God? Will we become kingdom builders by becoming sending churches?

When will we become sending churches? Are our eyes open to the despair and chaos that exist around us? Have we noticed that the walls of the kingdom are in danger of falling down and that the very fire of hell has burned them? Have we become brokenhearted because of the despair of our people? Have we come to the place of weeping, praying, and fasting? It all begins here. If we really want to see God build his kingdom here, we must repent. For it is only when we repent to God that he is obligated to work in our midst. Have we taken ownership of the part we each play towards sponsoring churches, or is someone else doing all the kingdom building?

Let us determine to build the kingdom through open eyes, a God perspective, and personal ownership. When we calculate the enormous task of the world evangelization that has become the responsibility of this generation, we must depend upon a sweeping move of the Holy Spirit. Otherwise there will be no success. Nearly four billion souls around our world remain unacquainted with the Good News and the true saving power of Christ. We have used satellites, video, and shortwave radio to reach them. Although progress has been made, it is only by becoming more apostolic and by the planting of new churches that we can hope to see the world turned upside down for the Lord. We need a continually growing army of men and women with all types of spiritual gifts to reach billions of unreached peoples in our generation. In these days God will not call just twelve apostles to change the world. Instead, he will establish a vast company of apostles who will be supernaturally empowered. The Holy Spirit will be poured out upon the entire church in a brand new dimension, allowing the church finally to accomplish its mission. When the next great move of God hits Earth, we will see arising another company of sending and going people.

Here is a short "sending church prayer" that may help as churches move forward in becoming sending organizations while sponsoring new church starts.

A Sending Church's Prayer

Oh Lord, possess us with your Holy Spirit
So that we cannot remain idle.

Remind all of us that we still must go,
Still must send,
Still must reach out to the lost!
As we go we will pray the Father,
Preach the Son,
Speak to the lost, and sound praises to your name.
Keep a burning light within us,
So we cannot stop planting new churches!
Remind us again and again that sponsoring new churches
Allows us to serve you, Oh Lord, on the edge.
For it is there that we have the most exciting and
Rewarding adventure that any church could ever have.

Doing missions means sending the brethren out to start new churches. The Gospel of John describes the sending of the Son by the Father: "As the Father has sent Me, I also send you" (20:21). This is absolutely the correct model and also our grounds for continuing to build a mighty force to accomplish the Son's mission.

Chapter 8

The Multisite Church

An Alternative Approach to Reaching New Communities

Church consultant and congregational change leader Lyle Schaller uses the following story to illustrate a paradigm shift that is fueling the multisite church planting movement in this country.

Yesterday. *"That's the First National Bank at the corner of Main and Washington, and directly across from it is First Church, where we have been members since we moved here thirty years ago. The college is up on the hill, our hospital is about a half mile to the west, and our doctor has his office in that building over there."*

Today. *"That's the First National Bank, but I haven't been there for years. We do all our banking at a branch supermarket where we buy groceries. We're members of First Church, but we go to their east-side campus, which is near our house. We have one congregation but three meeting places—a small one on the north side, the big one out where we live, and the old building downtown here. The old college on the hill is now a university. This is their main campus, but they also offer classes at three other locations. We're members of an HMO that has doctors in five locations, but my primary-care physician is in a branch about a mile from where we live. I've never been in the main hospital except to visit a couple of friends."*[1]

---

[1] Lyle Schaller, *Discontinuity and Hope: Radical Change and the Path to the Future* (Nashville: Abingdon Press, 1999), 174–75.

The preceding narrative illustrates the direction our world is going—institutions are growing larger and smaller simultaneously, blending the strength that size offers with the comfort and convenience of smaller, closer venues. The multisite church is a response that seeks to reach a generation that values the blended benefits provided by much of society.

A growing number of churches today continue as one congregation with one vision, one staff, one treasury, one membership roster, one governing board, and one name. But these churches may have three, four, five, or more worship venues each week. Schaller notes, "Several satellite congregations have discovered that their off-campus ministries are the most effective channels for reaching skeptics, agnostics, nonbelievers and inquirers at the very earliest stage of their faith journey and from a financial perspective, this may be the most cost-effective approach to evangelism."[2] Additionally, many multisite churches are finding greater evangelistic response and attendance at their extension sites.

The Multisite Phenomenon

The idea of one church with many satellites is not new. Elmer Towns challenged a group of church planters to consider using satellite and geographic expansion of their then-present church plants back in 1984. The idea of satellite congregations was promoted widely during the height of the Church Growth Movement by Elmer Towns, Charles Chaney, Lyle Schaller, and others. The current multisite movement, however, has been fueled not by theory but by successful examples.

For some, the multisite approach is but a pragmatic response to need. Jim Heaton, executive pastor of Westside Family Church (Kansas City, MO) notes that by the late 1990s their church was running five services and was out of seating room and parking space. A sixth service was not an alternative, and previous attempts to plant new churches had failed. For Westside, going multisite was a sound approach enabling them to realize their God-given mission.

At the 2004 meeting of the American Society for Church Growth held at Fuller Theological Seminary, Dave Ferguson, lead pastor of Community Christian Church in Chicago, noted the following statistics in a presentation on the multisite church.[3]

- 1990 = fewer than 10 multisite churches
- 2000 = fewer than 100 multisite churches
- 2004 = 1,500 multisite churches

---

[2] Lyle E. Schaller, *Discontinuity and Hope: Radical Change and the Path to the Future* (Nashville: Abingdon, 1999), 174–79, emphasis added. See also Lyle E. Schaller, *The Very Large Church: New Rules for Leaders* (Nashville: Abingdon, 2000), 110–12, 135–36, 192–94; Lyle E. Schaller, *Innovations in Ministry*, chapter 6, "Off-Campus Ministries" and chapter 8, "The Satellite Option" (Nashville: Abingdon, 1994), 86–97, 112–33.

[3] Dave Ferguson, "Multisite Churches," a paper given at the American Society for Church Growth, Fuller Theological Seminary, Pasadena, CA., November 4, 2004.

These numbers changed dramatically starting in 2005, because that was the year the multisite movement moved from the fringe to mainstream. Starting in 2005, conferences on the multisite church quickly sold out, and newspaper reporters called pastors and began asking questions about what was going on. That same year, our seminary included a lecture on the multisite church in our sponsoring church conference for doctoral students. Other schools did as well. These things, and many other things, indicated to almost everyone that the multisite approach, although not an alternative to church planting, could serve as a strategic means of reducing the unchurched population, resulting in kingdom growth. What are the different models for this burgeoning movement?

Major Approaches to the Multisite Church

- *The Franchisee approach*: As much as is possible, these new worship communities are "cloned." There is a "branding" element in this approach, where the sermon, songs, and other aspects of the worship service are generally copied from the mother or originating church. These often take on the flavor of a company owned franchise.
- *The Licensee approach*: These multisite churches are similar to ones following the franchisee approach, but they are not identical. About half of the elements are similar, but there is more contextual freedom. For example, there might be the same biblical text, but there might be a different presentation. One could envision this approach as being something like a privately owned franchise. In these cases, the site or "regional campus" might have its own budget, worship teams, and youth programs. Other components, including the message (often using a one-week video delay) and children's programs, may be clones of the main campus.
- *The New Venture model*: In this approach, the ultimate objective to starting the off-campus site is a new church plant. New venture models seek to start churches intentionally once the off-campus site demonstrates adequate maturity.
- *The Encore model*: In this model, an encore presentation of the service is held in another location. For example, holding a worship service on Saturday, and then doing the same service again on Sunday at another location using the same team. An encore approach may find the "main" service held at a local movie theater, then using the same team, an "encore service" might be held later that day at a local high school.
- *The Satellite model*: In this approach, a main campus might have dozens of satellite congregations meeting in various locations, including apartment buildings, homes, office buildings, and schools. This method may include features of what is called the cell church, with the difference being that the members of satellite churches usually are not expected

to come together in large celebration services, as is the case with cell churches. If most of the attendees never worship at the main campus, the churches are functionally satellite multisite churches rather than cell churches. (The Yoido Full Gospel Church in Seoul, South Korea, is an example of this.)

- *The Déjà vu model*: This model, which is similar to the franchisee approach, seeks to incorporate the elements of the original service to provide worshippers a familiar feeling and presence to the main campus worship.

- *The Third Place model*: From a book of the same name,[4] the third place model recognizes that for most people, their first place is their home, their second place is at work, and their third place is where they want to be—where they enjoy hanging out. Third places can be effective locations for multisite ministry. Going to where people want to be, such as theatres, sports cafés, coffee houses, community hang-outs, or other "third places" can reduce the barriers to the unchurched.

- *The Video Venue model*: Use of video or digital means to "cinematize" the church (and experience) including the worship and message in a second (or more) location. The use of tape delay allows for editing and involves less technology costs upfront. Often a church with multiple services will tape each service and use the best of the tapes. Some churches are experimenting with live feeds, which allow congregations to use the same worship guide and, if using two-way video, provide real-time interaction via video.

- *The Resurrection model*: Going into a dead or declining church and starting a multisite service. This model is becoming a popular and timely response to the thousands of church buildings that are vacant or host to declining congregations. This approach works especially well when the main campus has a number of members or families near the new site who are willing to attend the "resurrection" multisite location. Those adopting this model might consider a "funeral celebration" for the old church, then launching the new multisite.

- *The Multicultural model*: These multisites will use the same sermon and program that have been translated into the language and culture of the community. This is a potential response to transitional communities and can build bridges among cultures.

A Nomadic Approach to Ministry

A recent study shows that among all churches nationwide, 86% have their own facility and the other 14% use rented or borrowed space in schools or other

---

[4] Ray Oldenburg, *The Great Good Place* (New York: Paragon Books, 1989).

facilities. Among churches of my denomination (SBC), an overwhelming majority of congregations (96.7%) meet for worship in a church building, and in most instances (93.7%) the congregation owns the building. Only 7.4% of all congregations indicated they shared building space for worship with another congregation.[5] Buildings by their very nature suggest something fixed and permanent.

Among multisite congregations, however, these numbers are almost inverted. Many multisite congregations seek to be nomadic, allowing them to follow the movement of people in a community. Using rented facilities such as schools, movie theaters, YMCA's, community centers, industrial parks, restaurants, and sports bars, the church is able to avoid the long-term obligations of an owned building. For those who are building-centric—who think of "church" as believers always meeting at a particular geographical address—the nomadic model of the multisite congregation is a dramatic paradigm shift. A book such as *The Nomadic Church: Growing Your Congregation without Owning the Building,* by Bill Easum and Pete Theodore, explores the concerns raised by those who equate "church" and "building." Of course, not all multisite churches are nomadic. They simply outgrow their facility and adopt the multisite strategy to maintain fidelity to the vision and mission of the mother church. But many do not want to have a permanent and enduring edifice and, for them, the nomadic option is worthy of consideration.

The Multisite Benefits and Challenges

Going multisite provides a healthy congregation a mechanism to build upon their good name while at the same time providing that "new church" excitement. Historically, the multisite church is more like the church we read about in the book of Acts and the letter to the Corinthians, one church meeting house to house or in multiple sites. The advantages to the approach are many, including having a brand new church as well as a trusted brand, having a generalist as well as a specialist church staff, having a new church vibe along with a big church punch, and less cost and greater impact.[6]

There are also some disadvantages, because the multisite church approach by nature will tend to reproduce both the positive and negative aspects of the main campus. Homogeneity, unorthodoxy, the specter of superstar-status preachers—these and other questionable things are all characteristics that can be reproduced in the extended locations. And some multisite advocates see this strategy not as "a way," but rather as "the way," going so far as to teach against church planting itself. Another concern is that the multisite strategy does not generally allow

---

[5] Philip B. Jones, *Research Report: Southern Baptist Congregations Today* (Alpharetta, GA: North American Mission Board, 2001), p. iv.

[6] Dave Ferguson, "Multisite Churches," a paper given at the American Society for Church Growth, Fuller Theological Seminary, Pasadena, CA, November 4, 2004.

full autonomy for the off-site congregation, thus causing tension between the locations.

One of the major liabilities of the multisite strategy has to be human frailty. Consider, for example, if the pastor experienced a moral failure. In that case, the ripple effect surely would negatively impact the off-campus sites as much as the main campus. Such failures have occurred recently on what seems like a routine basis. The main church might experience a drop in attendance, and so will the satellites, but all sites can survive the ordeal by demonstrating the strength of community that is a characteristic of the true body of Christ.

Chapter 9

Sponsoring Set Free Churches

"**M**ister, God loves you!" was the announcement of the seven-year-old as she ran up to Ron Thomas while he was digging through a trash bin in downtown Los Angeles. After her proclamation, the little girl returned to the picnic her family was enjoying only a few yards away. The simple truth of those words from the mouth of a little girl broke Ron's heart that day.

Ron grew up in a Christian home in Tampa, Florida. His grandfather was a preacher. He knew about God and Christianity, but he never knew God personally in relationship. While running away from a bad divorce, his journey from Florida to Los Angeles took a tragic detour into a controlling drug habit. Ron was a professional chef by trade, and he had been a hard worker all his life. Then crack cocaine took over. He was so far down he was even ashamed to see his own reflection in a window or mirror. He was ashamed of who he had become, but God was not done with him! After the little girl's reminder of God's truth, the Lord began to speak to his heart and break down the shell he had erected. The Lord then sent another messenger about a half hour later. Chuey was a worker from Set Free Church,[1] and he was in the park passing out flyers about the first outreach Set Free was hosting in Los Angeles. He gave Ron a flyer and said, "We can take you away from this place." That touched Ron's heart, as he decided not to go back to the box in the alley he called home because he knew he would be tempted to use drugs. That night Ron slept under a bush in the park. The next morning he was one of the

---

[1] There are several ministries and parachurch organizations, including prison ministries and singing groups, using the name "Set Free." The one that we (Rod, Don, and Tom) are writing about in this book was started in 1992 by Pastor Willie Dalgity as a mission of Bryant Street Baptist Church, Calimesa, California. The Set Free churches discussed in this book are incorporated as nonprofit churches under the umbrella of Set Free Churches, SBC. If readers would like further information about these congregations, please go to the Set Free Web site at www.setfreerocks.com.

first ones to show up at the Set Free outreach. When the invitation was extended for those who wanted to accept Christ, Ron was the first one to respond. When the pastor pointed to the bus for those who wanted to go to the Discipleship Ranch, a two-month-long discipleship and detoxification process, Ron was the first one at the bus. God had changed his life. Today, five years later, Ron Thomas is the pastor of Set Free Church, Skid Row, in downtown Los Angeles. Many of the people he once did drugs with are now Christians because they saw what God had done in Ron's life. Ron also started a Set Free Church in Compton, a city having the highest shootings per capita in all Los Angeles County. God is an awesome miracle working God!

God has always loved the poor, the needy, and the broken people of this world. David writes in Psalm 72:12–14, "For he will rescue the poor who cry out and the afflicted who have no helper. He will have pity on the poor and helpless and save the lives of the poor. He will redeem them from oppression and violence, for their lives are precious in his sight." God has always challenged true believers to care for the poor. "Pure and undefiled religion before our God and Father is this: to look after orphans and widows in their distress and to keep oneself unstained by the world" (Jas 1:27). On judgment day God will honor those who have ministered to the poor, needy, and broken:

> Then the King will say to those on His right, "Come, you who are blessed by My Father, inherit the kingdom prepared for you from the foundation of the world. For I was hungry and you gave Me something to eat; I was thirsty and you gave Me something to drink; I was a stranger and you took Me in; I was naked and you clothed Me; I was sick and you took care of me; I was in prison and you visited Me." Then the righteous will answer Him, "Lord, when did we see You hungry and feed You, or thirsty and give You something to drink? When did we see You a stranger and take You in, or without clothes and clothe You? When did we see You sick, or in prison, and visit You?" And the King will answer them, "I assure you: Whatever you did for one of the least of these brothers of Mine, you did it for Me" (Matt 25:34–40).

God cares for the poor and needy, and for this reason he has always raised up the church to minister to them. This has been true from the beginning of the church, when the early Christians took care of their widows and fatherless: "For there was not a needy person among them, because all those who owned lands or houses sold them, brought the proceeds of the things they sold, and laid them at the apostles' feet. This was then distributed to each person as anyone had a need" (Acts 4:34–35).

Two examples of how God has raised up his church to minister to the needy during periods of spiritual apathy were John Wesley, considered the father of the Methodist movement, and William and Catherine Booth, founders of the Salvation Army. God took hold of John Wesley in eighteenth-century England at a critical time in history. After the established church would not allow him to preach in their church buildings, he went to the streets and preached to the common laborers. When Wesley said, "Give me the multitudes and we will change the World," he meant give me the poor and needy, the outcasts of church society, and God will change the world through them. History suggests that if Wesley had not been obedient to serve and evangelize the common man, England would have probably gone the way of France and the French Revolution, where thousands of innocent people died in the chaos caused by the religious wars. A century later God called William and Catherine Booth to tend to the poor and needy of East End, London, resulting in thousands being brought into the kingdom. As they ministered to the forgotten poor of society, the Salvation Army was birthed. Since that time God has chosen to use both movements to impact millions throughout the world.

Today among Southern Baptists and others, God has blessed the Set Free Church movement to minister to the drug addicts, the homeless, the poor, ex-cons, bikers, and the outcasts of society. In the past decade thousands have come to faith in Christ and overcome addictions and a life of crime to become productive citizens and solid Christians. These churches are multiplying throughout the United States, and in the last decade over sixty-five Set Free churches have been established in metropolitan areas all across the country.

The Set Free Story

Willie Dalgity grew up attending church and accepted Christ at a young age, but he walked away from the church. A native of Yucaipa, California, Willie married his high school sweetheart, Marsha. At the time, like many "carnal Christians," Willie was busy running his own business and living his own life, without regard for the Lord. Still, God was not done with Willie quite yet. In 1980 God drastically touched and changed Willie's heart, giving him a hunger for Christ and a desire to please him. Through a growing relationship with the Lord, Willie became involved in ministry at Bryant Street Baptist Church in Calimesa, California. He served as a deacon there for several years, and in 1992 he was called to minister to needy people in the Yucaipa area. He started his ministry at Bryant Street Church on Saturday nights. As they outgrew that location, they were able to rent a store front in town. In May 1993 Pastor Willie and his wife Marsha held their first public worship service at the store front. They soon outgrew those facilities as well. The next year they were able to purchase the facilities of the old First Southern Baptist Church of Yucaipa. The Lord blessed their ministry and expanded it. Soon the church was running two Discipleship Ranches, one for men and one for women; operating several Discipleship Homes; and providing GED, parenting, and anger management classes. They set up training schools for machinists, mechanics, and silkscreen operators, along with classes for those wanting to enhance their computer skills. The church was called Set Free, and it also developed schools to train potential church leaders and pastors.

On February 16, 2003, they opened their new facility on Calimesa Boulevard, an eighteen thousand-square-foot building on three-and-a-half acres. The church remodeled the interior and transformed the former State Farm Insurance building into wonderful worship facilities containing a five hundred-seat auditorium, state-of-the-art nursery and toddler rooms, and a Kidz Zone for elementary age youngsters. They also have an onsite bookstore. Each Sunday, the church averages 400 to 500 in attendance at their combined 8:30 a.m. and 10:30 a.m. worship services. The "Encounter" youth service is conducted during both Sunday morning worship services in the remodeled garage/repair bay.

For the past five years the Set Free Church of Yucaipa has been in the top one hundred churches in annual baptisms throughout the national Southern Baptist Convention, the top ten in the state of California, and the leader in the number of baptisms among the churches of the Inland Empire Southern Baptist Association. The congregation celebrated their fourteenth anniversary as a church on May 1, 2007, by hosting their seventh Car and Bike show. Since their inception, more than seven thousand people have gone through their discipleship programs, and today an average of one thousand new or newly committed Christians go through the Discipleship Ranch each year. God has blessed Set Free and helped them see the multitudes here and elsewhere turn to Jesus Christ for salvation.

Set Free is also a church-planting movement. Since 1995 they have helped plant more than twenty churches in the Inland Empire, five churches in the San Diego area, three churches in Los Angeles, and six up and down Central and Northern California. They have also had the privilege of starting churches in Atlanta, Seattle, Denver, Kansas City, Nashville, and Great Falls. These churches are themselves already reproducing other churches. There are many other major cities where the need for a Set Free Church or similar fellowship is great.

The Set Free Strategy

Although all sinners are welcome, the target parishioners for Set Free churches are the homeless, drug addict, ex-con, hard-core biker, and generally the disenfranchised of society. These churches solicit the people who "fall through the cracks of society," the ones most churches do not know how to touch, let alone minister to. But Jesus loves them and died for them, and he is raising up these churches as ministers of love and grace. The banner that adorns the front wall of the Set Free Church of Yucaipa simply proclaims, "SINNERS WELCOME." Sinners from the worst circumstances of life to the richest strata of society are welcome. They are special in God's eyes; that is why Jesus came "to seek and to save" those which were lost.

Let me share two stories of those targeted by Set Free. The first is the testimony of Chuck Snyder in his own words.

I was living in a field under a tree with a brother named Damien. We were lying, stealing, and cheating to support our heroin habits. One night we were asking people if we could pump their gas or clean their windows for money for food. (It was a lie; we needed money for a fix in the morning). A pastor came by. He said he would buy us some food but would not give us money. We agreed. We started talking. He did not condemn us but invited us to church.

For the next four months, we talked several times a week. He told us about the ranch where people go to kick drugs and alcohol. In 1997 we were ready to go. We went to Set Free and talked with Pastor Victor. He shared about his life of drugs and living on the streets. He shared with us how the Lord had delivered him from a drug habit. He prayed for us, fed us, and encouraged us to go to the Discipleship Ranch. I did not think I could make it after three days, but with God's help, I did. God has been so good to me. He has restored my family and helped me to stay clean and sober since I came to Set Free Church.

Today, Chuck Snyder is assistant pastor of the Set Free Church in Muscoy, California.

Some years ago Marty Souter was walking down a street in San Bernardino wearing cutoff jeans, a shirt with one button, and no shoes. He had been on the streets doing drugs and "existing" for seven years. He had a broken arm from a fight with some guys he owed money for drugs. That night a friend drove by and asked him if he wanted to go to an outreach.

"What's an outreach?'

His friend said that they would give him a hot dog there. He got in the car and that night he heard a simple gospel message and gave his life to Jesus. That same night Marty went to the Discipleship Ranch. The next day they prayed over his arm at the Ranch. Two days later he was painting a house using his healed arm. From that start, God has visibly and spiritually changed Marty's life! He is now the pastor of Set Free Church, Riverside, California, and is the minister of missions for the national Set Free Church movement. He has traveled with me all over the United States to help established churches plant Set Free Churches in the inner cities of their communities.

What makes the Set Free model effective in the inner cities? What biblical principles are they applying to their church planting methods that helped make an impact in the drug culture of our inner cities? I would argue that God has blessed them because evangelism is the heartbeat of the movement. Everything that Set Free does is geared toward *evangelism* because they understand what Jesus is saying in John 4:35: "Don't you say, 'There are still four more months, then comes the harvest'? Open your eyes and look at the fields, for they are ready for harvest." They take seriously the words of the Lord that he came to seek and to save those who are lost. They take it seriously because they know that many of the drug addicts and homeless of our inner cities are right on the "edge" of heaven or hell.

One overdose, one bad episode, and they are gone into eternity. Moreover, they believe God is patient, "not wanting any to perish, but all to come to repentance" (2 Pet 3:9).

The Meeting of Felt Needs

Set Free is a ministry-based church, reaching out to people where they are hurting. The idea is to help meet immediate needs so that they can then tell others about a deeper, greater need, Jesus Christ.

As the church goes into the needy areas of the cities to plant churches, it finds a place to give clothes away, provide food for the hungry, shelter for the homeless, and care for the broken spirits. It is a 24/7 ministry. If a drunk comes out of the bar at 2:00 a.m. knocking on their door for help, there is someone from Set Free to minister to them. If a battered woman and her children call for help in the middle of the night, Set Free will be there to help them. If a druggie is strung out and needs help, Set Free is there for them. If someone has no place to stay, Set Free will invite them in and provide shelter.

As Set Free meets the immediate "felt" needs of hurting people, these people become more open to allowing the church to share with them what the real need is—a personal relationship with Christ. It is not enough to pat someone on the back and say, "God bless you," when down deep the person feels disenfranchised and unwanted by the world. In their experiences, even the Christian church has treated them with contempt. As Set Free members meet their needs, they can see that God and his people love them in a very tangible way. The ability to love them where they are and as they are is critical. For Set Free, the saying, "love the sinner, but hate the sin" is a way of life.

Saturation Evangelism

The book of Acts tells us that the early church saturated the city of Jerusalem with the gospel: "Every day in the temple complex, and in various homes, they continued teaching and proclaiming the good news that the Messiah is Jesus" (Acts 5:42). This is the model used by Set Free churches. In 1996 the Lord led Pastor Willie Dalgity to start a church in San Bernardino, a city of 300,000. Approximately 30 to 40% of the people in this city live under the poverty level. Consequently San Bernardino is known for major problems with gangs, drugs, and crime. Pastor Willie and his church did not need to do a demographic study to find where their target group lived, nor did they require a detailed religious survey. Instead, they found out where Pizza Hut would not deliver after dark. That was where their target group lived. One Friday night, when they were doing an outreach in the Sunset district of San Bernardino, a policeman asked Willie what he and other church members were doing in the area. He said, "Don't you know that there was a big gang shoot-out last night?" Then he showed him the bullet holes in the wall behind where the band was setting up to play music. The only answer Willie could offer was, "This is where Jesus would be." That night seventy people accepted Christ and a church was born!

Saturation evangelism works in different ways. One way Set Free does it is to find a house or park with electricity to hook up their sound equipment. They then pass out hundreds of flyers inviting people to that location for free hot dogs and gospel music. Generally, on a Friday night, Set Free will play their music as loud as allowed and send members out into the community to invite people to the "party" where the music is being played. Using the PA system, throughout the evening members will share testimonies, play lots of music, and gather a crowd. The pastor will share a simple gospel message and give an invitation to accept Christ. Members mingle with the crowd and do personal evangelism. In the midst of this, often the Spirit of God moves in a powerful way with people coming to the stage to give their lives to Christ. Altar counselors are always available to help those who respond be sure of the commitment they made.

The evangelism effort is continued by doing daily follow-ups in the neighborhood. Set Free will usually do the Friday night outreaches for two months at a time in the same general area. It will find a place to give food and clothes away. It will rent a storefront building, perhaps bring people from the community in buses, anything to help get a church started.

Another aspect of saturation evangelism is that the planting of the church is a joint effort by all area Set Free Churches and often their sponsors. The churches in the area will help get the church started. They will send teams to do prayer walks and door-to-door witnessing, pass out flyers, and evangelism. They will bring their bands to play at the outreaches. They will send people to be a part of the church-planting team. In Set Free terminology, they literally do "takeovers" of communities.

The Discipleship Ranch

In a normal setting when one responds to a gospel presentation, we might say, "God bless you and we hope to see you on Sunday for worship." But when dealing with drug addicts or homeless or battered people, one has to take a far more intentional approach. In most cases these people do not know what they are doing in a few hours, let alone next Sunday morning. That is why Set Free will ask them if they want go to the Discipleship Ranch with them. If the convert agrees, they will take them that night. That is where the 24/7 approach is applied. If a person is coming down off a "high," they need personal attention. If they are lonely or scared or even suicidal, they need 24/7 attention and care. If they have accepted Christ, they need to start the discipling process immediately.

After Jesus raised Lazarus from the dead (John 11:43–44), he immediately instructed the disciples to "loose him and let him go." He still had the grave clothes of death binding his hands and feet and face. Today we need to realize that many

87

people in the inner cities are bound up with the "grave clothes" of hurts, pain, guilt, sinful habits, and destructive tendencies that have left them in the bondage of sin for years. Set Free understands this. The first step is to call people to come out of the graveyards, the places of death they have been living in for years. That is why the Discipleship Ranch is often a critical step in helping addicts overcome the past. The ranch is not a detox center, not a twelve-step-based program, nor is it a dude ranch. The Ranches owned by Set Free are where the "grave clothes" are unwrapped from the heart, minds, and bodies of the new believers.

At a Discipleship Ranch the new Christians are saturated with the Word of God, attending three Bible studies a day. They memorize Scripture daily, and if they will agree to stay for sixty days, they will memorize fifty Bible verses. They learn to pray together in community and cast all their burdens on the Lord. Set Free helps them build structure into their lives, where there has been none for years of addictive behavior. Discipleship Ranches are just a bunch of donated trailers out in the middle of the desert. The ranches are God's "boot camp" where people can start a new life, develop spiritual disciplines in their lives, and start walking with the Lord in a deeper and more meaningful way. There are no charges for anyone to come to the Ranch, and there is no waiting list to get people there. They will always find room for a new person. Although they can go day or night, they are asked to make a sixty-day commitment. A person can stay as long as he or she feels the need, and can leave at any time. The only requirement to go to the Ranch is desiring a heart change.

Discipleship does not stop after one leaves the Ranch. If converts choose to continue in the Set Free ministry, they can enter one of the "working homes" for free. After they get a job, they are asked to pay a program fee to help with the cost of rent, food, and utilities. While they are living in the working homes, or working on the church property, they are required to attend daily Bible studies and prayer time. All are taught how to do their own inductive Bible studies, and there is still a strong commitment to memorize Scripture.

Another aspect of discipleship at Set Free is on-the-job training. Jesus said, "As you are going, make disciples . . ." That is what they try to practice in the Set Free community, the goal of which is not just to develop followers but to develop leaders able to point the way out of darkness. Because of the emphasis on discipleship, the multiplication principle found in 2 Timothy 2:2—"and what you have heard from me in the presence of many witnesses, commit to faithful men who will be able to teach others also"—can be put into place at a faster pace than with most other church-planting models.

The Role of Faith

Due to the type of person Set Free chooses to minister to, their churches have little money, often no members with advanced education, few extraordinary abilities or talents, and a lack of resources many would think necessary for a church plant. All of this works against them. But the one thing working in their favor is that they do have faith in the Lord God Almighty who raised them up from death to life, changed them from the inside out, and gave hope where there was only hopelessness. The Set Free movement harkens to the words of Peter and John in Acts 4:13: "When they observed the boldness of Peter and John and realized that they were uneducated and untrained men, they were amazed and knew that they had been with Jesus."

How is faith lived out daily in the Set Free movement? New believers are taught that just as they received Christ by faith, they are to live every single day by faith. They believe what Paul wrote to the Colossian church: "Therefore as you have received Christ Jesus the Lord, walk in Him, rooted and built up in Him and established in the faith, just as you were taught, and overflowing with thankfulness" (Col 2:6–7).

If God leads them to step out in faith to start a church in a certain community, then that is what they do. They are not taught to look at bank accounts to see if it can be afforded. They do not consult demographic studies to learn if it is a logical or reasonable thing to do. For them, it is the call of God that matters. It is a faith issue, and if they sense he has called them to do it, they must do it. As they step out in faith and total obedience to God, remarkable things happen.

Set Free leaders learned from experience that the resources are in the harvest. As they go out in obedience to God, there will be people gloriously introduced to Christ. They will become the leaders of the new church. These new Christians will help them find a building, resources for food and clothing distribution, and places to do outreaches. The people they reach for the Lord out of the harvest field provide the finances. If Set Free waited until all the financial, personnel, and facility resources were provided, they would still be waiting. They have learned that God provides for all their needs through Christ Jesus our Lord, and that is the point of walking by faith.

The Set Free Church of Yucaipa feeds 350 people three meals per day on a daily basis. It also gives 100 pounds of food away daily to needy people and hot meals for 300 people each Wednesday night after church. They do all of this by faith, giving themselves for others and trusting God to provide. This ministry to the needy among us is duplicated by all the Set Free congregations, and they all hold to the faith principle that one can never out give God.

Sponsoring the Set Free Church

How can you and your church be involved in ministry to the poor, the needy, and the broken? I suggest sponsoring a Set Free church, or one that operates like it. Remember, a church can get involved at different levels, but it will never understand this ministry until they see it, feel it, and taste a bit of the Set Free flavor.

89

The leaders of the local church need to feel the heartbeat of the people at Set Free. They need to feel the uninhibited joy and thankfulness that so many of the people have because once they were dead but now they are alive. They need to feel the childlike faith that so many of the members exhibit in their daily lives. They need to observe those who have fallen in love with Jesus and are daily reading his love letter, the Bible, and believing the Word. They need to experience how Set Free prays, believing God will respond and rejoicing over his answers when he does respond. One can only know how to sponsor a Set Free church after one has attended their worship services, hung out at the Discipleship Ranch, and gotten to know several members.

The leaders of potential sponsoring churches should allow the people in their church to feel the Set Free passion by attending a worship service where attendees raise their hands in enthusiastic worship. They would benefit by visiting a Set Free outreach and hanging out with the people as they share Jesus with the homeless and the broken people of society. The first serious investment will be the time and resources required to make this visit happen. It is hard to see the passion of the new believers and to observe the Spirit of God moving in their meeting, and not have hearts set on fire for evangelism.

There are probably several people in your church who have been waiting for just such an opportunity to go out to the streets and minister to hurting people. Many church members come from very hard backgrounds and environments. Maybe they experienced the drug scene or made other bad mistakes. But they came to Christ and now they have a tender heart toward the dispossessed and hurting people in society. Perhaps they've always wanted to go out to the streets and engage in inner-city ministry, but no one has ever given them permission. This might be the time to introduce them to the Set Free fellowship. You might set a whole lot of your church members on fire for the Lord as they walk and work alongside the Set Free people.

Once you and others in the church have caught the vision and experienced the Set Free ministry firsthand, the next step is to inspire and challenge your church to get involved with planting a Set Free congregation in the urban area of your community. Challenge them by sharing your own experience or testimony with Set Free. Inspire the sponsoring church by allowing some of the people from Set Free to share their stories in one of your worship services.

Since the people in the church are at different levels of Christian maturity and commitment, the local congregation can get involved with Set Free at various levels. One of the most important and critical areas of inner-city ministry involvement is the participation of prayer teams. The battle we are facing is in heavenly places. Paul tells us plainly "our battle is not against flesh and blood, but against the rulers, against the authorities, against the world powers of this darkness, against the spiritual forces of evil in the heavens" (Eph 6:12). The only way to win the spiritual battle is with prayer warriors.

This is especially true in the battle for souls. When Satan controls people through drug or alcohol abuse or other destructive behaviors, he thinks he owns them. He controls them through abuse and brokenness. But he is a liar and he does not own them. He tries to convince people that they have sinned too horribly and too much, so much that God can no longer love them. There is no hope for them. But that is not true. In fact, God loves them so much he gave his Son to pay the price for their sins "so that everyone who believes in Him will not perish but have eternal life" (John 3:16). We need to win the battle for souls on the battlefield of prayer.

The sponsoring church can enlist prayer teams for the pastor and his family, and for other church staffers, because when they step out in faith to start a church in the inner city, they have a bull's-eye target on their back. If the enemy can knock down the church starter, then the church start will never happen.

As I have worked with church starters, I have learned they are mostly vulnerable in the areas of family, finances, and health. If the church starter gets wrapped up in any of these issues, it will wear him out and discourage him and his family. If they quit, the enemy wins. We need to pray for the family that God will protect them from fear, failure, and discouragement. And we must not forget to pray for the family's health, especially the children—that God will keep them healthy. Pray for the pastor's wife, that God will not allow her to get discouraged by financial pressures. Pray for the church starter, that he will not be allowed to get sidetracked by issues that do not matter for eternity.

This prayer team needs to have people committed to pray every day for the pastor and his family. They need to pray specifically, asking the new-plant pastor to share issues in his personal and ministry lives that can be supported in prayer.

Another team can pray specifically for the ministry setting of the inner-city harvest field where the church is located. That means on occasion going to that location to pray. This could be done once each month or, better yet, on a weekly basis. Some of the team members may not be able to go out each week, so one good alternative is to find a detailed map of the area to pray over the individual streets.

This team should also pray for the ministry opportunities that the church has in the inner city. They know when the services are being held, so specific prayer at those times should be lifted up to the Lord. If the church plant is having an outreach that week, there needs to be specific prayer for that event and for the people involved in the event. As the team communicates with the pastor, he will give them names of special people who need a touch from God. In this way, the ministry prayer team can target those prayer requests.

It is also important to have a crisis or emergency prayer team—a prayer team for those crucial and critical times that can occur at any hour, day or night. This team needs to be made up of dedicated prayer warriors who know how to pray passionately for desperate and decisive situations. They might get a call at 2:00 a.m. asking for prayer for a woman who has been severely beaten by a drunken boyfriend. Or they could get a call to pray for the newborn baby of a drug addict, or for a family that was just notified their thirty-year-old son died of an overdose

91

on the streets. Members of this prayer team must be utterly willing and committed to pray at such crisis moments.

Additionally, the sponsoring church can develop a support team to deal with such things as providing supplies and materials. Members of this team know where materials can be found in their particular community. They are the "supply" lines for those on the front lines in the inner city. A support team is needed especially if Set Free is starting a church in a city where they have no local connections. One such city was Denver. A few years ago Set Free was asked to go to Denver to plant a church. Pastor Marty Souter and I went there to explore and prepare to send a team. We met with Howard Waller, missions minister at Bear Valley Baptist Church, who then introduced us to a support team he had developed. They had been doing community ministry for a number of years in Denver, so this team had already developed connections with the food ministries, with the prisons and local jails, with the homeless coalition, and various other social services in Denver. That was the team that helped Set Free get started in Denver, and that team still supports the Set Free Church there. In a few scant years the church has grown from nothing to several hundred in attendance.

In a local setting where Set Free has regular, ongoing contact with their sponsors, the sponsoring churches can be very helpful in supporting the ministry in a myriad of ways. For example, they can provide clothes. Probably everyone in a middle-class church has more clothes in their closet than they really need or could ever wear. Instead of giving them to the local thrift store, the sponsoring church can have a team collect and coordinate the distribution of clothes through Set Free. The clothes team can also coordinate donations for clean and warm clothing, especially during the winter months. There can be a strong and lasting impact on a poor family by providing clothes when that family has only one set of clothes per child. For a man who sleeps out in the cold all night, one can provide a warm-hearted ministry by giving him clean and dry socks. By giving clean clothes to a man who has worn the same clothes for six months, it is possible also to give him some of his self worth back.

Another way to support an inner-city ministry is by supplying food. Set Free churches want to feed the souls of people on the streets. They are there to share the Word of God with them; but if they want to show the love of Jesus, they sometimes need to feed stomachs before offering real spiritual food.

Many of us cannot go out in the streets, but we can provide food. Set Free was starting a church up in the Hesperia-Victorville area of the high desert in Southern California. First Baptist Church of Hesperia, which was sponsoring the new plant, has a great senior citizen ministry. Many of the ladies in that ministry had a compassion for the hurting people on the streets of their community. They were not strong enough to go out on the streets, but they could cook. Because they are located at an altitude of 2,500 feet and the wind blows all the time, it can get very cold at night during the winter months. On Friday nights when Set Free got out in the streets to evangelize and minister to the needy, the ladies in the senior ministry would cook up large pots of homemade chili to be served at the outreaches. That was a very significant part of how the Set Free Church in Victorville was started.

Still on the topic of food, a sponsoring church can provide food items in bulk quantities for the Discipleship Ranch ministry. That is a much needed ministry as there are on any given day between 150 and 200 people needing three meals a day on the various Set Free ranches. Not long ago, I was leading a Bible study at one of the men's Discipleship Ranches. One of the major prayer requests was for food, because they were just about to run out. They were not sure if they would have enough for dinner that night. So we prayed for that need along with several others. After the study a truck backed into the yard to unload cases full of chili bean cans. The driver simply said, "God told me to bring these out to you today." That was an obvious answer to prayer and only one example of how God meets needs. One of Set Free's favorite sayings is "beans and rice and Jesus Christ."

A sponsoring church can collect food items from its members and distribute them to the local Set Free ministry. In this way they are sharing with hurting and needy people in the community. Remember that the desperate and the homeless are hungry every day, not just at Thanksgiving and Christmas.

Here are some practical reminders about how to work with a food ministry: First, do not donate food items you yourself would not eat. Let us not have the patronizing attitude poor people will eat anything. Treat people with dignity and with respect and donate the kind of food you would be happy to have on a daily basis. And second, do not donate food items requiring a lot of cooking or preparation. Giving a frozen turkey is a wonderful idea, and it will feed a family for a long time. But if that family has no place to cook or store the turkey, we are not helping them in the best way possible. Instead, give food items with pop-off tops that serve one-meal helpings or that can easily be heated in a microwave oven. As we minister to the needy, we can be practical and helpful if we just use some common sense and try putting ourselves in someone else's shoes.

Supporting inner-city ministry can also be done by providing Bibles, tracts, or training materials. As Christians, we believe that the Word of God is "sharper than any two-edged sword, penetrating as far as to divide soul, spirit, joints, and marrow; it is a judge of the ideas and thoughts of the heart" (Heb 4:12). If we really believe this, we should feel compelled to get Scripture out on the streets for those who need to hear God's voice.

- Your church can collect extra Bibles not being used by members, or it can purchase cases of Bibles in bulk at a reasonable price. Those who minister on the streets will pass them out all over the inner city of your community. And the sponsoring church can also gather gospel tracts to share with inner-city Christian workers to distribute in various outreaches and street witnessing opportunities. The Set Free ministry alone has seen many come to accept Christ as Lord and Savior, more than fifteen thousand in the last ten years. But that is just the beginning in a new Christian's walk. Now they need to be discipled.

93

- Churches can also provide discipleship training materials for community inner-city ministries by, for example, offering Sunday school material for children's ministry. This material could be for new adult believers or for on-going discipleship training.

One of the best ways to engage churches as church planters and sponsors of urban work is to provide short-term mission teams. These teams can be assembled in a variety of ways, such as short-term teaching assignments for those who have a gift for teaching on different Bible subjects. There are a variety of subjects that could be taught on a weekly basis, and the classes would serve dual purposes. The first would be to wet the spiritual appetite of the non-Christian, and the second would be to strengthen new believers. A person can teach a five-week course on biblical stewardship, for example. Inner-city people need to know how to handle the money they receive just as anyone else does. This course can be taught at different levels—the gospel can be brought into the lessons so nonbelievers can hear about God's love, and it can also lay a stronger foundation for the new believer.

Another way is to consider assembling a short-term evangelistic team to share the gospel on the streets and perhaps hold evangelistic services. The evangelistic services can be held at the church plant facility or on a street corner. Of course the main purpose for this team will be to bring people into the kingdom, but that is not the only purpose. It will also give sponsoring church members a valuable hands-on experience with witnessing and evangelism, and, one would hope, set some people on fire for the Lord.

Some church members may be hesitant to go street witnessing, but they can be involved in another type of team—a short-term ministry team. On a team like this, they can handle things like giving away food or clothes at a specified location. As they encounter needy and hurting people of the inner city, they can observe the joy these people get from receiving clean, warm clothes, and the sponsoring church members will be touched and challenged to share the love of Jesus. People on the streets are hungry for more than just physical food.

Or church members can be challenged to do one-on-one mentoring as a way to become involved with inner-city ministries such as Set Free. Think what the lasting impact would be on a new believer's life if a member of the sponsoring church would spend one or two hours a week with them. Maybe the one being trained and discipled just needs to get over the hump and win a victory over the cycle of despair, defeat, and destructive behavior. And the kicker is that a one-on-one mentoring ministry will always bless the discipler as much as the disciplee.

As sponsoring churches become more involved with the Set Free-type ministry, they will find that sometimes ministry is a messy thing. One sees and hears many things better left unseen and unheard. But the sponsoring team will also see broken lives transformed by the power of the resurrected Christ, and they will experience the amazing grace of God that can and does change lives.

CHAPTER 10

Sponsoring Ethnically Diverse Churches

According to the 2005 U.S. Census Community Information Survey, Hispanics comprised 14.5% of the national population (41.9 million), black Americans 12.1% (34.9 million), Asian Americans 4.3% (12.5 million), and those of other races approximately 9% (25.7 million).[1] The need to sponsor new ethnic and foreign language churches is great.

Sponsoring an ethnic church is a strategic and practical way to be involved in world missions in your backyard. Over the past decade in America, we have seen that white English-speaking Anglos no longer represent the majority population in many cities. Thus, the opportunities and need for sponsoring ethnic churches are readily evident in many regions. Sponsoring an ethnic work usually is less threatening to most congregations than sponsoring a same-language new church plant in the same geographical area. Among new churches in North America, the Southern Baptist Convention reports that approximately 60% are foreign language, African-American, and ethnic congregations. During any given week, these churches share the gospel in more than 217 languages.[2]

Although the vast majority of today's church members are not infested with the sort of racial hatred and ignorance that led to race riots in past years, many have done little to actually cross the barriers of language and race. This can be done through church planting. Sponsoring an ethnic congregation often involves

---

[1] US Census Bureau, 2005 American Community Survey, http://factfinder.census.gov/servlet/ DTTable?_bm=y&-geo_id=01000US&-ds_name=ACS_2005_EST_ G00_&-mt_name=ACS_2005_ EST_G2000_B02001, accessed March 21, 2007

[2] Richard Harris, "Assisting in Church Planting," *On-Mission* magazine (Spring 2004): 14.

navigating cultural differences, in addition to language and social-economic differences. Consider the following true case study:

When the need for a new Asian language church was announced at the associational fellowship meeting, Pastor Tom immediately volunteered his church, TBC, to serve as the "mother church" and host of the new congregation. Although Pastor Tom's congregation was relatively small, his enthusiasm and offer seemed logical because many of the targeted Asian community lived within walking distance of TBC. Due to the changing demographics of the community, space was no longer an issue. In the 1970s TBC had been tight on educational space and parking. At present, the church had plenty of both. Also in their favor was the fact that TBC had no debt and had recently called Tom, a missions-minded pastor.

After meeting with the associational leaders and the associational missions committee, a traditional sponsoring church agreement was adopted by both the sponsoring church and the mission.

Next, Pastor Tom, the leadership from the new Asian work, and the associational leadership met for a tour of the facilities and prayer. During the tour Tom pointed out rooms that were available to the new work as well as those that were off-limits. He also proudly pointed out the new photocopier and other office supplies. Tom told the Asian church planter to "feel free to use the copier and office supplies. Just supply your own paper." This culminated with Tom handing the Asian leaders two sets of keys to the church building and leading in a season of prayer.

Over the next several weeks, Pastor Tom and the church planter sat together during the weekly associational fellowship. Each week testimony was given to the growth in the new Asian church plant. Several new believers had been baptized in a combined service, bringing excitement and joy to both fellowships. Everything seemed to be going great until one day neither Tom nor the church planter attended the weekly associational fellowship. Later that week, Tom asked the association to find a new meeting place for the Asian language mission.

Apparently the church planter was having difficulty finding resources in his language, including Bibles. Convinced that each family in the community should have God's Word in their language, the pastor downloaded the New Testament from the Internet. He then proceeded to photocopy the entire New Testament on the new photocopier. When the copier overheated, instead of waiting, the church planter unplugged it, replugged it, and kept making copies until terminal meltdown occurred. When the church secretary arrived to prepare the bulletin, the machine was broken. A service technician determined the cause to be abuse, and this was not covered under the machine warrantee. The sponsoring church terminated their association with the Asia mission and insisted that the new work meet elsewhere. Although another meeting place was found, it was miles from where the people lived and the new church lost members and momentum that unfortunately were never recovered.

Thorough communication is one of the greatest challenges churches face when sponsoring ethnic churches. In the situation above, seemingly small issues, such as the use of the copier and office supplies, were not spelled out. The agreement also failed to address whom the church planter was to call in case of problems. A contextualized approach to working out a sponsoring covenant is included in the appendix to this book.

Often cultural barriers are as challenging as the language barrier. For example, among most Chinese people, gifts of knives and clocks are associated with funerals. In the Czech culture, the home is considered very private. To drop by unannounced shows a lack of respect and very poor manners. In El Salvador, on the other hand, failure to drop by when one is in the neighborhood is an absolute insult.

When I worked with one ethnic church start, repeated failures by the new church plant to comply with the sponsoring church's reporting requirements resulted in a formal meeting between the church planter, the associational, state, and national convention leadership, and the sponsoring church. During a break in that meeting, the national missionary shared a critical insight. The sponsoring church was making a request the mission pastor was unable to accept. In his culture, however, to say no to an elder (someone much older or in authority) was strictly taboo. In the church planter's mind, the greater sin was saying no to the leader of the sponsoring church rather than failing to turn in his monthly reports. Once the problem was identified, the host church was able to rephrase the sponsoring agreement using terminology promoting communication and contextualization and not merely compliance.

Sponsoring ethnic churches certainly does not have to be fraught with difficulties, and many churches find sponsoring ethnic congregations to be the best way toward becoming a missional church. Let's consider three models to sponsoring ethnic work.

The Nesting Model

The story above illustrates the nesting model for church planting. In this model, the ethnic congregation meets in the sponsoring church facility. The nesting model is most appropriate when:

- The community is early in the process of transitioning from one ethnicity to another.
- The sponsoring church is nearby a concentration of another ethnic group.
- The sponsoring church has facilities that are adequate for multiple congregations to meet at the same time. This can include multipurpose rooms, fellowship halls, large classroom areas, chapels, and gymnasiums.

- The sponsoring church is stable but not growing. In many cases, the sponsoring church will be a church on the downside of the growth curve, but still having a viable fellowship and active congregation. Such churches may be experiencing a demographic shift or "suburban flight." If the church is growing, space and scheduling issues will need to be carefully addressed.

The nesting model provides several strategic advantages for the sponsoring church and the church start.

- Start-up costs usually are minimal. Generally the new church starts under the legal and administrative umbrella of the sponsoring church. Church materials and staff salaries, if required, are the primary expenses. The host or sponsoring church should anticipate incidental costs, however, including higher water, gas, electric, and phone bills, along with the higher cost of supplies and office machine wear-and-tear.

The challenge of the sponsoring church is balancing the financial support provided with the goal of helping the new congregation develop autonomy. Charles Brock says the goal is to realize the five selves: self-supporting; self-propagating; self-governing; self-expressing, and self-teaching.[3] If this is true, then the sponsoring church must avoid providing so much support that the new work becomes dependant on the existing work. The other extreme is placing too much financial burden on the new plant too soon.

The Legacy Model

When Valley Baptist Church in Bakersfield, California, was launched in the late 1980s, it represented the merger of two existing churches (with a major infusion of cash resources). This meant that one of the buildings was not going to be used. Since one facility was located in a transitional area of town that was becoming predominantly Hispanic, the new church decided to launch a Spanish language congregation. Today Primera Iglesia Bautista is a leading Hispanic congregation in the Central Valley of California.

Leaving an ethnic church behind when the mother church relocates or disbands can be an effective missional and highly practical approach to our ever-changing communities. The Legacy Model is appropriate when:

- Churches merge, leaving one facility unused by the new congregation.
- Churches relocate, especially in situations where the church is following the demographic shift of their community.
- An association or denomination is deeded a building when a congregation disbands.

---

[3] Charles Brock, *Indigenous Church Planting: A Practical Journey* (Neosho, MO: Church Growth International, 1996), 27.

- A church expands and is no longer using the chapel or auditorium and can give that section of the campus to an ethnic congregation.

There are challenges to the legacy approach. Several years ago a friend gave me a classic Porsche. The acquisition costs were $2,600, which I did not have at the time, and the restoration costs were estimated at $30,000. Over the three-year period I owned this car, the cost of ownership far exceeded my ability to pay for a proper restoration. Eventually the car was sold (for less than I had invested) to someone with the resources needed to restore it the right way. The challenge of the legacy model is that without adequate planning, the new congregation may be strapped to a building or location that does not fit their vision or strategy. They may not be able to afford the utilities, the building maintenance, or the insurance. The facility may not meet the needs of the community, and this is especially true of older buildings. Many older church buildings have small kitchens and fellowship areas, whereas most ethnic congregations require large fellowship areas if they are to grow. Additionally, in some communities, adults hold two or three jobs in order to make ends meet. These adults, although willing, cannot be counted on to spend time on building upkeep or renovation.

The Intentional Piercing Model

A third model for sponsoring ethnic churches seeks to pierce the darkness through proactively penetrating ethnic communities and establishing congregations there. Often the motivation to plan an ethnic church is birthed by a burden placed upon the heart of a person or group of people. As the burden is shared, the vision is acted upon. The result is a plan that involves intentionally sponsoring a new church inside the ethnic community. If the congregation is unable to undergird the new work spiritually and financially, consider securing multi-congregational support for the church planting project. Establish a coordinating counsel with leaders representing each congregation, and don't forget the strong evangelistic witness such a cooperative endeavor promises.[4]

Preparing for Challenges

Whatever the approach to planting ethnic churches, often the greatest challenge is finding qualified church planters. Many different problems could be mentioned. Sadly there are some who live in other countries seeking church planting positions in order to come into the United States legally. I have personally worked with two such individuals who obtained R1 (Religious worker status) visas whose English skills endeared them to the sponsoring church. But once in America, these church

---

[4] Ken Davis, "Multicultural Planting Models," *The Journal of Ministry and Theology* (Spring 2003): 116.

planters sought out existing churches and abandoned the church plant. In both cases, the sponsoring churches felt deceived (which they were) and ripped off. Both have been reluctant to sponsor another ethnic plant.

Another frequent problem is the underfunding of ethnic church planters. Often the financial package for church planters is far less than what a reasonable and prudent person would endorse. And yet somehow, congregations will approve such a woefully underfunded package when the church planter is from an economically disadvantaged ethnic group or community. But utilities cost the same, as do food, child-care, and other basic essentials. Items such as a car and home insurance often cost more, especially if the planter is renting. Some insurance companies are now basing their premiums on credit ratings, which can hurt those without a solid credit history. The cost of living for an ethnic church planter can therefore be surprisingly high. And if the spouse works and has English-language difficulties, minimum wage jobs may be all that are available.

The Baptist General Convention of Texas is currently conducting a comparative salary study of ethnic churches.[5] The underlying concern is that many ethnic pastors are under compensated. I think most of us know how the study will conclude, but what I want to say is that the worker is worthy of his wages, and the church has the responsibility to raise the bar of ethnic church planter salaries. If the church planter is not currently a citizen of the United States, or has a work permit, recognize that it will take months, maybe even a year or more, to work through all the immigration issues for the planter and his family. It may also cost thousands of dollars. If the church is employing someone on an R1 visa, a livable wage, including heath care and other benefits, will be required.

Another mistake is to equate language with culture. When I lived in Porterville, California, a community that was more than 60% Hispanic, our church voted to sponsor a Spanish-language church plant. We called a pastor from El Salvador, with the assumption that if he speaks Spanish he will relate well to the community. Little did we realize at that time all the cultural barriers existing between immigrants from northern Mexico and those from South America. In some cases, the ethnic planter is a true missionary, with the gift of crossing barriers, but this is not always true. Thus it is important to discuss these potential barriers before committing to the support of an international church planter.

Finally, the greatest barrier to overcome in establishing ethnic plants is often the one inside the hearts and minds of our members. Consider a personal experience:

> Soon after the church I pastored sponsored her first foreign language congregation (using the nesting approach), I began hearing murmurings about the "filth" the new ethnic congregation was leaving in the sanctuary after services on Sunday afternoon. At the next business meeting, a church member said that "we either have them pay to clean up the church

---

[5] For more information about this study, contact the Intercultural Mission Network of the Baptist General Convention of Texas at www.imissions.net.

each week or kick them out." When asked for specific examples of the "filth" the mission congregation was leaving, our congregation was told of dirty disposable diapers, food containers, and even beer cans being found in the sanctuary following the ethnic service. That week I met with the pastor and shared this concern. It hurt him to think such carelessness was being demonstrated by his small but growing congregation, and he promised to speak about the matter to his congregation the following Sunday.

That next week I received his report. First, they had no young children, so the diapers were not theirs. (It turned out the diapers were left by one of the 11:00 a.m. Anglo church attenders.) As for the beer cans, one of the men attending the new ethnic mission found two empty beer cans on the church grounds. Concerned they would be a poor witness and eye sore, he placed them in a bag with other trash, such as food containers from a nearby fast food restaurant, which he also picked up around the church grounds. Unfortunately, when he responded to the invitation to join the mission, he forgot to return to his seat and thus he left the bag of trash waiting in the pew.

We need to see people with the eyes of Jesus. Only then can we truly look beyond race, language, culture, or social status to see the great worth and value of crossing barriers and planting ethnically diverse churches.

CHAPTER 11

The Church Split

My friend Phil Langley likes to say that church splits are simply churches that are pregnant and don't know it. As a director of missions and former state church extension director, Langley has seen dozens of churches start through splits. These "unplanned pregnancies" can benefit from the love, care, and responsible parenting given to any unplanned pregnancy. Church splits, like unplanned pregnancies, will not benefit from fault finding and finger pointing, but they will benefit from a biblically based process that includes confession, repentance, honesty, and faith.

Dan Reiland is the executive pastor of Crossroads Community Church in Lawrenceville, Georgia. He suggests one way to look at a church split is observing it as a poorly handled church-planting project.[1] Although many would argue that church splits should be avoided at all costs, such thinking does not appear to acknowledge the human tendency towards downgrade. Some church splits arise when a church begins to shift from its biblical moorings. Others can occur over conflicting personal convictions. An example of this is found in Acts 15:39 when Paul and Barnabas split over the issue of taking John Mark on the second missionary journey. "There was such a sharp disagreement that they parted company, and Barnabas took Mark with him and sailed off to Cyprus." Was this a good thing? Christian history suggests the result was two missionary teams going out instead of one.

The point is that in terms of outcome, there is a fine line between a church split and a church plant.[2] Some call this fine line "splats." Splats are splits that become church plants. Church growth authority Elmer Towns suggests several reasons when a church split is justified. One thing that justifies a church split is if the church is

---

[1] Dan Reiland, "The Anatomy of a Church Split," *Equipping Leaders of Today's Church*, vol. 2, no 17 (September 1, 2001), cover story.

[2] Ibid.

not baptizing new believers. If new converts are not being baptized, this is clear evidence the church is not winning souls.[3] In this case, the "called out" have become the "home-bound," and the church has become little more than an inner circle or club where the original vision has been compromised. Members who leave this kind of church to start a new church plant should have little remorse for leaving.

A second reason identified by Towns is when biblical doctrine has been compromised. The authentic New Testament church is to be bound together in stability by the harmony of doctrine.[4] Although we will never find a church where every member (or even two members) agree on everything, failure to uphold the major historical doctrines of the church are legitimate grounds for a split. The plenary inspiration of Scripture, the virgin birth, the primacy of proclamational evangelism, and so on, are doctrines that should never be open to concession.

A third acceptable condition for a split is impurity. Towns writes,

> When a church permits obvious sin to persist in the congregation with no attempt to correct it, the blessing of God will be taken from that church. However, a split is justified only when sin keeps a church from fulfilling its basic purpose in life. The following cautions are in order: (1) Every church has some evil present, for no man lives without sin. Therefore, no group of people is completely pure. (2) If a church is attempting to deal with its sin, a young hothead should not try to split the church. (3) Sin will usually exist in fringe members. This is not a basis for a church split. A split is justified when there is obvious compromise in the pastor, deacons, or workers. [5]

We should know the truth about church splits, and we should know that some studies demonstrate church splits can result in healthy, growing churches.[6] When the split does occur, both parts tend to flourish, especially during the initial stages.[7] One survey demonstrates that splits are more likely to succeed than intentionally planted churches! Towns identifies four strategic advantages when new churches are created from a split:

1. They have financial commitment.
2. The new plant has a solid core of people.

---

[3] Elmer Towns, *Getting a Church Started*, 3rd ed. (Lynchburg, VA: Liberty University, 1993), 75.

[4] Towns, 74.

[5] Towns, 76.

[6] 2000 Anabaptist Church Planting Survey, http://www.newlifeministries-nlm.org/online/aec01 clapp-4.htm, accessed March 5, 2005. From the report:

It is interesting to note that about a fifth of the new congregations in this study were the result of a split from an existing congregation. Differences in perspective on what the church should be doing caused division, which was no doubt painful at the time. Yet those congregations in our study which have split off from existing churches appear to have attained new life and strength. Our study was not designed to secure information about the churches from which the new congregations split. The comments offered by survey respondents do not suggest that those churches have been destroyed as a result of the split.

[7] Robert Logan and Steve Ogne, *The Church Planter's Toolkit*, audio tape, 1991.

3. The new church has committed and mature Christians.
4. The new group is closely knit around a cause.[8]

Towns also points out potential disadvantages:

1. Usually a church split leaves a poor reputation in the community as well as among other Christians.
2. Bitterness may hinder the ministry.
3. New churches may be established for a reason other than evangelism.
4. People who could not get along with others in the old church will cause problems in the new church.
5. There is usually strong opposition from the old church.

A healthy church that takes a split under its wings can alleviate or reduce such potential disadvantages. In much the same way that a marriage prior to the birth of a child reduces the stigma for an out-of-wedlock pregnancy, a healthy sponsoring church can help a new church weather the pain of a split. The pain is not eliminated, nor is any sin that led to the split being condoned. But the God of forgiveness has promised that he will make "all things work together for the good of those who love God: those who are called according to His purpose." This promise is predicated upon two conditional clauses. The first is that the those who have caused or experienced a "bad" situation are in a love relationship with God. The second is predicated upon being "called according to His purpose."

Christians can, and do, fall out of the perfect will of God. When we act in his permissive will, we find ourselves living, as Paul wrote, in the flesh. When we repent and return to God, we once again will enter his perfect will. The problems and pains of the past, however, those resulting from being out of the perfect will of God, will remain. The promise of Romans 8:28 is the redemption of the situation for ultimate good.

Some years ago our family relocated to Minnesota to be involved in PRAXIS, a seminary-related summer-long church planting experience. After this, I accepted the call to copastor a church in Hibbing, Minnesota, a church that was a split from my home church. The pastor and a group of members departed from the original church over conflict issues that arose and escalated while I had been to seminary. In taking this position, I believe I acted in the permissive will of God rather than his perfect will. Over the next year I worked bivocationally as the new church experienced slow growth. By the end of the year, the church purchased property, began paying the staff, and held a service of reconciliation with the congregation from which they split. Both churches continued on for more than a decade, but today both have ceased to exist.

The pain over the fate of these churches is only a memory now. The tragedy is that no witness exists in the areas these churches served in northern Minnesota. Of course many of the converts reached through these churches went on to serve other evangelical churches in the community, and most of those who relocated

---

[8] Towns, 75.

have remained faithful to Christ. Towns summarizes my feeling about this experience well:

> In spite of all the unfortunate church splits, God has used many to his glory. People have been brought to salvation who would not have otherwise been reached. Communities have been evangelized . . . missionaries sent out . . . God causes even the wrath of man to praise his name (Gen. 50:20).[9]

Adopting a Church Split

One of the most loving ways to deal with unplanned pregnancies is through adoption. When a church splits for a justifiable reason, the process of adopting the new work as a sponsor is easier than when the split results from ungrounded accusations (which would be a violation of Matthew 18), personality differences, and jealousies. A church may want to think twice before entering an unjustifiable split as it becomes an accessory to sin. On the other hand, a justified church split is worthy of a healthy sponsor. Rieland writes, "Perpetual growth was not what God had in mind. Reproduction, however, is what God had in mind for all living things. Whether it is an oak tree, a human being, or an elephant, they were all designed to reproduce their own kind. A church is a living organism and no different in design."[10]

Get the Whole Story

In the Old Testament book of Esther, a clear contrast can be seen between Haman, who planned to kill all the Jews, and Mordecai, who saved King Ahasuerus's life. Mordecai refused to bow down and pay homage to Haman. When Haman tells the king about Mordecai, he gives the king less than the whole story and labels all Jews as disloyal subjects.[11] In contrast to the half-truths Haman told the king, Mordecai communicated the whole story, along with supporting documentation, to Esther and to the king.[12]

Dan Reiland writes that "emotions may be flying high; people can be hurt; and of course, the crusaders will be looking for allies. Do your best to rise above the clutter and seek the truth..."[13] Interviewing members on both sides of a church conflict will provide a clearer picture of reality than hearing from just one or two persons from one side. Consider inviting a denominational leader or others who can help provide a clear picture of the split.

---

[9] Towns, 74.

[10] Reiland, "The Anatomy of a Church Split."

[11] Esther 3:8.

[12] Esther 4:7–8a.

[13] Dan Reiland, "Surviving a Church Split," *Equipping Leaders of Today's Church,* vol. 2, no. 18 (September 15, 2001), cover story.

Count the Costs

Churches are communities, with networks of relationships that permeate at every level. Over a period of years, families may have members attending several different churches in a local community. In all likelihood, if your church is the result of a split, it has members who do business, go to school, and live next door to families involved in the split. The moment word gets out that your church is sponsoring a new work that is a split from another church, certain assumptions will be made.

Communicate

For those experienced in ministry, there is no surprise the apostle Paul included gossipers in the same list as homosexuals and other vile sinners who will not inherit the kingdom unless they are washed, sanctified, and justified in the name of Christ. Gossip can ruin people and churches, and it can be the downfall of new church plants. One way to reduce gossip is to openly communicate plans for new church sponsorship. If the new church you sponsor is a church split, the importance of communication is even higher. Using the Sunday morning worship service as a means of communication works for many church leaders. Remember that whenever the number of people involved in a project extends beyond the church staff, the likelihood of gossip grows. The old phrase "nip it in the bud" (stop it before it grows) is *apropos*. Truth is always the best weapon against gossip. It is highly appropriate for church leaders to communicate their truthful intentions to both sides of a congregation being split, and to pray for the spiritual vitality of the whole church.

Finally, after the official split, it is only natural that many in the new plant will maintain close friendships with those from the old church. These networks, like dysfunctional families, are often perplexing but they should not be discouraged. They are simply a reality the church leader must recognize.

Leadership Issues

The new side of a church split may or may not have a church planter or pastor. Often the leaders who come with the church split are members who filled a leadership vacuum that may have existed in the previous church. Others may have what might be called "uneducated enthusiasm." The church sponsoring the new split should clearly define the lines of communication it wants followed. Unlike a traditional church plant, where the leadership lines are fairly easy to identify, the church split may bring a "family chapel" style of leadership, with a "church boss" such as a patriarch or matriarch, or other behind-the-scenes influencer.

Recognize the Difference

Sponsoring a new church involved in a church split is different from sponsoring a brand new church plant. The membership generally will be believers who have many years of church experience. Most understand how a church is organized and have clear expectations of what the church should look like. Many are committed to biblical stewardship. Therefore, unlike previously nonexisting churches, the church coming out of the church split is often ready to begin implementing programs and committees immediately.

Most church splits do not attempt a dramatic and large launch, preferring to use traditional growth methods such as door-to-door outreach, Sunday school evangelism, revivals, servant evangelism events, and traditional advertising. This means start-up funds will usually be limited.

What the Sponsoring Church Can Do

Financial support may be needed to rent a facility or purchase property. Beyond that, in many ways a church split is similar to a family experiencing a divorce. Things one assumes will be there suddenly are gone. Office equipment, serving sets for the Lord's Supper, baptistery, sound system, worship instruments, music, and the pulpit are often high on the list of felt needs for the new church. By helping the new church acquire these items through short- or long-term loans or gifts, the sponsoring church can tangibly assist the new congregation.

In some states the new church will benefit from the "covering" provided by sponsorship. The sponsoring church can help the new work by providing liability insurance and bringing them under the constitution and bylaws of the sponsoring church until such time the new church takes wing and flies.

Many churches born as splits will benefit from a healthy role model. Involving new church members in activities at the sponsoring church that model church health and vitality will serve the dual purpose of building bridges between the two congregations and providing ministry opportunities that usually are beyond the capability of the new church.

Help the new church extend the right hand of fellowship to other local pastors, churches, and denominational leaders. Introduce them around. Remember that the sponsoring church is providing a legitimacy for the new church created out of a split, as well as introducing the new church leaders to your network of relationships and resources. Sometimes a simple call to a respected pastor or area leader inviting them to lunch with the new church leaders can have lasting benefits.

Wrapping It Up

Nearly every fellowship or denomination in existence today arose out of a church split in the past. And remember that Christianity as a nascent movement was considered nothing more than a split-off from Judaism. God often creates something new to take us where we would not go otherwise, so if your church is called upon to assist a new church resulting from a split, recognize that not every split is bad. Just as Paul recognized John Mark as a valuable member of his team, even after he and Barnabas sailed off for Cyprus, the church split can result in a valuable new ministry for God's kingdom.

CHAPTER 12

The Multiple-Sponsor
Approach to Sponsoring

Perhaps the best example of an outwardly focused ministry is when a church or group of churches cooperate together to plant a new church. While there are few churches claiming to be internally focused, plenty of them are around. They focus on getting everyone to come to "their church," their chief desire being to generate activity.[1] Rusaw and Swanson write that "if all the human and financial resources are expended inside the four walls of the church, then no matter how 'spiritual' things may appear to be, something is missing."[2] Truly missional churches that take a serious approach to hands-on mission through the sponsoring and planting of new works are strong internally, but they are always inclined to reach out.

A friend living in the Seattle area of the Puget Sound is in my view one of the greatest developers of church planting partnerships ever. He is always creating sensible ways to draw together various churches to partner together for the cause of church planting. Gary Irby reminds us well that "any partnerships flow out of our mission and are a part of a comprehensive plan."[3] He says that any good partnership has at least five teams:

- A Prayer Team
- A Recruiting/Assessing Team
- A Training and Coaching Team

---

[1] Rick Rusaw and Eric Swanson, *The Externally Focused Church* (Loveland, Colorado: Group, 2004), 16.

[2] Ibid.

[3] Gary Irby, Address: State Summer Leadership Meeting & Church Planter Missionary Forum, World International Conference Center, Atlanta, GA, July 28, 2002.

- A Focus-on-the-Community Team
- A Partnership Development Team[4]

Any successful multiple-sponsor approach starts with all parties beginning in prayer, remaining in prayer, and continuing proactively in prayer throughout the length of the plant's successful establishment. The Bible says for us to "pray to the Lord of the harvest," and there has never been a better way to do that than by beginning a new church plant. Why is multiple-sponsor partnering the most effective method of church planting? A primary reason is the critical resources the sponsoring partner can offer: finances, people, and emotional support. These three elements are essential for a new church to get a healthy start and grow into an exciting established church for God's glory. Under this method there are several models, and the model a sponsoring church chooses to employ depends a good deal on its life circumstance. A church's life circumstance involves its readiness to sponsor another congregation, its membership and facility size, the population base in the targeted planting area, how recently the sponsoring church has experienced a major change, how close it is to the planting area, and the loyalty of the pastoral and church leadership towards the church planting effort.

Understanding Sponsoring Terms[5]

There are some terms that need to be defined and understood when entering into the multiple-sponsor approach to church planting. A few terms might escape our grasp until we begin working with the idea of churches cooperating together to create a new church, but here are a few important ones:

Mother-Daughter Sponsor

The mother-daughter sponsor is the term used by many denominations to refer to the main or lead sponsor. The "mother church" is often called the primary or full sponsor since it is the major supporter of the new church plant. This primary sponsor is responsible for the day-to-day guidance of the new work as well as ongoing prayer, financial support, and Christian fellowship. The primary or full sponsor accepts the call to lead in the planting of a new church, and by functioning as the primary sponsor, the mother church recommends the new work to the local association and state convention. The mother church also works with the church planter to provide regular supervision, coaching, and mentoring. The primary sponsoring church conveys a sense of legitimacy to other area churches that the new work is a vital part of God's plan for kingdom expansion. Depending

---

[4] Ibid.

[5] The Church Planting Group of the North American Mission Board uses the terms *primary, clustering*, and *supporting church sponsor*. The list included in this chapter deals with the larger Christian community and the popular terms used to address this key issue.

on a church's level of commitment, it would assume the primary role of encouraging, coaching, supervising, resourcing, and financing the new church plant. And though the daughter work is accountable to the mother church, the primary sponsor might continue to enlist the help of other partnerships.

Secondary Sponsors

The secondary sponsor is also a supporter of the new work, but usually it functions in a secondary rather than the primary role due to practical matters such as geographic proximity to the new work. Like the primary sponsor, the secondary sponsor participates in the ongoing prayer, financial, and fellowship support of the new church. It participates in the financial support, but usually the secondary sponsor is not the go-to church for finances. The secondary sponsor is a church demonstrating the same high level of interest in church planting but might be unable to shoulder the full financial responsibility for a plant at this time. Thus, it seeks to partner with another church and functions in a secondary role. Typically this means it is willing to assist in financial and other areas, and to offer ministry support, but it is not able to provide a full range of resources for the church plant. Rather, it works alongside the mother church and provides resources where needed—depending on the full approval of the primary sponsor. Wise church planters seek secondary sponsors to help in areas where money or resources are still needed, without further taxing the mother church as the primary sponsor.

Cluster Sponsor

A clustering church sponsor is when three or more churches begin working together to sponsor and plant a new church. A clustering partner is a church choosing to join another church or churches to begin a new work, and there are several ways a clustering church can participate as a sponsor:

- A clustering church can work alongside a primary sponsor to support the new work through financial and physical resources, as well as personnel.
- A clustering church can also work with other clustering churches to plant a new church.
- A clustering church can work alongside a church planter to support the new work in financial and other ways.

Many churches have a firm commitment to church planting, but they prefer to work with other churches when starting a new work. By working together as a cooperating cluster church, the new plant benefits from a new work assistance team providing a broad base of support. Often a sponsoring church is not able to provide sufficient resources for a new church alone, so acting together as cluster partners is a proven way to secure solid support and ongoing leadership.

Supporting Partner Sponsor

A supporting sponsor is a church willing to provide short-term ministry activities or physical support to a planting church, cluster churches, or directly to a new church plant.[6] Many churches begin sponsoring new churches in this way, by first becoming a supporting partner sponsor. This is the way for almost every church across this land to participate in kingdom expansion through church planting. It is true that often churches exploring their participation with mission work may not be willing or able to make the long-term investment and commitment required of a primary sponsor. As an alternative, the supporting partner sponsor can remain active as a missionary-minded church by engaging in project-based support of church plants. Usually they do not take a lead role in planting a new work, but they play a valuable support role through one-time financial gifts, missions trips, and ongoing prayer support.

Partner Sponsor

This term is used to refer to two churches working together to sponsor a new church. Where a clustering sponsorship usually means three or more churches working together, a partner sponsor is a cooperation between only two churches.

Multisite Sponsor

The multisite sponsor is a congregation remaining under the umbrella of the original church until it gains the necessary strength to spin off. Though there are some churches that never spin off and operate as a single church in two locations, after three or more years most do become independent congregations with their own church building and their own leadership.

Adoption Sponsor

An adoption sponsorship is when a core group of people already meeting for worship are open to being taken under the wing of an established church. Usually this happens within the context of a church restart or refocus, and the membership of one group is absorbed into another. Many missions-minded congregations find this to be a great model to begin the work of church planting and sponsoring. Far too many people in churches all across North America think that the most essential component of a new plant is a church building. By using this adoption model, churches often are more willing to come on board because they see a tangible core of people and they can think of ways to get involved helping the new church

---

[6] *Partners in Church Planting*, Church Planting Group, North American Mission Board is available by contacting the Equipping Team at 770-410-6237 or contacting Church Planting Group Resources at cpgresources@namb.net or calling 1-888-749-7479 Select #1.

planter. Some very strong multisite sponsors have used this method as a means to further the cause of Christ all over an entire region.

Splat Sponsor

I remember going to the county fair when I was a kid and all of the excitement it would bring to the area while it was there. As kids we would all make plans to meet at a certain place and time. For days we would converse at school about the fun we were going to have and what rides we were going to take. But I was interested in another thing. I would go out into the midway and look for the tiny booth where you could make splat art. I loved that booth as a child. Every year I would beg my parents to let me do another splat art project right before we left the fair. Do you remember splat art? It was that booth in the midway where you would drop five or six colors of your own choosing (avoid the grey unless you wanted an ugly painting) and watch a small ugly piece of cardboard miraculously turn into something beautiful as the attendant turned on a little motor and those pre-selected colors spun across the card and created a beautiful vibrant mosaic. The splats, suddenly under centrifugal force, turned into an incredibly bright painting. To me as a kid, it was just amazing.

A church mired in conflict can experience its own sort of splat art. This is where a possible church split is turned into a plant. Most churchgoers have probably seen this. Let's say the pastor does or says something that alienates a particular group, or a power broker and his cronies block a much needed change, or a high maintenance special interest group is excluded from a church decision. The end result could well be that the once popular pastor, who could do no wrong, is fired. Within a very short time a small group splits off and begins a new church. When an impending church split results in a viable creation of a new church plant, the result could be termed a "splat," which stands for a split turning into a plant. A splat may leave some former church members hurt and confused, but the honest end effect is that a healthy reproducing church is born out of the difficult circumstances. The Lord can make something good out of even a bad situation.

Some Critical Milestones for the Sponsoring Churches

Milestones are perhaps the best barometer in sponsoring new churches. Careful attention should be given towards carefully thinking through the critical milestones for the new work. One author said that "a common mistake made in most church plants is to be driven by the calendar instead of milestones." A milestone in a new church is the achievement of a major result or goal signaling that a turning point has been reached. Milestones are essential for ensuring the launch of a healthy church, and they are nonnegotiable in that they have to be achieved to ensure a successful church plant. Milestones measure progress and determine the appropriate time for launching a healthy new work. Some milestones are transferable from one healthy church plant to another, while others are unique to a specific context. J. David Putman lists twelve critical milestones that should be given attention in a new church plant. They are:

1. Determine church planting readiness.
2. Develop an intercessory prayer team.
3. Select and define the church planting context.
4. Develop a partnering church network.
5. Arrange financial support.
6. Develop a core group.
7. Develop a planting team.
8. Discover a shared vision.
9. Establish community presence and evangelistic penetration.
10. Launch public ministry.
11. Develop and implement an assimilation process.
12. Mobilize and multiply the body.[7]

The writer of Proverbs states, "A house is built by wisdom, and it is established by understanding; by knowledge the rooms are filled with every precious and beautiful treasure" (24:3–4). The following list will be helpful for thinking about the kinds of milestones one must reach in a successful new church plant. Under each stage of sponsoring are things one must do or consider doing. The list is not exhaustive, but it is designed to encourage reflection. It is important to make these milestones personal to your project.

STAGE 1: Developing Vision

- Articulate your vision of sponsoring a new work.
- Determine how to share it with your membership.
- Pray for clarification of the vision.
- Take a day away from it all to let it incubate within you.
- Talk to other sponsoring church leaders.
- Read books on sponsoring and attend appropriate training.
- Describe what the new church might look like.
- List the benefits to the sponsoring church.

STAGE 2: Portray the Vision

- Make a list of the key leaders who share your vision.
- Develop a sermon series on the vision for a new work.
- Share the timing with the entire congregation.

---

[7] J. David Putman, *Critical Milestones for Planting Healthy Churches*, can be downloaded from the Church Planting Village at www.ChurchPlantingVillage.net. Used by permission, NAMB.

- Share the dream with area association leaders.
- Share the dream with state denominational leaders.
- Search for a qualified and gifted church planter.
- Pre-assess the planter (no exceptions).
- Assess the planter (no exceptions again).
- Bring the church planter on location.
- Begin working on a sponsoring church strategy plan.
- Find a qualified coach and mentor for the sponsoring church.

STAGE 3: Prepare to Coach and Mentor

- Attend training with state convention leaders.
- Prepare yourself emotionally for the journey.
- Rework the sponsoring church strategy plan.
- Send the church planter to basic training with an agency like NAMB.
- Select a qualified mentor for the church planter.
- Send the mentor along with the planter to basic training.
- Present the sponsoring church strategy plan to the association leadership.
- Present the sponsoring church strategy plan to state leadership.
- Determine and resolve funding issues.
- Put a prayer strategy in place at the sponsoring church or churches.
- Determine the level and extend of recruitment needed from the sponsoring church or churches.
- Clarify expectations between the church sponsors and new church plant.
- Refine the sponsoring church strategy plan.
- Clearly understand and identify key milestones.

STAGE 4: Send Out the Church Planter

- Plan a commissioning service.
- Schedule the commissioning service.
- Celebrate the release of the church planting team.
- Attend the first preview service for support.
- Attend the launch service of new church plant.

STAGE 5: Develop a Church-Sponsoring Resolve

- Evaluate the health of the sponsoring church or churches.
- Identify key areas needing to be stabilized.
- Focus on stabilization.

- Get regular reports from the new work.
- Provide opportunities to build depth into your own people.
- Include stats from the new work in your reporting to show impact.
- Develop the sponsoring church's recovery strategy.
- Schedule some time away for the sponsoring church pastor.
- Celebrate those called to stay with the new work.

STAGE 6: Look toward the Future

- Begin looking at other areas to plant another church.
- Prayerfully consider how you will be involved in the next plant.
- Stay open to potential church planters.
- Be aware of opportunities to plant in other areas.
- Prepare the church financially for the next launch.
- Set a target date to plant the next new work.
- Dream the dream again and enjoy the journey!

The most important decision in planting a new church is finding the right church planter, one with a high level of leadership ability. The second most important decision a sponsoring church or church planter can make is identifying the church planting location. Here are a few things to consider in selecting the location of the new work:

1. Look for a growing population with a vibrant feeling of expansion.
2. Look for a changing population that might offer a new wave of growth not yet explored within the ministry context.
3. Look for an unreached population group within the target area not being reached or ministered to.
4. Look for a receptive population.
5. Look for a compatible population that fits the church planter and those assisting in the new work.

It is absolutely vital that there be an alignment with the church planter, the core group, and those from the sponsoring church or churches helping with the new work. The greater the compatibility, the greater the potential impact! When it comes to sponsoring new works, most church leaders want to know the timetable. When could they be ready to plant a church? The readiness for a church to sponsor another church has more to do with church dynamics and attitudes than with anything else. When the following dynamics are present in a sponsoring church, it has a strong potential to become a successful sponsor:

- A burden for those without Christ.
- A willingness to step out boldly in faith.
- A vision for its region or beyond.
- A spiritual maturity.

- A generous spirit that has been demonstrated.
- A kingdom mind-set (turning outward not inward).
- A positive level of health in the sponsoring church.
- An unselfish spirit.

When you assess yourself and your church in each of these areas, you may be more ready to sponsor a new work than you think. It takes all kinds of churches to sponsor all kinds of churches to reach all kinds of people.

The Benefits of Planting New Churches for the Spin-off Church

When a spin-off church becomes actively involved in planting new churches, there are many positive things that happen within the sponsoring church:

1. Partnering keeps the church fresh and alive to its mission and vision.
2. Partnering reminds the church of the challenge to pray for the lost.
3. Partnering enables the church to assimilate other people into the kingdom that it would not otherwise.
4. Partnering creates a climate open to birthing a variety of need-meeting groups within the sending church.
5. Partnering provides evangelistic vitality and activity.
6. Partnering encourages the discovery and development of new leaders.
7. Partnering encourages the discovery and development of latent leaders.
8. Partnering encourages coaching, mentoring, and apprenticeship in ministry while providing a renewed understanding of how we are all part of a unified church planting team.
9. Partnering provides an occasion for the sponsoring church members to become personally acquainted with church planting missionaries.
10. Partnering builds on the past and insures a healthy future.
11. Partnering minimizes the tendency toward a self-centered ministry.
12. Partnering provides an education in missions and serves as a stimulus for young people's dedication to Christian service.
13. Partnering provides a visible proof that God is still working through people and that people still respond to his Great Commission.
14. Partnering provides a new opportunity for personal involvement in missions.
15. Partnering challenges our faith as we see God's hand moving and working among people in the target area.

117

When Not to Sponsor the New Work

I met my wonderful wife Cheryl and fell in love with her while we were both in college. She was finishing up her business degree at a university near the church where I served as the youth minister. I was a year ahead of her and served our church during her last year of school. We got married and moved to northern New Jersey for a few years where we both worked and I helped start new churches in the New York City area. Then off to seminary we went. Our prayer during this time was that the Lord would allow us not to begin a family until I graduated with my seminary degree. During those three years we grew in our love towards one another and made plans for having a family one day. We knew that it would be better if we waited until I was out of school and working again full-time in the Lord's work. God was so faithful to our prayers, and we were blessed with the news that we were going to have our first child the fall after I graduated! Having children was never an issue; it was just the timing of things. We knew this was something we wanted to do. Looking back I realize we were so utterly unprepared for having children and becoming parents. It was hard when we first decided to have children, yet we have been so blessed by having both our son and daughter in our lives. Being a parent is a challenge and such an awesome blessing.

Let me focus this illustration and apply it to the sponsoring of a new church plant. Just like Cheryl's and my decision to hold off having children right away (even though both families wanted instant grandchildren), sometimes there are times when it is better to hold off sponsoring that baby church. Cheryl and I were better off waiting, and there are some times better than others to parent a new church. Timing for the sponsoring church can be just as crucial as for a young couple deciding when to begin a family. Even when the sponsoring church feels the timing is right, it will never be completely ready to give birth to a new work. Therefore, realizing there are really no perfect times, the real goal is to identify those optimum times to begin a new work.

The Fraudulent Four

There are four fraudulent ideas about sponsoring a new church. These fraudulent four concepts very often deter a church from considering the participation in a partnering church movement. Ask anyone who has not planted a new church what the fundamentals of planting are and you will quickly see their misunderstandings and misgivings. Simply stated, most existing churches do not know how to plant a new church. The following fraudulent concepts have dissuaded many churches from planting a healthy New Testament church.

The Fraudulent Concept of Crowd

This is the belief that only A-type churches can parent. The reality is that churches of any size can participate in partnering and sponsoring a new church plant. It is true that not all churches can use the primary sponsor model, but every church can get involved in sponsoring in some way. Some churches could become clustering sponsors and work with three or four others to start a new church. Still others could get their missional feet wet by participating in one-time activities to help the new church get started. Size really has very little to do with sponsoring a new work. Willingness is the thing that counts. Church planting first and foremost springs from a heart for missions.

Sadly, some missional vigor tends to get lost at the expense of building bigger churches instead of planting new ones. Yet, pastor after pastor will say that when their church reaches a certain size, then it will be time to plant a new church. Often, once they reach that certain magic size, a case of amnesia sets in. Churches that plant churches are not focused on turnout, but rather on reproduction and multiplication. Without question, any church running one hundred or more attendees on their primary worship day can plant a new work. And any church smaller than that can participate in church planting through one-time activities and assistance in the local association of churches.

The Fraudulent Concept of Season

"If only you asked us when we were younger, we could have been of assistance. But now our church is just too old to plant a church." This thought that a church is too old to sponsor a new church is fraudulent. Perhaps their biological clock has ticked too far past the time where they could reproduce? They believe the younger the church is, the easier it is to move toward sponsoring a new work. In reality, an older, more established church can and should parent. Sponsoring a new church can become a great unifier for even older established churches to become more missional. Younger churches usually have built within their initial strategy the idea of reproducing and planting other churches, and so it is easier for those churches because they do not need to drag the dead wood with them. But, again, older churches should definitely be sponsoring younger ones.

The Fraudulent Concept of Standing

Many people think a church could never sponsor a new work until it first has purchased its own tract of land, constructed a building, added more ministerial staff, or reached some other stated goal. This fraudulent concept could extend forever. When would a church ever be ready? I have a personal "things to do list" at home that always seems full; it never gets truly completed. Churches have similar lists, but if they are not mindful of their responsibility to missions and evangelism, they will never become a mother congregation of a daughter church plant. They might want to, but the to-do list never gets completed. They just never get around to it. How many great congregations across our land have said, "We can't sponsor a new work because we are in a building program right now"? The point is that there will always be that one more thing to do on the "things to do" list. Stop looking at the list and start looking at the Lord's "I want you to do this" list! It is a both/and question, not either/or. If we plant new churches while at the same time growing the sponsoring church, God will truly bless both ministries.

The Fraudulent Concept of Expertise

I have often heard this kind of statement: "I just don't know how to lead such a task, so we better wait for God to provide someone who does." The church leadership decides it will not become a sponsoring church because they do not have enough guidance, teaching, comprehension, insight, education, or the right experience. But no church group or pastor has to be an expert in church planting before they get involved in sponsoring healthy New Testament churches. A lack of experience should never keep us from willingly sponsoring a new church. There are just far too many resources available to help all churches become excellent and fruitful sponsors. All churches, from novice to expert and from big to small, can experience the blessing of creating and sustaining new church works.

Like most fraudulent concepts, these four do have some partial foundation of truth. But they have gained undeserved momentum over time and have now become unnecessary hindrances. Which of these fraudulent concepts stand in the way of your church sponsoring a new work? Become a sponsoring church today. No church should be left behind.

Five Red Flags to Sponsoring a New Work

I was on the Emerald Coast in Destin, Florida, just after a major hurricane devastated that portion of the panhandle. As I walked on the beach one evening after dinner, a warning flag caught my eye. There are two types of red warning flags one usually sees posted in these situations. The first one is the single red flag that warns of hazardous undertow conditions. The second is the double red flag warning of extremely dangerous undertows and swift currents. Swimmers should not be in the water when either one of these flags is flying. Once the yellow or green flag is posted, it is once again safe to go into the water.

I was there to lead a partnering church conference with five of our mission-minded associations and their local churches committed to sponsoring new plants. The thought came to me that there are also red warning flags when it comes to sponsoring churches. What I mean is, there are legitimate times when it is healthier not to sponsor a new work. The flags are not meant to discourage Christians from planting, but they are motivations to do everything possible to prepare to sponsor the new church for God's glory. These caution flags are not affirmations for neglecting our corporate duty to grow the church, but they are signals where to avoid the hazardous undertows and dangerous currents that can drag us under.

A Much Too Hasty Change

There are various types of changes that can occur in an existing church that are capable of stalling and undermining church planting efforts. To move too rapidly in the face of these changes could hurt the chances of birthing a successful plant. An example of one such major change would perhaps be a church relocation project. Another could be a recently completed building project. Perhaps the church has just experienced a pastoral transition either coming or going. That would be another example of a time when it would be ill-advised to try accomplishing a new church plant. Another critical one is when a large number of people leave the church due to a split, ongoing job transfers, or a recession in the local economy. It takes time after these rapid transitions to prepare the church for adequately sponsoring a new work. Often unwise leaders want to reverse a sagging momentum or create a manufactured excitement by rushing the church into such a sponsoring campaign. Under such conditions it is highly likely both the sponsoring church and new work will suffer.

Spiritual Soil That Remains Unfocused and Unprepared

It takes an incredibly unselfish and mature church congregation to sponsor a new work. It takes an incredibly selfless pastor to encourage a church-planting movement. A church cannot be planted in an appropriate way unless the sponsoring church has a solid understanding of the biblical charge to plant churches and grow the kingdom. Healthy churches plant healthy churches, so spend time getting focused on the Great Commission of church planting.

Have you ever broken a pair of glasses? I did recently and had to go three days while a new pair was made. Everything was fuzzy during those three days. Sometimes the local church can become fuzzy by turning inward instead of outward, and by serving ourselves instead of others. Churches that are part of the greater worldwide church planting movement have made the missions-minded decision to become and remain indefinitely pregnant. If the congregational temperature for spiritual reproduction is low, the first need is to begin preparing the sponsoring church. Once the spiritual soil is focused and prepared, then it is time to move to the higher ground of church planting.

Negative Lay Leadership

Even when the apostle Paul was confronted by continual negative opposition, still he never stopped preaching the Good News of the kingdom. It is vital for pastors who sense God's leading to become part of a worldwide church-planting movement to understand that there will be opposition. Do not doubt this. And opposition will come as often from within as from without. It is critical that sponsoring church pastors move their lay leadership forward in a steady and careful way. They need to be growing forward, not groaning forward. There are many different types of lay leaders, and most of them need to be developed. Many are pessimistic about anything not inwardly focused. In this case, the pastor might need to begin developing the initial leadership team to assist in becoming the nucleus for developing a church mind-set that is positive to church-planting missions.

No Multiplication and Reproduction Mechanism in Place

A church needs to have in place certain mechanisms allowing for regular reproduction and multiplication. Every church built on New Testament principles must have a systematic and sequential plan to continually preach the gospel. Churches everywhere in this country and around the world become actively involved in accomplishing the Great Commission through church planting. There are five places in the New Testament where the challenge of the Great Commission is presented, and in all cases sponsoring and starting new churches is the natural outcome of the Great Commission command. One can usually determine if a local church has a reproduction mind-set by noticing whether the congregation displays an internal example of reproductivity—for example through small groups and Bible study classes. When this is lacking, it will be difficult valuing reproduction and multiplication as a methodology or strategy for increasing Christ's influence into the world.

Unhealthy Spirit within the Entire Fellowship

An unhealthy church needs to focus on getting healthy. Healthy organisms have the ability to reproduce themselves, so if a church has an unhealthy spirit, the goal is to go beyond health to reproduction. And in fact one of the best ways to develop and maintain church health is through reproduction. Perhaps the greatest miracle of God's wonderful working power is still seen today in the birth of healthy Bible-preaching and soul-winning evangelical churches.

Wrapping It Up

There is a multiple-sponsor approach to establishing new church plants, but there are some real cautions about when not to sponsor a new work. If a potential sponsoring church has even a single red warning flag, it may be a wake-up call to make sponsoring a new plant an impending goal. But church planting should be done by everyone. "Not right now" does not mean "our church will never do it."

Part 4

Understanding the Phases of
New Church Development

There are a number of reasons why sponsoring churches and new church plants avoid doing strategic planning. It is not the exciting part of the journey, but it is crucial to any long-term success. Some church planters avoid strategic planning altogether. Where planters are resistant to church development, it is usually because it is just plain hard work.

CHAPTER 13

Getting the Church
Ready to Spin
Where the Spin-off Strategy
Rubber Meets the Road

Traveling is one of the things I enjoy most. I am always amazed by the people the Lord allows me to meet and in many situations actually lead to Christ. Traveling is fun and adventurous—if you forget about airport waiting times. My wife and I have been blessed by the trips we've taken because we see the world as a book, and those who do not travel are only reading the first page. A traveler sees what he sees, while the tourist sees what he has come to see. I prefer being a traveler any day.

Just as there are various types of travelers in life, there are various types of church sponsors and church planters. At least four of these types should be avoided. In his book *The Success Journey,* John Maxwell mentions several tongue-in-cheek examples of travelers,[1] and I have revised his examples with my own list when it comes to getting the church ready to sponsor.

Mark the Martyr

Mark is the one we all know. He is quick to tell you it's not really his fault that he is getting nowhere on sponsoring a new work. He doesn't make any definite growth plans because he is too busy focusing his time and energy on changing things not really within his power. He frequently blames others for his lack of

---

[1] John C. Maxwell, *The Success Journey: The Process of Living Your Dreams* (Nashville: Thomas Nelson, 1997), 74.

church success, and he seems to be more concerned with finding justification for failing than with grabbing hold of occasions to advance. When an opportunity to sponsor a new church plant comes Mark's way, he will tell you just how difficult things are and why he could not even think about sponsoring a new church.

Status Quo Sammy

Sammy isn't worried too much about the past, and he doesn't want to think very much about the world to come either. He is focused on the present. In fact, Sammy loves the present so much that he is willing to do almost anything to maintain the status quo. When it comes time to consider the planting and sponsoring of a new church, he dislikes change so much he just can't think about all the hard work and effort it would take to do such a thing. So he remains faithful in the status quo, avoiding change in any event, and he is so satisfied with things as they are that he wants to keep them that way.

Whimsical Walter

Walter loves to plan, and he spends a lot of time doing just that. When he develops plans to sponsor a new church, it is always glorious. The problem for Walter is that he never turns his whimsical plans into accomplishment. Often he has great ideas, but on the other hand he doesn't want to take any dangerous actions. Walter is not willing to pay the price required to get off the dime and move forward to successfully sponsor and plant a new work.

Premeditated Paul

Finally there is premeditated Paul. I like this guy! He focuses the majority of his time on the current, doing his best to take full advantage of his latent talent. But the reason he is so effectual today is that he spent much time yesterday in preparation. As a result, he focused on his purpose—that of sponsoring a new church—and he is unabashedly moving his church in the direction of sponsorship. Paul is sowing seeds both inside and outside the congregation that will benefit the church and the growth of God's kingdom.

What separates a premeditated Paul from all the others when it comes to sponsoring a new church? The answer is that he has a clear church sponsoring strategy and has set some specific goals that are both timely and attainable. A clear and straightforward strategy allows the sponsoring church and church planter to know where they are going and how they are going to get there. A church sponsoring strategy shows in a transparent way a sense of mission and purpose for the new work. It gives both the sponsoring church and the church planter a get-up-and-go mentality to accomplish something significant for the Lord. Strategy helps both to create progress indicators and to focus not on mere activity, but on solid accomplishment.

127

All of the partnering preliminaries have been accomplished and now it is time for the expedition. It is time to apply the rubber to the road, to develop a significant strategy of embarkation, and then, with God's help, to accomplish the task you've been given. This may be the sponsoring church's first real church planting strategy, so let me give you something to consider. While you create this new work strategy, remember to set clear goals for the new work plant that are just out of reach but not out of sight. If you will remember this, it will save you from becoming engrossed with meaningless activity day in and out that frankly produces nothing.

Why Develop a Strategic Plan for Your New Work?

Stephen Macchia writes that in becoming a healthy church,

> strategic thinking and planning help us integrate the will of the Holy Spirit, our own church's uniqueness, and our ongoing responsibilities as leaders to develop a Christ-centered church. It lays down the tracks in a systematic fashion so that the train we are traveling on together doesn't go off course and land in the woods. It identifies what you will do together as a church; how you will live out your strategy; when you will accomplish stated goals; where you will focus your energies; why you will do what you do; and with whom you will partner to accomplish the tasks ahead. It integrates a clear understanding of your past ministry activities and accomplishments and bridges you through your present realities into an exciting future. In addition, the strategic planning process helps each church and leader identify the right things to be done and the right way to execute them. The process builds a sense of unity among all participants at every level of the discussion. It reinforces the need to be proactive rather than reactive in your ministry pursuits. It maximizes your effectiveness in the utilization of time, resources, coordination, and communication within the leadership team and throughout the church. Finally, it helps you measure your effectiveness by providing a baseline from which to grow and a target you hope to hit.[2]

Before developing any strategic church planting plan, the whole process must be bathed in prayer. Ask God to reveal the direction he would like you to lead the new church. Pray that his ways and your ways do not clash, for God's glory must be realized, not yours. Ask the Lord to bring health to your sponsoring church and great effectiveness to your Great Commission ministry as you launch into this new plant. Besides personal prayer, recruit members of your congregational prayer base to seek God's wisdom as you begin to plan this whole process.

---

[2] Stephen A. Macchia, *Becoming a Healthy Church: Ten Characteristics* (Grand Rapids: Baker Books, 1999), 163–64.

Simply put, strategic planning determines where a church plant is going to be located, how it's going to get there, and how everyone will know whether or not it ever got there. The focus of a strategic plan is usually more broad than narrow; it's on the entire church plant's effectiveness and not minor portions of the plant. It is either "we are successful in planting this new work" or "we are not successful." There are a variety of perspectives, models, and approaches used in strategic planning, and the way a strategic plan develops depends on the nature of the sponsoring church leadership, the culture of the new church target area, and the expertise of both the sponsoring church and new work planners.

There are several strategic planning models, including goals-based, issues-based, organic, and scenario planning.

Goals-based planning is probably the most common model, and it starts with a focus on the new work's mission, values, and vision goals. Has the new work moved toward the overall mission? Have the strategies used achieved the desired goals? Has the action planning (who will do what and by when) been effective?

Issues-based strategic planning often starts by examining whatever issues face the new work, what strategies need to be to addressed, what action plans have or have not been completed, and so on.

Organic strategic planning is a bit more fluid. It might start by articulating the new church's vision and values, and then developing the appropriate action plans to achieve the vision while adhering to those values.

Much of the day-to-day strategy development for new church starts uses the goals-based strategic-planning form. It is the most common strategy-planning device for working out the road map of the new work launch. Strategic planning is creating a vision of the future for the church and then managing it towards that God-given and God-guided expectancy, always operating under a missional umbrella and focusing the sponsoring church's new work effort. It is an effective process for aligning short-term decisions with long-term goals. Strategic planning answers the three biggest questions:

1. Where are we today?
2. Where do we want the new church to be in the future?
3. What should we be focused on today, in order to make it more likely we will be where we want to be in the future?

Strategic planning is a simple but necessary process that energizes the sponsoring church while helping the new church prepare for ministry. It bridges the gap between long-term vision and day-to-day achievable tactics for the new work. Here is a quick outline of things to consider when developing a new work strategy plan.[3]

---

[3] Additional help can be obtained by going to www.ChurchPlantingVillage.net and downloading the *Preparing Your New Work Proposal* by Lewis McMullen.

Keeping the Cart behind the Horse:
A Process of Strategic Planning[4]

Identify the Target Group

- Will you target non-Christian people?
- Will you target unchurched non-Christian people?
- Will you target people like yourself?
- Will you target receptive people?
- Will you target needy people?

Gather Information on the Target Group

- Who are the people in your target group? (Demographics)
- What do the people in your target group want out of life? (Psychographics)

Construct a Profile Person

- Who lives in your target area?

Determine the Kind of Church That's Necessary to Reach Your Target Group

- What kind of pastor should lead the new church?
- What kind of people should form your core leadership group?

Location of the Target Group

The second step in designing a ministry strategy is to discover where the target group is located in the community. The majority of people in the world today now live in cities.

- Determine where in the world you want to plant a church.
- Determine where in the United States you desire to plant a church.
- Determine where in the city you want to plant a church.
- Do a feasibility study of the target community.

---

[4] Further development of this idea can be found at: Aubrey Malphurs, *Advanced Strategic Planning: A New Model for Church and Ministry Leaders* (Grand Rapids: Revell, 1999). Additionally, if you go to www.mapphursgroup.org you can download a resource entitled *The Advance Strategic Planning Method*, 2001. This is perhaps the best available visual guide for doing strategic planning.

Reaching the Target Group

Another step in developing the broad ministry strategy is to consider a specific strategy to reach the unchurched where they are.

- Designing a strategy to accomplish the Great Commission.
- Developing a program to accomplish the strategy.
- Whom has God provided to lead the programs?
- What are the best programs to implement the strategy?
- What are some programs that have proved effective?
  - † Targeting the relational community
  - † Direct mail
  - † Telemarketing
  - † Community service
  - † High attendance Sundays
  - † A prayer ministry
  - † Servant evangelism
  - † Media
  - † Special events

Benefits of New Work Strategic Planning

Strategic planning serves a variety of purposes in the sponsoring church process, including:

1. Clearly defining the purpose of the new work and establishing achievable, realistic goals and objectives consistent with that mission in a predefined time frame.
2. Communicating those goals and objectives to the new work's constituency.
3. Developing a sense of ownership of the plan by both the new work and sponsoring church.
4. Ensuring the most effective use is made of the new work's resources by focusing the resources on the key growth priorities.
5. Providing a base from which progress can be measured, and establishing a mechanism for informed change when needed.
6. Bringing together everyone's collective best while building a consensus about where a new work is going.
7. Producing greater efficiency and effectiveness in the plant and keeping the focus clear.
8. Providing the glue that keeps the sponsoring church and new work moving forward together toward an agreed-upon objective.
9. Solving major problems along the way.

The Implications of Strategy Planning

Here are some obvious and not-so-obvious implications that should be considered:

- Strategy planning depends on many variables, such as location and resources.
- Strategy planning is dynamic and fluid.
- Strategy planning should reflect the unique challenges of each setting.
- Strategy planning is determined by the Holy Spirit.
- Strategy planning possibilities are infinite.
- Strategy planning may change when any one variable changes.
- Strategy planning cannot be determined before the context is examined.
- Strategy planning formation is a spiritual process.
- Strategy planning development is learned as we study others who have contextualized successfully.
- Strategy planning options increase with increasing knowledge of our team, our setting, and our values.
- Strategy planning variables mean little without an understanding of church planting principles.
- Strategy planning development takes faith in the Holy Spirit rather than human ingenuity.
- Strategy planning formation should be a team process.
- Strategy planning formation can be overwhelming unless we trust in God.
- Strategy planning formation can be reduced to one simple axiom: follow the Holy Spirit.[5]

It is absolutely essential that the sponsoring church commit to the planning process. Aside from the church planter, no single ingredient is more vital to a good outcome than a solid commitment to the process by the sponsoring church and its key leaders. Sponsoring church leaders must sincerely want the planning process to make a difference for the new work. They must also be open to change. Sponsoring church leaders must be willing to permit and participate in open discussion of sensitive and controversial issues as they prepare for the new ministry launch. Additionally, besides the commitment to the planning process, sponsoring church leaders must also invest time in regularly planned meetings to gauge and follow up on the whole process.

When Should Strategic Planning Be Done?

Scheduling for the strategic planning process depends on the nature and needs of the new work. Consider these guidelines:

---

[5] Gary Bulley, *Developing Your Contextualized Strategy: Skill Development Module B-7* (© North American Mission Board, 2001) available at www.ChurchPlantingVillage.net.

1. Strategic planning should be done when the new work is just getting started. The strategic plan is usually part of an overall launch plan, along with evangelism, financial, and operations plans.
2. Strategic planning should also be done in preparation for a new major venture from the sponsoring church.
3. Strategic planning for the network of sponsors should be conducted at least once a year in order to be ready for new opportunities and challenges. As soon as the new work is up and running, once every two to three years is sufficient.
4. The full strategic planning process should be conducted at least once every three years. As noted, these activities should be conducted every year if the new work is experiencing tremendous target area changes or significant growth.
5. Each year the new church plant action plans should be updated.
6. Note that during implementation of the new work strategy plan, the progress of the implementation should be reviewed at least on a quarterly basis by the sponsoring church and denominational agency working with the planter. Again, the frequency of review depends on the extent of change in and around the new work.

A Simple Strategy Planning Self-Diagnosis[6]

Rate on a scale of 0 to 5 the following statements.

1. I understand the importance of strategic planning.
2. I can identify several key principles of strategic planning.
3. I could explain to another pastor how to involve his church in a strategic planning process.
4. I know the difference between values, vision, and strategy.
5. I can identify the key issues in any church planting strategy.
6. I know the difference between goals and action plans, and I understand the role of each.
7. I know how to involve others in strategic planning.
8. I know how to present goals and strategy in a way that informs and motivates others.
9. I know how to create ownership in my strategy.
10. I have developed a church-planting strategy.
11. My strategy effectively addresses the gathering of new people and evangelism.
12. My strategy effectively addresses the assimilation of new people into the life of the church.

---

[6] Ibid.

13. My strategy effectively addresses the unique cultural context of my target community.
14. My strategy effectively addresses decision-making and administrative processes.
15. My strategy effectively addresses discipleship and leadership development.
16. My strategy is flexible enough to adjust to new issues and information.
17. My strategy is unique and not a formula borrowed from another situation.
18. I understand that strategy development is never finished.
19. I believe I can effectively understand and critique church planting strategies from a variety of contexts.
20. I feel more comfortable with my strategic planning abilities than I did before I picked up this book.

Add your scores together and grade yourself as you would for a test in school. The following scale will help you assess your progress:

85 – 100 > Great! You should have no problem meeting these key expectations.

70 – 84 > Good, but briefly review the areas where you scored low until you feel that you have it down.

50 – 69 > Making progress. Review all of this and talk with your mentor regarding areas of concern or misunderstanding. Agree on a plan to further address key issues.

30 – 49 > Need help. Discuss again with your mentor the entire church planting process. Address key areas and develop a plan to become proficient. Pay attention to areas of anxiety and weakness as you revisit these issues.

0 – 29 > Ouch! Start over.

Use this diagnostic as a tool to assess your understanding and comfort with church planting. Be honest! This is for your benefit, so note the points where you scored low and revisit those areas. Maybe you will have to reread something, discuss an issue with your mentor, or phone an experienced pastor. The important thing is that you feel you have a handle on this area of ministry.

Nine Common Causes of Failure in a New Work

Failure is a topic most of us would rather avoid when it comes to planting churches and strategies. But ignoring obvious (and subtle) warning signs of plant or planter trouble is a surefire way to end up on the wrong side of the new church survival statistics. Here is a list of nine causes of failure based on my own personal experience as well as informal discussions with planters and sponsoring churches across North America. The idea is to learn what not to do and increase the odds of new work survival.

Not understanding your target area, your prospective field culture, and the habits of your target area households

Two telling questions should immediately come to mind: Who are the people who live within the prospective target area? And why would they want to spend their life doing community and church work with you? You should be able to clearly answer both questions in one or two sentences. Without target area profiles of individuals, the sponsor and the new work will not survive.

Choosing a target area that isn't very fruitful

Perhaps the target area you've chosen is the hardest area in the country to plant a new church. Even though it is possible to generate lots of activity, the growth never materializes to the extent necessary to sustain an on-going church plant. It takes more than a solid idea, a good plan, and a spiritual passion to keep the new work in business. What does it take? It takes the right match between the plant and the right target area. An example of this was my church plant in the southern end of Boston. Here I was, a strongly conservative preacher in a land that was highly liberal. Because I was not that experienced yet in my ministry, I did not realize just how hard it would be to develop a church start with people usually at the opposite end of the spectrum of my convictions and beliefs. You take a southern boy, put him in one of the Yankee states, and allow him to work like he did in the south. What will happen is he will get frustrated and the work will suffer—all because of a failure to connect with the target area.

Failure to really understand and clearly communicate what you are doing as a church planter and new work

Clearly define your new church and its value to the area. What do you and your new church do that can help or benefit others? Ask yourself if you are communicating this effectively. Does your target area connect with what you are saying? Almost as important, how are you saying it?

Inadequate funding of the new work

One reason for developing a church planting strategy for the new work is that funding always follows strategy. If you don't have enough resources in reserve to carry you through the weather, calendar cycles, or downward trends of seasonal ministry, your prospects for continual success are not very good. Developing a realistic funding plan is vital in connection with any new work strategy planning.

Failure to anticipate or react to changes in the target area

Don't assume that what you have done in the past will always work. In many church plants, what God allowed in a previous plant just will not work in a new one. Therefore, realistically challenge the factors that led to your past church planting success. Do you still do things the same way despite new cultural demands and changing times? What are other successful plants doing differently? Those who fail to anticipate and react to the cultural and lifestyle changes in their target area end up as obsolete church plants and church planters.

Failure to define what you are offering the target community

Trying to do everything for everyone is a sure road to failure as a church planter. Spreading yourself too thin diminishes the quality of the new work. The community you target often pays excellent rewards for excellent results. Excellent results come from doing what you do well and then doing it over and over again. If you selected well, the target community will respond affirmatively.

Keeping your new work plant in order

Slow and steady wins every time when it comes to church planting. It's hard to believe that too much early growth can work against you, but there have been many cases where this proved true. To serve the target area well, focus on delivery of quality, follow-through, and follow-up. Often denominational leaders seek the fast and furious when launching large new works. Huge sums of money are expended only for these leaders to discover it is not the preferred strategy for a successful and fruitful plant. One can launch large, to be sure, but huge sums of money will not determine the effectiveness of the new church plant. Only God's blessings determine that.

Poor management of the new work

Management of a new church plant encompasses a number of activities, including planning, organizing, leading, delegating and communicating. The cardinal rule of new work management is to know exactly where you stand at all times. A common problem faced by many successful church planters is the new church growing beyond their management skills. Usually the gifted planter is not necessarily a gifted administrator, and there is sometimes the need to bring someone alongside to manage the day-to-day operations.

No planning by the planter and just winging it

If you don't know where you are going, you will never get there. No clear picture of church planting success will lead to the status quo. To grow and be successful means actively working on new growth and evangelism. As the saying goes, failing to plan is planning to fail.

Wrapping It Up

We don't make the church grow or reproduce any more than pulling on a stalk of corn would make it grow. Paul plants, Apollos waters, God gives the growth. We sow, water, weed, fertilize, and fence the crop, but we rely on the church's own God-given potential to reproduce. An obedient, Spirit-filled church *has* to reproduce at home or abroad. It's her very nature; she is the body of the risen, life-giving Son of God.[7]

There are a number of reasons why churches sponsoring new churches and new churches themselves avoid doing strategic planning. It may not be the exciting part of the journey, but it is crucial to any long-term success. Yet some church planters do all they can to avoid this step. Laziness may be one reason for this resistance to strategic planning, because developing a comprehensive strategy is time consuming and just plain hard work. Another reason is that some church planters fail to see the actual benefits of the planning process because they have not thought things through. There are still others who fear the risk of failure, and strategic planning shows failure for what it is. Overconfidence from experienced planters is a reason some refuse to develop such a plan. But if a church planter is not willing to do the necessary new church strategy planning, the sponsoring church should refuse support and think about sponsoring someone else. There is always a price to be paid, and the question in the strategic-planning area is, are you up to the task and are you willing to do the hard work that is necessary?

---

[7] George Patterson, *The Spontaneous Multiplication of Churches in Perspectives on the World Christian Movement: A Reader*, ed. Ralph W. Winter and Steven C. Hawthorne (Pasadena, CA: William Carey Library), 604.

CHAPTER 14

The Joys and Realities
of Parenthood

When my wife and I found out we were going to be parents, we took several steps to prepare for this life change. One of the first things we did was to set up an appointment with our doctor. Over the next few months we attended prenatal classes at the local hospital and subscribed to *Parenting* magazine. Even the basic topics of conversation changed from cars and fishing to diapers and parenting. At that time I also became aware of habits and actions in my life that needed to change before the baby came.

About the same time, a college acquaintance was also preparing to become a first-time father. His approach, however, was to change as little as possible. He continued to spend money on himself. When it became uncomfortable and impractical for his wife to join him on his weekly trips to the lake or mountain, he left her at home. In short, his preparation for parenting was lacking.

There is no question that sponsoring a new church should bring change, because in some ways church starting is like having a baby. It will never be done if one waits until the sponsoring church can "afford" to do it. This chapter will cover some phases the new church will likely go through, and the role of the sponsoring church during these phases. Just as in human development, the phases of a church's infancy, childhood, and adolescence will vary with each individual church. Over the years, having children has changed our values. Before I had children, my dream was to become a millionaire by thirty. After our first child was born, my dream changed dramatically—for the better!

The World Health Organization reports that the global child mortality rate has dropped from 25% in 1950 to 7% in 2000.[1] In poor countries such as Niger, how-

---

[1] World Health Organization, Press Release #67, 12 October 2000.

ever, the child mortality rate is 33.5%. According to the WHO, the underlying factors are economic problems, civil strife, and a poor choice of interventions to try reducing deaths among children. These same factors existing in the sponsoring church can also lead to a high mortality rate among new church plants. When this happens, the joy of parenthood can rapidly turn into a nightmare. A study conducted by J. D. Payne at Southern Seminary clearly showed that finances are the number one concern of church planters. There is case after case of sponsoring churches approving building programs while the mission pastors of plants they sponsored were struggling far below poverty level. While no sponsoring church is the perfect parent, some need to remember they have a young mission church to raise.

Church planters who have gone through Basic Training for Church Planters will have developed a draft of an action plan for the new work. Though this rough action plan will often benefit from the input and refinement of the sponsoring church, this intervention is not a linear process. Each developmental life-phase has unique attributes that can be summarized through the following biotic phases of development.

The Phases of Parenting a Church Start

Conception

As noted earlier, church plants tend to be either of the planned or unplanned variety. The conception phase begins with the dream or vision for the new church plant. During this first phase the sponsoring church begins taking an active role in helping provide the greatest chance for viability and health for the expected baby. For each of the phases, the potential mileposts for the church planting team and the sponsoring church have been identified.

CONCEPTION PHASE	
Church Planting Team	**Sponsoring Church Role**
Planned Conception	• Actively seek or adopt the vision for the church plant.
• Clarify the vision—share the vision until it is a shared vision.	
	• Put together a mission committee (and planter search committee if needed).
• Identify your ministry focus group.	
• Identify the church planting team members.	• Learn as much as possible about the Ministry Focus group.

139

- Initiate frequent contact with the sponsoring church.

- Work with sponsors in developing a covenant.

- Continue to recruit additional team members.

- Use discovery tools to help planting team understand their roles.

Unplanned Conception

- Seek counsel from associational or state leaders.

- Identify whom the new church will be able to reach effectively.

- Confess and repent of actions that might have contributed to the split.

- Seek God's help in the building of the new church and his vision for the work.

- Consider enlisting partnering church(es) to help.

- Use discovery tools to help team leaders understand their roles.

- Identify possible fears or objections that will be raised that might thwart the vision God is giving.

- Begin developing the sponsoring covenant with the church planting team.

- Identify and remove reproductive barriers.

- Seek to create a positive environment for reproduction among the membership.

- Identify potential members who feel called to work with the church planting team.

- Initiate contact with associational or state church planting leaders.

- Develop partnering prayer network.

- Commission the planting team.

- Commit to a support package.

- Pray for the seeds of this new work to fall upon the good soil.

- Avoid pushing too hard or becoming overbearing, thus aborting the dream.

- Encourage leaders to network with other sponsoring churches or to join a Multiplying Church Network (MCN).

Prenatal

The prenatal phase follows conception. During the prenatal period, the sponsoring church assumes the role of a pediatrician. Again, consider the evolving role of the sponsoring church during this phase.

PRENATAL PHASE

Church Planting Team	Sponsoring Church Role
• Begin core group development— continue recruiting members throughout this phase.	• Work with the church planter in finding strategic location.
• Identify core values.	• Prepare budget and secure resources.
• Develop written vision, purpose and mission statements.	• Meet at least monthly with the church planter.
• Develop and put into action a new work prayer network.	• Join or develop a multiplying church network.
• Secure resources.	• Conduct a sermon series on church planting.
• Identity and secure a strategic meeting place.	• Provide small group ministries with information about the new start.
• Attend basic training for church planters.	• Attend mentor training if you will be the church planter's mentor.
• Join or develop a church planting network.	• Deploy members who feel called to work with the church planting team.
• Plan preview services.	• Promote prayer for the new work.
• Secure tax identification number(s).	• Help with administrative and logistical questions.
• Set up bank account.	• Host a "baby shower" for the new work.
• Identify core group members' gifts and roles in the new work.	• Offer to help with and evaluate preview services.
• Conduct preview services.	• Take time to meet with the associational missionary or church planting missionary.
• Organize publicity for the first public service.	• Consider beginning financial support during this period.
• Begin financial support of the new work through core group tithes and offerings.	
• Begin cooperative mission giving.	

Birth

The third phase, birth, is the time of the first public worship service and the period immediately following. The focus should be on celebration and worship. This phase truly tests the ability to assimilate the skills developed during the prenatal period.

BIRTH PHASE	
Church Planting Team	**Sponsoring Church Role**
• Conduct one last preview service.	• Celebrate with the mission church following the first public worship.
• Consider hosting a prayer retreat or vigil just before the first service.	• Encourage concentrated prayer for the birth.
• First public worship. A time of joy and celebration.	• Provide encouragement and assistance with immediate follow-up.
• Begin modeling stewardship through support of worldwide missions.	• Host a dedication service for the new church.
• Immediate follow-up begins.	• Continue prayer support with an emphasis on prayer for the viability of the new work.
• Send prayer partners birth announcements.	• Begin monthly review of reports with the church planter.
• Complete the first monthly report.	• Contact the denominational leadership with an update.
• Review the first service with associational missionary and sponsoring church leaders.	
• Make adjustments as needed.	

Infancy

The fourth phase is infancy, and the focus here shifts from anticipation and expectation to implementation and growth. This phase is a time for either rapid growth or fragile dependence for the new work. The sponsoring church will need to respond appropriately to either condition. During infancy, the new work is developing the structure, leadership, and programs envisioned in the strategy plan.

INFANCY PHASE	
Church Planting Team	**Sponsoring Church Role**
• Rapid growth should be taking place.	• Providing positive reinforcement and modeling for the new work.
• A time of teething pains. Do not be afraid to discuss problems and concerns with the sponsoring church leaders.	• Remember that seemingly small hurdles may appear to be huge barriers for the new church.
• Maintain weekly contact with your prayer team.	• Continue to have regular contact with the church planter and its leadership.
• Revisit the strategy plan frequently.	• Avoid comparing the new work to other new churches. This is counterproductive.
• Determine which of the emerging "personality" characteristics of the church are positive and which may be detrimental. Make corrections as needed.	• Provide weekly "snapshots" of the new work to the congregation.
• Ensure leadership reproduction is taking place.	• Pray for the healthy development of the new work and for its immerging leaders.
• Enjoy discovering your unique identity.	• Provide leadership development opportunities for the new work.

Childhood

The fifth phase is childhood. During childhood the new church will likely make some dumb and immature mistakes. It is important for the sponsoring church to remember that young children rebound quickly from mistakes whereas it takes the members of the mother church longer to put things behind them.

CHILDHOOD PHASE

Church Planting Team	Sponsoring Church Role
• Easily distracted from the goals and objectives set during the prenatal period.	• Revisit the goals and objectives of the new work with the church planter each time you meet.
• Avoid the tendency to mindlessly copy what other new churches are doing.	• Encourage grace when the new work makes a mistake.
• A time of high energy. Make sure the team is not suffering from burn out.	• Communicate to the congregation the milestones that are achieved.
• Evaluate the role of prayer during this phase. It is easily overlooked.	• Ask questions rather than give answers.
• Conduct a planning retreat with the leadership team.	• Begin praying about partnering with another new work. (This is similar to family choosing to have more than one child.)
• Mistakes will be made. Short memory of mistakes.	• Support and encourage the new church's early attempts at independence.
• Observe and celebrate milestones.	• Consider a special celebration service with the new work to observe a completed milestone.
• Lead out in short-term mission projects.	
• Don't become so active that you forget to have contact with the sponsoring church.	
• Have fun.	

Adolescence

Veteran parents know that the adolescence phase in their child's life can be looked forward to with anticipation or dread. The same is true in church planting. A common complaint of sponsoring church leaders is that the mission church begins making decisions without consulting them first. Adequate preparation in the earlier phases can ensure a smooth transition into and out of adolescence.

ADOLESCENCE PHASE

Church Planting Team	Sponsoring Church Role
• A time of self-awareness. The church has a clear identity.	• Provide increased autonomy and prepare to let go.
• Recognize a tendency towards rebellion against the "established" churches and tradition.	• Decrease support and encourage new ideas.
• Prepare for self-support.	• Don't avoid contact with the church planter.
• Meet with associational leadership regarding membership and constituting.	• Revisit the sponsoring covenant with the new church leaders.
• Seek to communicate to the congregation the value of interdependence over independence.	• Provide information regarding constituting and incorporating.
• Model increased dependence upon God for the church's needs.	• Discuss reproduction values with the new church leadership.
• Schedule a constituting service.	• Highlight the accomplishments of the new work publicly and encourage prayer for the work as they prepare for autonomy.
	• Work with the new work and associational leadership in planning a constituting service.

Maturity

The final phase is maturity. During this phase the sponsoring church will let go of the new work as a sponsoring or parenting church and instead assume the role of a sister church. Following this phase, both congregations should be involved in reproduction.

MATURITY PHASE	
Church Planting Team	**Sponsoring Church Role**
• Conduct the constituting service.	• Help plan and participate in the constituting service celebration.
• Evaluate the church planting process just completed.	• Evaluate the sponsoring process just completed.
• Develop and engage in a process for reproduction.	• Plan for additional sponsoring opportunities.
• Become a sponsoring church for another new work.	• Celebrate.

Wrapping It Up

Successful spin-off churches recognize that the success of the new work depends on their success in appropriate parenting. Treating a church plant as a child during its adolescent phase can result in painful relationships, unnecessary or irrelevant meetings, and a sense of disconnect. By using these tables, it is possible to identify the developmental phase of the new church as well as the appropriate role and actions for the sponsoring church. Granted, as in real life parenting, the unexpected is inevitable. During those times, drawing upon the experience of leaders whose spin-off efforts have been successful is a time-proven approach.

CHAPTER 15

The Upside of the Downside
Overcoming the Hardships
in Sponsoring

A re you and your church determined to fulfill your God-given destiny as a sponsoring church? God has a great plan and an exciting purpose for every church and every pastor holding up the cause of missions through the sponsoring of healthy new churches. But that plan is not going to come to pass without a little hardship, and without some kind of opposition. And how we handle the tough times of life will either break us or make us! Your troubles can either make you better, or they can make you bitter. They can thrust you forward and cause you to grow stronger, or they can overwhelm you and cause you to just shrink back.

It has been said that you will never make God angry if you sponsor new churches. Sponsoring the birth of a healthy New Testament church is a God thing. Instead of standing strong and fighting the good fight of faith, far too many sponsoring church leaders and church planters get all pessimistic and vinegary when things don't go their way. And then they settle for mediocrity. But God is looking for sponsoring church leaders and church planters who have what has been called a warrior-like mentality, planters with their minds made up and who are unwavering about living in victory.

We all need to understand that sometimes God allows certain things to happen to us to allow for learning and maturing. Even if we want to, we can't run from everything that is hard. And anyway, it's the hard times of life that help us develop character. That is when God's doing a work in us, stretching us and getting us ready for advancement. If everything were always easy, if we never had to reach for our faith, then we would never reach our full potential. So when times get tough, instead of getting disheartened, we need to view those hurdles as opportunities to grow. and advance. Responding wrongly to our hardship only prolongs the anguish! The wisest thing we can do is to learn how to respond correctly.

Here are some tough questions regarding the sponsoring of new church plants:

1. What will you do as a sponsoring church leader or church planter when you hit a brick wall so big you can't see any way around it?
2. How will you handle the discouraging down moments of the new church?
3. How will you prepare yourself for situations testing your leadership as a sponsoring church leader?
2. Which of the many promises of God will you hold close during those times of hardship? Are you ready to learn how to overcome the hardships you face as a sponsoring church or church planter?

David said God enlarged him in his times of distress. I like the way the psalmist put it:

> When I call, give me answers. God take my side! Once in a tight place, you gave me room; now I'm in trouble again; grace me! Hear me! ... Complain if you must, but don't lash out. Keep your mouth shut, and let your heart do the talking. Build your case before God and wait for his verdict (Ps 4:1–4, *The Message*).

Your Hardships Can Be Your Greatest Asset!

Your hardships can be the thing that leads to your next advancement. My own experience is that in the midst of challenges as a pastor and church planter, the Lord would often open up a great opportunity for our church not only to conquer challenges but—while seeking God's hand in the midst of hardships—to discover our next place of sponsorship! Hardship refines fervor and fervor fuels vision! It's the struggle that gives us strength, and no one develops spiritual muscles without some kind of resistance. We have got to be determined when times get tough. We have to show the enemy we're going to outlast hi n.

Have you ever had a spiritual pity part, over a situation when your feelings were hurt? We can either keep feeling sorry for ourselves or we can ask God to turn the hardship into an opportunity. I can testify that hardship offers many striking opportunities for personal improvement and growth. We serve a God who specializes in doing the impossible, and he does this every day. Someone has said, "If you want to launch big ships, go where the water is deep!" Dream big, and then as a sponsor lead your new church to be all God is calling it to be. But remember, God never promises a life free from hardship. In church planting, hardships often reveal a new adventure in sponsoring.

Even though Goliath was twice his size, David looked him straight in the eyes and said, "Look. I know you may be big, but the God in me is much, much bigger." He then proclaimed, "This very day I will defeat you and feed your head to the birds of the air." That's the kind of attitude successful spin-off churches need to have. When we face our Goliaths in life, whether it's slow growth in a church plant, trouble in a relationship between sponsoring church coach and planter, financial difficulty, or whatever that hardship is, we need to look it straight in the eyes, and say, "I will defeat you. I'm not going to give up. I know God is enlarging me in this time of distress."

I think about churches I have planted. Most church plants that explode in growth do so out of the pits of hardship before moving upward and onward. God uses struggle to enlarge vision. He uses hardship to usher us into a whole new era of ministry. And what the enemy means for evil, God can turn around to use to his advantage. If we did not know how to handle hardship the right way, none of that would happen.

Sponsoring church pastors and planters of new church works respond in different ways in the midst of hardship, and some ways, such as the following, are clearly unhealthy:

1. *Some use the wrong source for self-worth.* Some sponsoring churches or planters identify so closely with the new work that they see it as a reflection of their own self-worth. Remember the promise of God when he said, "I will build My church" (Matt 16:18). Our self-worth comes from God and God alone.

3. *Some expect everyone to share their own personal dream.* Most sponsoring church pastors or church planters believe they have higher highs and lower lows than other types of ministers. How many pastors of existing churches welcome the pastor of a new church plant only thirty minutes away? Planting a new church is a great goal, but it is not everyone's dream.

4. *Some allow broken promises to get them down.* Are you harboring negative feelings toward people who have not stepped up as they promised?

5. *Some partners and planters fall into the sin of comparison.* Comparison is the thief of joy for the sponsoring church or plant church because it causes us to deny the God who has uniquely called us to sponsor or plant particular churches. Understand the truth from Jesus' parable of the sower in Matthew 13 that no two sponsoring churches and church planters have the same soil condition. For some the soil is so ready, the crop pops up above even our wildest imagination. Others have rocky soil that requires more time to get ready before the harvest can begin. The point is that if you play the comparison game, you will always be the loser. It is wrong to expect the same results in kingdom work as others are having.

6. *Some have the wrong motivation for church planting.* It is an unworthy motive to want to do our own thing to prove our self-worth or significance, or to advance a personal agenda, or to wield power over a group of people. We need right motives, such as compassion for the lost and a desire to expand the kingdom.

7. *Some allow their personal lives to become imbalanced.* Far too many church planters seem to use their work as an excuse never to be home. Planting a new church is a run-far-run-fast effort, but in no way should this work sacrifice family life on the altar of church planting.

We learn things about God in hardship we can't learn any other way. God could have kept Joseph out of jail (Gen 39:20–22), kept Daniel out of the lions' den (Dan 6:16–23), kept Jeremiah from being tossed into a slimy pit (Jer 38:6), kept Paul from being shipwrecked three times (2 Cor 11:25), and kept the three young Hebrew men from being thrown into the blazing furnace (Dan 3:1–26). But God allowed those problems to happen, and as a result every one of the people mentioned was drawn closer to God as a result. You will never know that God is all you need until God is all you have! Many sponsoring churches or planters become bitter rather than better, and never grow towards Jesus. A lot of sponsoring churches or church planters become negative and sour, giving up before they ever make it to their Promised Land. God does not send the trouble, but he will use any hardship we face to take us to the next level. We just need to do our part and keep standing strong.

There are two kinds of faith, a delivering faith and a sustaining faith. Delivering faith is when God instantly turns something around. Most of us have seen that happen, and it's a wonderful thing. But I believe it takes a greater faith and a deeper walk with God to have sustaining faith. Sustaining faith is when you say, "God, I don't care what comes against me. I don't care how long it takes; it's not going to get me defeated. It's not going to get me down. I know you're on my side. And as long as you're for me, who dares even to be against me?" The courage that comes from sustaining faith is what is needed to be a sponsoring church or church planter!

When you have that kind of sustaining faith, the adversary doesn't stand a chance. And really, it's not so much our adversities that cause our problems, but rather how we respond to our adversities. You can have a relatively small problem that can defeat you. I have known many church planters over the years who have had huge problems, and yet they're happy because they display an attitude of sustaining faith. They actually believe God can and does change things! Sponsoring church pastors and church planters need to come from that breed. We want warriors and not whiners, sponsoring churches or church planters that have the never-say-die perspective and who are determined to live in victory. They know they are the victors and not the victims. They live out Romans 8:31, which says, "If God is for us, who is against us?" We need confident warriors standing with the apostle

Paul and confessing confidently, "I am able to do all things through Him who strengthens me" (Phil 4:13).

When we face hardships, we should remind ourselves that the thing trying to overwhelm us could be the very thing God uses to advance us.

I have fallen and can't get out!

On a podcast a while ago, I heard a story about a farmer who had this old mule. One day, unfortunately, this mule fell into an empty well. The well was about forty or fifty feet deep, and this farmer was so very disappointed, because he loved that old mule. But after studying and analyzing the situation, he realized it was going to be impossible to rescue that mule. The well was just so deep and too narrow. And the poor animal was just crammed down at the bottom. And as much as he didn't want to, he figured that neither the mule nor the well was really worth saving. So he decided to fill the well up with dirt right then and there and put the mule out of his misery. The farmer called some of his friends over to help him out, and one shovelfull at a time they begin to put that dirt into the empty well. When that old mule felt that dirt hit his back, and he realized what they were trying to do, he threw a fit. He screamed, he kicked, he yelled, and he hollered. I am sure he thought, "Poor old me. I've fallen into a well and nobody is even going to help me out." But as the mule just sat there having a pity party with the dirt getting heavier and heavier on his back, all of a sudden a brilliant thought hit his mule mind. He decided when he felt that dirt hit his back, instead of letting it bury him he was just going to shake the dirt off and step right up. Shake it off and step up. And so, shovel by shovel, blow by blow, crash by crash, time after time, he would shake it off and step up. No matter how the mule felt, no matter how tired he got, he just kept shaking it off and stepping up. You know, after he did that for three or four hours the old mule was able to step jubilantly over the wall of that well and walk out to freedom. The very dirt that tried to bury him actually saved his life. All because of the way he responded to his hardship.

Throughout life we are all going to have some dirt shoveled on us. We have to decide if we'll fall down in a pit of self pity and be buried underneath our problems, or if we're going to be like that old mule and shake it off and step up. When times get tough, let's not whine and feel sorry for ourselves. Have that soldier mentality. Be determined. Learn to shake it off and step up. It is well documented that Thomas Edison failed thousands of times trying to invent the electric light bulb. That did not dissuade him. He didn't give up. He just kept shaking it off and stepping up. We have all failed plenty of times and had a plethora of setbacks. That does not mean we can't get back up and go again. The Bible says, "Though a righteous man falls seven times, he will get up" (Prov 24:16). God will raise us up so if we get knocked down, we don't have to stay down and get buried underneath the dirt. Let's shake it off and step up.

Nobody had more unfair things happen to him than Joseph. He just had to keep shaking it off and stepping up. His brothers were so jealous of him they wanted to throw him into a deep pit and leave him to die. Eventually they sold Joseph as a slave, and eventually he worked for a man named Potiphar. Potiphar's wife attempted to seduce Joseph, and she was frustrated when he resisted. She falsely accused him of attempted rape, and he was unceremoniously thrown into prison for a crime he didn't commit. Once again, Joseph just shook it off and stepped up. He kept doing his best. Before long, he was put in charge of that whole prison.

How many times must Joseph have thought, "God, what are you doing in my life? Here I'm doing my best—trying to serve you—but one bad thing after another keeps happening to me." He must have gotten discouraged. But Joseph had that warriorlike mentality. He may not have realized it, but God was doing a great work in him. God was getting him prepared. Scripture says that as he sat there in that prison, in those chains of iron, Joseph's soul entered into that iron. In other words, he developed the strength and perseverance that made his soul as strong as that iron.

Tough times are ahead for sponsoring churches and church planters, so tough we might think nothing good is happening. But we must keep on persevering and doing the right thing even when the wrong thing is happening. Like Joseph, we will emerge with a greater strength, a greater determination, and with more resolve than ever before. Isaiah 41:10 says, "Do not be afraid . . . I will strengthen you; I will help you. I will hold on to you with My righteous right hand." God hardens us to difficulty when we keep shaking it off and stepping up. We're growing, getting stronger. Those things that defeated us in the past won't take us down anymore. God has hardened us to difficulty. Think of Joseph's life. He was a prisoner in iron chains, and some twenty years later he was the governor of all the affairs of Egypt. In sponsoring and planting new churches, that thing overwhelming us now just might supernaturally be used by God to advance us tomorrow.

None of what happened to Joseph would have happened if he hadn't had sustaining faith—that willingness to go through hardship and to shake it off and step up. Some partners and planters feel just like Joseph. Unfair things happen, and life hasn't gone our way. We're tempted to think it's never going to get any better. But no, start shaking it off and stepping up. Somebody rejects you? Shake it off. Somebody offends you? Shake it off. If you suffer a setback, shake it off. As long as we are shaking it off and stepping up, the enemy cannot defeat us. Remember that many times our greatest challenge leads to our greatest opportunity. It happened that way for Joseph and David. Maybe the turmoil and messiness of life are so difficult or delicate that it's hard to see any purpose to it right now. That's when we've got to learn to be like Joseph and say, "God, I don't understand why all this is happening to me, but I do know you're a good God, and you said you'd take the evil and use it to my advantage. You said you would enlarge me in my times of distress. So Father, I thank you that this hardship is leading me one step closer to my divine destiny as a sponsoring church or church planter."

A man was an executive with a large home improvement business, with retail stores all across the country. He was high up in the company. But one day, there was a corporate restructuring, and out of the clear blue his position was eliminated and he was laid off after thirty years of helping build the company from the ground up. It was the most trying time of his life—the greatest setback he had ever suffered. But instead of sitting around feeling sorry for himself and mourning over what happened, he decided he was going to shake it off and step up. And so he got a few of his friends together, and they started their own home improvement store, and they called it the Home Depot. God blessed that business and it took off. Today, his old company is no longer even in business while Home Depot is all over the globe. His greatest hardship turned out to be his greatest opportunity. Had that hardship never come, he wouldn't have been able to get to his divine destiny.

What we may think was the worst thing that could have ever happened to us is one day going to seem like the best thing. We'll look back and think, really, that wasn't so bad. After all, if it had not happened, where would we be today? Hardship has a way of pushing us to our divine destiny, and sometimes we need a push.

It's a lot easier to stay in the comfort zone, but God wants us to be growing continuously. Sometimes a hardship will be used to apply pressure to keep us moving forward. Who knows our gifts and talents better than God? He put them into each one of us and knows what we are capable of and how far we can be pushed. He's going to push and prod us into our godly future. Most of us would be amazed what we could achieve when God puts a little pressure on us to move from the safe zone to the faith zone. Corrie ten Boom, who suffered in a Nazi death camp, explained the power of being in the faith zone. "If you look at the world, you will be distressed. If you look within, you will be depressed. But if you look at Christ, you will be at rest."

Don't give in to short-term thinking. Stay focused on the end result. Bear Bryant, the famous coach of the University of Alabama football team, had a experience that highlights this theme:

> One time Alabama was up by six points, and there was only about a minute or so left in the game. He called his quarterback over and said, "I want you to play it very safe and just go in there and run simple running plays to protect the ball, and to run out the clock so we can win this game." So the quarterback went back to the huddle and called the coach's play. But his best friend and wide receiver said, "No. Don't run that play. That's what they're expecting. Throw me a pass." The quarterback agreed. They snapped the ball and he threw that pass. But the star defender and fastest runner on the other team intercepted that ball and took off toward his goal line. Now this quarterback, who was not known

for his speed, took off after that player, chased him down from behind, and tackled him on the five-yard line to save the game for Alabama. After the game was over, the opposing coach came up to Bear Bryant and said, "What's this about your quarterback not being able to run? He caught my fastest guy." Bear Bryant said, "You've got to understand. Your man was running for six points. My man was running for his life."

The eleventh chapter of Hebrews describes the terrible opposition faced by some past heroes of faith—from jeers and flogging to torture and death itself (11:32–40). We are going to face obstacles in our church-planting work because the more worthwhile the dream, the more opposition and setbacks there will be to face. How we handle these attacks will determine more of our success in ministry than anything else we do. Prevailing faith must be tested faith! It is a testing God uses to refine and develop us for a greater kingdom future. Those with prevailing faith learn how to hold on steady in the storms.

When a Church Planter Fails

One of my doctoral students came into the program after a successful ministry as an international church planter. His next two church plants in Missouri, however, both failed. His experience was the foundation for his doctoral project exploring unsuccessful church planters and how to prepare them to stay in the game.[1] His study demonstrates the depth of the pain and discouragement experienced by church planters whose plants fail.

Usually the symptoms of an unhealthy church plant are evident. Unfortunately they are also often unheeded until it is too late. For example, the planter might "pull away" from his coach, mentor, or supervisor. What were once regular reports to the sponsor, now become sporadic. Sometimes the relationship between planter and sponsor disintegrates to the point where the sponsoring leadership, upon hearing the news the plant has failed, simply wash their hands of the experience. Although it is tempting to chalk it up as a learning experience, leaders of successful spin-off churches recognize the redemptive nature of the death process.

A network of ministering relationships is required when the church planter fails. More than ever a network of relationships is required. Recognize that the planter is likely battered emotionally and spiritually at this point. Providing job assistance, transition assistance, and counseling can aid the planter's transition to other ministry opportunities. Some of the best planters I have worked with experienced failure in their early plants. Just as Paul did not write off John Mark, remember that God may well be using this experience to equip his servant for another (successful) plant.

---

[1] Richard Smith, "The development of a plan for restoring unsuccessful church planters and preparing them for possible redeployment in church planting ministries," D.Min. dissertation, Midwestern Baptist Theological Seminary, 2005.

Wrapping It Up

For five years I have been faithfully working on and adding features to my waterfall. I learned my way into this project one step at a time. It is a huge waterfall with eight deep pools dropping into one after another from a height of twenty feet, ending in one final large pool below. It is spectacular during the spring time when all of the exotic water plants have just been placed back in the water garden from winter storage. While all of those plants have been in winter hibernation, they have been busy and quite fruitful. I just finished dividing each of these magnificent plants into more underwater pots so they could be expanded into the mystic water landscape. Now if I left the previous pots of the late summer and early fall as they were when I placed them in storage, they would eventually become stagnant and no longer reproduce. But because I carefully took the time to expand the foliage, by early summer my waterfall has doubled and even tripled its ability for reproduction—all because in March I took the time to carefully reproduce and divide the plants. If I had just kept filling the previous pots, in a short time my plants would have become root bound and died.

I feel blessed as a result of my labor and proud of my horticultural accomplishments. It is the law of the harvest blessing for plants to reproduce and add beauty to the landscape. There is also a law of the harvest blessing when it comes to the sponsoring of new churches. As a sponsoring church invests in a new plant, the existing church needs to let go, divide, and watch the multiplication begin. Remember, there is help available. Keep the dire needs of the world always in mind and not on hold while you search for the right time to sponsor. Get ready for an adventure, and don't wait too long for the next season to reproduce, because the hand of God might pass you by and remove the opportunity and blessing of a new church start.

I have learned that in every hardship there is an opportunity. Our greatest frustrations are God's greatest opportunities. And the opportunity often comes in the middle of the challenge of church planting. We can accomplish amazing things when we have some hardship as a sponsoring church, because it is in those times of distress that God enlarges us.

Two men were out in the woods one day, and all of a sudden a huge grizzly bear appeared about thirty or forty feet in front of them. They both froze in their tracks. One guy whispered to the other, "What are we going to do?" The other guy said, "We're going to run for our lives." The first man said, "Are you crazy? We can't outrun a grizzly bear!" That second man responded, "I know that. I don't have to outrun the bear. I just have to outrun you."

God will at times use a little hardship and allow pressure to push us, to stretch us, to get us out of that comfort zone. Becoming a spin-off church will stretch pastors, church members, and church finances. But God knows just how much we can handle. In those times of challenge as a sponsoring church, we need to remind ourselves that God is broadening us and our ministry. In the struggle, we are getting stronger. Without any kind of hardship, we would never be the people God really wants us to be.

Stand strong and fight that good fight of faith. Don't be a whiner. Be a warrior! When things don't go our way, let's learn to shake it off and step up, and not get buried beneath the dirt. God wants us to live in victory, and if we do our part as church sponsors or church planters, handling hardship in the right way and the right attitude, God will turn hardship into a stepping stone for advancement. What the adversary meant for evil, God will use that very thing to take you closer to your divine providence. Be courageous. Remember Isaiah 43:1, which says, "Do not fear, for I have redeemed you; I have called you by your name; you are Mine." We don't serve a far-off and disconnected God who encourages us safely from the sideline. He enters the fray with us, and he will never leave us alone. Let's refuse to allow the roller coaster of hardship to keep us from sponsoring new church plants.

CHAPTER 16

Leaving a Legacy

There are many ways to measure the greatness of men. Some are great because of incredible talents. A baseball player like Ozzie Smith, perhaps the greatest middle infielder around, was blessed with incredible talents. Peyton Manning, the great quarterback of the Super Bowl-champion Indianapolis Colts, is also considered great because of his superior athletic talents. There are some people called great because of their wealth and possessions. Some can be called great because of the buildings they have built or because of the service they render to their community and the world. Most ministers want to leave a mark or legacy in their particular place of ministry. They don't want this in an egotistical way, but when one stands before our heavenly Father, he wants to hear, "Well done thy good and faithful servant!"

Something within us desires to leave a lasting impression. A pastor who sponsors many new works while fulfilling the Great Commission shows that a legacy is more than a particular pastorate in a particular place. Rather, the legacy comes from the understanding that the sponsoring of new churches can make a huge kingdom impact. A legacy of sponsoring healthy church plants encompasses the past, present, and future, and it forces us to consider where our individual church has been, where we are now, and where we are going. Leaving a legacy of healthy New Testament churches is a journey from daily service to kingdom significance.

Jesus commissioned us to go and make disciples of all nations. Many Christians around the world are convinced that discipling the nations will only be achieved by having a church, which is the shopping window of God, in walking distance of every person on the globe. The church must again become the place where people see the body of Christ, where his glory is revealed in hands-on, down-to-earth, right-next-door, unable-to-ignore, living-every-day-among-us terms.[1] How do we want to be remembered when our ministries come to an end? Is it the seeds we planted each day that make up our own unique legacy for the Lord? What will others says about our legacy after we are gone to glory? Will it be the wit they remember, or just how great of a communicator we were? Will it be our kindness towards others, or our generosity? The only way we can measure our ministry is the legacy we leave after this life is over. We need to nourish church planting movements that plant and water other church planting movements. Part of discipling the nations is to reproduce the form in which Jesus chose to express himself while on earth, and that is the local church.[2]

Surely the greatest legacy we could leave for the Lord Jesus when he calls us home is the new church plants we have been involved with around this country to reach the lost for the kingdom of God. Whether we recognize it or not, we are all leaving a legacy of some sort. What could be more important than starting new Bible-believing churches all over this land that connect with the unchurched and non-Christian population in an effort to lead them to Christ? Those who come after us will inherit what we do today, for both good and ill.

I am reminded of the story of the little girl whose mother could not decide whether she should attend her father's funeral or not. The girl and her father had been quite close, but all her family and friends felt it just would be too much for her. But the little girl surprised the whole family. When they went to the funeral home, it was she who talked of the beautiful flowers, and it was she who said, "A lot of people loved my daddy, didn't they?" It was she who was the most sensible when they saw the body for the first time. "That isn't my father," she said. "That's just the place where he lived awhile." She was the most calm person at the funeral, and she lifted the faith of all the others by reminding them with quiet confidence that her daddy was happy in heaven. This composure did not happen by accident. Because he and his daughter were so close, the father talked to her a lot about God and about death and about what happens to those who love the Lord when they die. He left a legacy to his family that enabled faith in even a little one.

When George Washington Carver was a student at Iowa Agricultural College, now Iowa State University, he and a friend planned to go as missionaries to Africa. But as his agricultural studies progressed, Carver, a devoted believer, began to sense a different calling from the Lord. God was working in him so that he could use him in a new way that would make a huge impact on this nation. Shortly thereafter Booker T. Washington asked him to join the faculty of Tuskegee Institute in Alabama. As a matter of prayer he wrote to Washington in 1896 and said: "It has been the one ideal of my life to be of the greatest good to the greatest number of my people possible, and to this end I have been preparing myself for these many

---

[1] Wolfgang Simson quoted by Jim Montgomery in "His Glory Made Visible," in *Perspectives on the World Christian Movement: A Reader*, ed. Ralph W. Winter and Steven C. Hawthorne (Pasadena, CA: William Carey Library, 1999), 608.

[2] Ibid.

years."[3] He pledged to do all he could through the power of God to better the conditions of African-Americans in the racially segregated South.

George Washington Carver's sensitive heart and willing obedience to God bring to mind the experience of Samuel when he was living with Eli the priest. Samuel responded to the Lord saying simply, "Speak, for Your servant is listening" (1 Sam 3:10). During Samuel's lifetime of distinguished service for the Lord, he honored God by listening to and obeying his call. The result still to this day is a rich legacy and lasting example for others to admire and follow.

A life lived for God leaves a lasting legacy. In an age when generally everyone lives for the moment and is enamored of erecting their own memorials, Samuel's greatness is a worthy goal. We need a revival of ministers in our churches, in our communities, and around this nation who will leave a legacy of church planting and sponsoring for others. Here are a few key ingredients in leaving a lasting legacy.

To Leave a Legacy Requires a Great Dream

In the Scripture, King David had a dream of building a great house for God (1 Chr 22:1–16). This was to be a magnificent, marvelous temple of the Lord. The reason for the king's high resolve was clear. The people of God under his most successful reign had prospered. They lived in their cedar homes and enjoyed a high quality of life for that time. To David, it was inconceivable that God should have no house when his chosen people were so magnificently affluent. For too long the ark of the covenant knew no settled resting place. David thought it was time to do something glorious for God.

Must God look with disfavor upon a people who spend their best on their own comfort while bringing him the second best? Could we be doing that in our respective attitudes toward the sponsoring of new church plants? Or could we dream of how we and our churches could reach a greater number of people for Christ through the sponsoring of new works?

At what rate are we as the Christian church expanding the kingdom of God? I thought about this some years ago. Our church was making it happen in our local setting, but we were not really making a huge numerical difference concerning moving men and women out of darkness and bringing them into the glorious light of salvation. Yes, we were baptizing. In fact, a few times we either led our state in youth baptisms or in total baptisms. But were we making any headway against the lostness of North America? No, we were not.

I heard the statement that church planting is the single most effective evangelistic methodology under heaven. I believed it, and I was faced with what I was going to do about it. God began to challenge me to leave a legacy of church

---

[3] David McCasland, *Daily Bread Devotional Guide* (Grand Rapids: Radio Bible Class, Tuesday, February 1, 2005).

planting. I wanted to be a part of a church-planting movement so much I became willing to make sacrifices in order to contribute to what that movement might look like. I do not believe it is going to come through the "bigger is better" syndrome of modern generations, but rather through starting smaller churches all over this land. The average size of the mainline church in our country is just below two hundred members who are active in worship and weekend events. How can small congregations make a great impact? By leaving a legacy of new churches sponsored and planted.

One Plus One Equals Two

One plus one equals two, and two plus one equals three, and so it goes. Starting new churches can be simple arithmetic, the addition of binary numbers. Suppose we added thirty new saints to God's kingdom this year through our church. Praise the Lord! If we ministered there for the next twenty years with the same results, we would have led six hundred people to salvation. That would certainly be good; but what if we learned how to stop adding and start multiplying?

Two Times Two Equals Four

What if we continued to lead thirty people to the Lord in our local church each year while at the same time sponsoring new church plants? What would be the result if we sponsored and planted a new church once every three years? Let's take a look. In twenty years the ministry would bring six hundred people to a knowledge of Christ. Then, through the new church plant and in the same time line, the number would climb up to twelve hundred. The baptismal rate would soar as well. This would be an impressive legacy, but let's go on.

Three Times Three Times Three Times Three Equals Eighty-One

Introducing twelve hundred souls to Christ would be amazing, but could our influence for the kingdom of God be even greater? Imagine if our churches could catch the vision of planting new churches once every three years, and then lead their sponsored daughter churches to do the same thing. If each church reached twenty persons for Christ per year, you could practice hyper multiplication and reach 43,740 people for Christ in twenty-one years. Imagine. All from practicing a multiplication mind-set.

The Significant Seven in Multiplication

What if we could step this up a little bit more? Imagine that ours is the originating church, and we have planted seven new churches that in turn have started seven new churches, which in turn started seven more new churches. Remember, each of our churches led six hundred people to the gospel over a twenty-year period. Then each of all these churches started another seven churches that in turn started another seven churches in this twenty-year period. What would be the results? Let's take a look.

If six hundred people embraced Christ through the first church plant over the next twenty years, that would be an additional twelve hundred names in the book of heaven. Now each church commits to plant seven new churches within this twenty-year period, resulting in forty-two hundred new Christians through our efforts. Then these seven other new churches start another seven new churches. Now the result jumps up to 29,400 who would be Christ-followers as a direct result of our legacy and mission mind-set. Now those same seven new churches would then plant their seven new churches as well in the same period of time. What would be the result? The result would be an incredible legacy. All of our new churches would account for 205,800 men, women, boys, and girls living in heaven for eternity as a result of taking seriously God's leading to become a spin-off church. Which approach makes more sense—addition or multiplication?

King David's dream was to build a great house for God, who had blessed his people with wonderful affluence. David had another motivation that was more personal. It was God's goodness to him that led to the worthy dream of honoring the Lord with a magnificent temple. A great man wanted to do a great thing for a great God. The problem with many of us is that we have stopped dreaming of great things. We are so inundated with the rush and frenzy of our lives that in many Christians the dream has all but died. We are trapped by the possible, the feasible, and the practical. What a shame so many of us have lost the capacity for dreaming and can never escape the present. This limits human planning and encourages us to be inert in society. The status quo is the opposite of biblical faith because biblical faith is no sedative that lulls people into accepting things as they are. It is faith that dreams of the future.

In the Old Testament the faithful dreamed of the messianic age. In the New Testament they looked forward to the coming of the Lord, and without fear they marched out to conquer the world for Christ. Just as David dreamed of building a glorious house for God, we too must dream in order to leave a significant legacy for the kingdom. As pastors and church planters, we lead our lives among God's people, and that is where we will leave our legacy.

We desperately need to dream about some tomorrows. The one who makes a real contribution in our time, either to men or God, is the one who never looks back with reminiscence, nor around with cynicism or surrender, but ahead with expectancy. It was George Bernard Shaw who said, "Some men see things as they

161

are and say, why? I dream things that never were and say, why not?" And the dream ought to be of a great thing. Those who think our dreams of technology are enough to assure a great future need to recall Henry Thoreau, who watched men put up something they called telegraph wires. When he asked what they were for, he was told they would make it possible for people in Maine to talk with people in Texas. Thoreau's famous observation was: "But what if the people in Maine have nothing to say to the people in Texas, and the people in Texas have nothing to answer to the people in Maine?" We can certainly have some tremendous means for some awfully small ends, and for this reason the dream ought to be of something only God can do. The cause has to be great for us to leave a legacy through the sponsoring and planting of new works.

Leaving a Legacy Requires a Level-Headed Modesty

Of course there are limits to what any one of us can do alone, and when it comes to God's work we should never be going it alone. The Lord's work does not move forward unless there is unity in the body of Christ rather than division and strife. This means there are some things that disqualify us for planting new works for God. The person interested only in what they themselves can accomplish on their own is limited indeed in the good that can be achieved. The beginning of real legacy building is allowing people to be coworkers together to strike blows for the kingdom.

It is scary to think of letting perhaps the most gifted members in church go out to plant other churches, especially in the day of hierarchical churches. But I have learned as a pastor and church planter not to seek control of my members in an effort to lessen any chance of their leaving or of their open rebellion. Wise pastors know that by letting their people go, they will get the greatest commitment. If anything great is to be done, we must do it together. I depend on you and you depend on me, and together we build churches for God. When pastor-leaders steal from others the opportunity to make a kingdom impact through starting new churches, they steal some of the legacy those others might have left. We would all be healthier and more Christian if we could get over our sense of being indispensable and learn to share the load. People commit to causes, not to plans.

Paul had the right idea. He never considered the churches he built to be limited to what he could do, not even when Christians were divided between him and other preachers. Rather, he said, "I planted, Apollos watered, but God gave the growth." The change in verb tense here in 1 Corinthians 3:6 shows what he meant. I planted, Apollos watered. Both did their work once and for all. But God was causing the growth. It is amazing what one man or woman can do who does not care who gets the credit for it. We are all limited by talent, by circumstance, and by opportunity. But if we are willing to do our part and humbly leave the rest for others, if we are willing to plant trees we shall probably never sit under, there is no limit to what we can do with God's help.

To Leave a Legacy Requires a Sense of Urgency

The important thing is the cause. It must be big enough for us to want to advance far beyond our means and abilities. And there must be an urgency to the cause. This sense of urgency is required of church planters and pastors because they have to be forward-looking people. They must be concerned about tomorrow's churches today, and also concerned for those who will inherit the church. A pastor who leaves a significant legacy is a custodian of the future, and it is his job to ensure we leave these future healthy churches in solid shape. Yet many churches that could greatly impact the kingdom of God through sponsoring new churches are often hostages to the present. They are focused only on what is happening this year in this particular community. The day-to-day pace of growing one church keeps them from ever trying to do more for the future. Coping with the urgent ministry needs of the present robs them of the blessings of a future-oriented perspective.

David was interested in building a house for God. He wanted to build it on the very spot God heard David's prayer and turned away pestilence from the people. This was not too far removed from the end of his life. In perfect submission to the will of God, David gave up all thought of finishing the building and prepared something for another to accomplish after him. He gave his energy to the cause. He set his servants to work cutting stones. He prepared the nails for the doors of the gates. He brought brass and cedar trees in abundance. He collected an almost unbelievable amount of silver and gold. And after his hands could do no more, and after his body was cold, only then did the cause come to fruition. The temple rose to the glory of God, and the world has not yet built anything to surpass its magnificence.

David built a house he never entered, and yet he left an unmatched legacy. There are thousands of places across our land that need new churches. Who is willing to do something great, to make a contribution that they might never live to see in final form? Churches plant churches, and on it goes. Who will give towards the cause one will not personally benefit from? Yet this is not our work. It is the work of our Lord. Who will offer commitment, self-forgetfulness, and investment in the sure confidence that nothing done for our Lord is ever finally lost?

God will use pastors all over this land to leave a legacy of churches planted. There is no greater gift one can give to the family of God than that of church plants. One hundred years from now, will anyone know who any of us were? Will our churches be known for bequeathing anything significant? We don't have to be wealthy, well known, or abundantly talented to leave something meaningful for others. Some of the most inspirational legacies have been left by pastors and people outside of the history books and newspaper headlines.

The best way to begin creating a sense of urgency for the future is by being more mindful in the present. This is true of sponsoring new churches, too. It is easy to lose sight of what is happening all around us, to be myopic, to refuse to see and hear what is going on outside our small circle. It is important to be still and stop the frantic pace for a while so God can start doing something new in our lives. Get away from that computer. Turn off that cell phone. Put aside those e-mails, and don't forget to look at the future. Consider the exciting process of leading the church to become a sponsoring reproducing church. Every church birth I have witnessed has been a miracle and an exciting thing to watch happen. Church planting does not drain off energy and resources needed to keep the mother church healthy and growing. In fact, it amplifies and enhances the growth of the original sponsoring church when it begins to be involved with planting new works.

Tips for Leaving a Legacy

- Accept that your church will leave a legacy. That means you want to leave something significant behind after you are gone.
- Regardless of church size, recognize that it can leave a lasting legacy.
- Pastors and members must forgo their ego for investing in only their church and begin to invest in others.
- Sponsoring church pastors need to have a passion for church multiplication as a God-given means of kingdom growth.
- Pull the weeds. Trying too many things can get you into a rut, so trim your church activities to a comfortable range to foster strong growth.
- As a spin-off church, finish what you start.
- Find your niche in sponsoring. Each church can find a niche that will put their talents to use in a fulfilling way.
- Stop and smell the roses. One day I realized that I spent so much time pulling weeds in my rose garden, I hardly noticed the roses anymore. While crawling on my hands and knees, I broke off a branch. On it was a beautiful rose. It took only a minute or so to see that rose, smell that rose, stand up and look at the whole garden, and then get back to work with a new point of view. Sponsoring churches need to stop and smell the roses of God's blessings every now and then, and then get back to gardening.

A church is significant if it impacts areas other than its own.

Results are what count, not perfection. I used to think that everything had to be done perfectly. The major problem with that idea is that no one has enough time to do everything perfectly when it comes to sponsoring new churches. It is all right to do most things reasonably well as a sponsor. Good enough is usually good enough. It is about growing the kingdom of God, not about developing a new set of commandments. Concentrate on growth in the new plant. Perfection will come in glory. I am not excusing sloppy work, but I am saying to consider the final results. It is results that count.

Grasp the big idea that our own legacies are built upon the legacies of those who have gone before us and those who minister beside us. Sometimes the person who leads the orchestra must turn his back on the crowd.

In the final analysis, being a spin-off church is one of the most strategic and biblical means of leaving a legacy of faith and faithfulness.

Most effective people can see how to work towards completing a given task. They are able to see beyond the dream. In the area of church sponsoring and planting of new works, those who have the ability to visualize the end are the ones who will succeed. While most of us don't know where we're headed, those who leave a legacy of planting churches plot several generations down the road—and then live backwards. Just how many things are we and our churches involved in that will outlive us? How many things will God allow us to be part of that will last far beyond our lives? Legacy leavers prepare the way for the next generation. The churches we pastor were planted either by us or someone who has gone before us. Someone prepared the way, and we ought to be thankful.

What are we going to do to help set the stage for the next generation of new churches? How are we going to reserve funds for the future expansion of the gospel through the sponsoring of churches?

Those who leave a legacy are flexible while looking to the future. Legacy churches look way beyond themselves to lay foundations for a glorious future. It takes a lot of courage to realize your dream while you leave a legacy. I personally want to leave something for those who come after me. I want to leave a legacy full of one-of-a-kind gifts, the churches I have been part of as a church planter and key member. Sponsoring churches is our laboratory, and we ought to use it to conduct as many experiments as possible. The sponsoring church's mantra should be "we might fail to successfully sponsor a new work, but we will certainly learn how to successfully sponsor a new work." As my father used to say, "It doesn't matter if you try and try and try again. It does matter if you try and fail, and fail to try again." Leaving a legacy by sponsoring significant new works is not just wishful dreaming. It is the result of determined daily doing. We will never know (until eternity) whose life we reached for Jesus' sake. Leaving a legacy demands that a piece of our hearts be left behind with others always in mind. Isn't that what legacy means, a gift left behind?

Wrapping It Up

Leaving a legacy takes time. We need to challenge ourselves and our members to think about benefiting the church universal over the long haul. What about challenging Christians to account for church planting in their wills and trusts?

Part 5

FINDING THE RESOURCES

*There are various reasons churches should consider
sponsoring a new work. But sooner or later, once the
decision is made to become a sponsor, someone will
ask how much it will cost. There is never a simple
answer to this question. We should ask what we would
want in a church we attended. This kind of question
will help get at a clearer picture of what it will take to
sponsor a new plant.*

— Tom Cheyney

Chapter 17

The Sponsoring Church's Most Critical Ingredient
Finding the Right Church Planter and Team

Has God called us to plant new churches? If so, what gifts are needed and who will make up the church-planting team? How will you find these individuals and persuade them to join the church-planting team? The first step is that those who have been given the vision for the new work begin to pray, and God will begin to do part of the work in bringing together the best team for the assignment. "Unless the Lord builds a house, its builders labor over it in vain" (Ps 127:1). If your spin-off strategy involves your church selecting the church-planting team, start with a small group whose primary role is to seek the face of God for wisdom and direction. Seeking God's face should not go without saying; we do not want to rush ahead of the Lord. And it is actually fairly easy to become disconnected from God from the very beginning of the sponsoring process by not allowing sufficient time in prayer and fasting. In Acts 13:1–3 Barnabas and Saul were set apart for the mission work God called the church of Antioch to do. After much prayer, fasting, and the laying on of hands, they were sent out. This should be our model still today.

The Bible implies that among the first actions taken by the apostle Paul was to share the vision God had given him with the rest of his traveling missionary team. "After he had seen the vision, we immediately made efforts to set out for Macedonia, concluding that God had called us to evangelize them" (Acts 16:10). A church planter needs a team because, unless he has one, he will be limited severely in his efforts as long as he works alone. A single planter may start a worship service where he leads in worship and delivers the message. But a congregation, by scriptural definition, performs several vital functions, including Bible study, worship, evangelism, fellowship, discipleship, ministry, and missions. A lone church planter cannot possibly lead every function as effectively as a team. A biblically functioning church plant requires a team effort, and due diligence is required in developing such a critical unit to expand God's kingdom. Although the Bible does not define the roles for all of Paul's missionary team, we do know that Silas was identified with the apostle in a healing ministry because he was imprisoned with Paul when the slave girl who was following them was healed of her demonic spirit (Acts 16:16–21). The initial step of putting together a church-planting team is so critical to the success of the new church that many pastors and church planters become paralyzed in the process. The good news is that there are many groups and agencies available to assist in the practical "how-tos" of finding the right church planter and church-planting team.

A team is "a group of people bound together by a commitment to reach a shared goal."[1] Thus, a team can be a group of professional football players striving to win the Super Bowl, or it can be a group of Sunday school teachers pouring their lives into middle school students. It can be a group of people starting a church to carry out Christ's Great Commission in their community and around the world. After receiving God's clear direction and go ahead, and along with the congregation's official blessings to move forward, ask God who should comprise the team. The Lord's ability to supernaturally bring together a team has always amazed me. I've seen it hundreds of times and still marvel at it.

When sponsoring church leaders begin praying like this, they will often find talented individuals aboard the team they never even would have considered. Now, what are the practical things a sponsoring church can do to begin putting a church-planting team together?[2]

So I Need a Church-Planting Team. Now What?

"Two are better than one because they have a good reward for their effort. For if either falls, one will lift up his companion. But woe to him who is alone when he falls, for he has no one to help him up. Again, if two lie down together, they will keep warm; but how can one be warm alone? Though one may be overpowered by another, two can withstand him. And a threefold cord is not quickly broken." (Eccl 4:9–12)

---

[1] Gene Wilkes, *Jesus on Leadership* (Nashville: LifeWay Press, 1998), 215.

[2] A great primer for any sponsoring church leadership team would be to attend a Building a Powerful Ministry Team workshop. This information can be found by contacting the Next Level Leadership Network at the North American Mission Board or by going to: www.namb.net/nextlevelleadership.

Harry Truman was often quoted as saying, "It is remarkable how much can be accomplished when you don't mind who receives the credit."[3] For a church planter to be most effective, he must develop a "whatever-it-takes, no-matter-who-gets-the-credit" attitude. In his book *Second Wind: Memoirs of an Opinionated Man*, Bill Russell said this of his former Boston Celtics championship team (which won eleven championships in a thirteen-year period): "By design and by talent we were a team of specialists, and like a team of specialists in any field, our performance depended both on individual excellence and on how we worked together. None of us had to strain to understand. We had to complement each other's specialties; it was simply a fact, and we all tried to figure out ways to make our combination more effective. All work is for a team. No individual has the temperament and skills to do the job. 'The purpose of a team is to make strengths productive and weaknesses irrelevant.'"[4] What a powerful statement. When was the last time your leadership team sat down to think of ways to make your combined roles more effective?

According to Gene Wilkes, building a TEAM involves four steps: (1) Togetherness, (2) Empowerment, (3) Accountability, and (4) Mentoring.[5] First, a church planter must create a sense of togetherness on the church-planting team. I have a coffee mug that says "Together Everyone Achieves More." And that is exactly right. Most people long to be a part of something far greater than themselves. Again, as Peter Drucker rightly notes, "The purpose of a team is to make the strengths of each person effective, and his or her weaknesses irrelevant." Churches have been doing shared ministry for more than a century, so the idea of team work is not new. In fact, Jesus himself ministered through a team (Mark 6:7). Perhaps the apostle Paul was most known for his team work. His fellow workers varied at times, but he was seldom found alone. There was a core group always assisting him in spreading the gospel among the Gentiles. Paul stood at the center of a web of relationships extending around the eastern part of the Mediterranean while his co-laborers constantly came and went.

- Luke was the author of Acts and Paul's "fellow worker" (Phlm 24).
- Barnabas was part of Paul's original team (Acts 11:22–30).
- John Mark was added to the team on the first church-planting trip (Acts 13:2–3,5).
- Epaphras played a significant role in reaching the Colossians with the gospel and probably in both Laodicea and Hierapolis as well. The apostle called him "our much loved fellow slave. He is a faithful minister of the Messiah on your behalf" (Col 1:7).

---

[3] David McCullough, *Truman* (New York: Touchstone, 1992), 564.

[4] *Next Level Leadership Network: Building a Powerful Ministry Team Workbook* (Alpharetta, GA: North American Mission Board, 2002), 40. Last sentence quoting Peter Drucker, *Managing the Nonprofit Organization* (New York: HarperCollins, 1990), 152–53.

[5] Ibid., 219.

- Epaphroditus was a loyal companion and messenger whom Paul described as "my brother, co-worker, and fellow soldier, as well as your messenger and minister to my need" (Phil 2:25).
- Onesimus was an escaped slave (of the Christian Philemon) whom Paul led to the Lord. Paul describes him to the Colossians as "a faithful and loved brother, who is one of you" (Col 4:9).
- Silas is described as a "faithful brother" (1 Pet 5:12) who accompanied Paul through much of his second missionary journey and was with him in Antioch, Philippi, Corinth, and Thessalonica (Acts 15:40).
- Timothy, one of Paul's converts and the son of a believing Jewish woman, was certainly one of the best known of his teammates. "This is why I have sent to you Timothy, who is my beloved and faithful child in the Lord" (1 Cor 4:17). Timothy accompanied Paul on his second and third missionary journeys. During his last imprisonment in Rome, Paul summoned his spiritual child, although we are uncertain they were able to connect before Paul's execution (Acts 16:1–3).
- Titus was another of Paul's converts and a good friend. Paul calls him "my partner and co-worker serving you" (2 Cor 8:23).
- And in Acts 18 we see that others were added to Paul's team in Corinth.

Paul's approach was simple and uncomplicated. It was to win them, build them, and then send them. That is still the best way to plant churches today. Win converts to the Lord in the local church. Disciple the new Christians and mentor them so they are equipped for the journey. Then send them out with the blessings of both the sponsoring church and the new plant. Watch God bless not only the new work, but the sponsoring one as well. Paul multiplied his ministry by multiplying leaders, not by gathering followers. He started with a few potential coworkers, and he committed his life to helping them reach their leadership potential. Because he did, the first-century church experienced exponential growth such as the world has never seen.

The essence of successful partnership is synergy, working together and being compatible as kingdom participants. It is the idea that the outcome of the whole is far greater than the sum of the parts. It's as simple as this: two people working together can accomplish more than what each can accomplish individually. Acting together in a combined way brings the leveraging of assets, abilities, and strengths. To leverage assets effectively and create synergy, however, each participant must be working towards the same goal. The resources for this step will help the various partners achieve the "good reward for their labor" as seen in the above text.

According to Dennis Mitchell, director for men of the strategic readiness team within the Church Planting Group of the North American Mission Board, only 5.2% of Southern Baptist churches are sponsoring new works. Many more churches want to be involved, but they are unfamiliar with the processes. A survey of pastors and church staff from thirty-eight churches in California revealed that not one had received training in college, seminary, or through their continuing leadership development programs to prepare them to lead their congregations to plant a new work. The main point is that the church planter will be limited seriously in his efforts as long as he works alone.

Planting Teams Are the Best Way to Plant Churches

Church-planning teams are superior to individual efforts for many different reasons, including these seven:

- First, teams involve more people, thus affording more resources, ideas, and energy than would be possessed by an individual.
- Second, teams maximize a leader's potential and minimize weaknesses. Strengths and weaknesses are more exposed in individuals.
- Third, teams provide multiple perspectives of how to meet a need or reach a goal, thus devising several alternatives for each situation. Individual insight is seldom as broad and deep as a group's when it takes on a problem.
- Fourth, teams share the credit for victories and the blame for losses, fostering genuine humility and authentic community. Individuals take credit and blame alone, which sometimes leads to pride or even a sense of failure.
- Fifth, teams keep leaders accountable for the goal, whereas individuals connected to no one can change the goal without accountability.
- Sixth, teams can simply do more than an individual.
- Seventh, Jesus did his ministry using teams.[6]

Has the Lord been working in your life and your church's life such that there might be a vision (and even location) for sponsoring a new church? Perhaps it might be right next door, or twenty miles away, or a thousand or more miles away. Now it is time to find out about the target area and begin writing names alongside the positional functions we mentioned earlier. Have you looked at that list each day in prayer? Have you heard yet from God not only on the planter to choose, but also the team that will come alongside the sponsoring pastor and lead planter to grow the new work? To get to that stage, there are six key essential considerations for the sponsoring church in choosing the team:

First, a godly spirit. The number one qualification for any person on a church planting team is having a godly spirit. Such passages as 1 Timothy 3:1–13, Titus 1:6–9, and Acts 6:3 set the standard.

Second, a clear vision. Any time more than one individual is brought together there will be a diverse set of ideas regarding vision. There is always potential for

---

[6] Gene Wilkes, *Jesus on Leadership*, 212.

disagreements, so both the sponsoring church pastor and church planter must be sure the entire team is aligned with their vision for the new work. The best way to do this is to keep the vision always before each possible team member. Unless everyone is "on the same page," the launch and future of the new work will be problematic.

When identifying a church planter and potential team member, ask the question whether the candidate fits the community that the sponsoring church is attempting to reach. And be sure the wrong people get off the team before you reach critical mass and the momentum gets going. At times we see people as team assets early on, and only later do we see they could make a better contribution elsewhere. But if for whatever reason they don't fit, then they should no longer be a part of the planting team. Eliminating someone from the team at such a critical time as the early starting of a new church will be difficult. But it will be necessary. All members of the team must be one-hundred-percent on board for what everyone believes God is calling them to do.

During the dry spells of planting work, a team member might come forward with their own solution to things. Perhaps it is a great idea, but if that member has been waiting for the opportunity to suggest their own agenda, then competing visions will arise. During these times the pastor and planter need to stand their ground according to the vision God has given them. It is much easier to handle potential conflicts on the front-end of the church plant, because otherwise, alternative visions will surface later at just the wrong time. Members of the team need to be committed to the dream. No way is the perfect way to do things, but the team must agree to do things the planter's way. Follow the leading of the Lord and gather the right people for your team; for the right team members will be an incredible blessing. And the right team will assist you in building the right church.

Third, a practical yearning. Each team member should be committed to the purpose of the team no matter the stage of the church plant—whether it's church planting, church renewal, or something else. His or her soul should yearn for the cause—even anguish over the cause.

Fourth, role clarity and function. This would include such things as the number of team members, their roles or assignments on the team, and their special giftedness. There are different types of teams. (a) The two-person team consists of a leader and a manager. The leader would be the one with the spiritual and natural gifts of leadership (Rom 12:8), and possibly the spiritual gift of faith (1 Cor 12:9), which certainly involves vision. The manager should be the person with the spiritual and natural gifts of administration (1 Cor 12:28). (b) The three-person team comprises a pastor, an evangelist, and a music specialist. (c) The three- to five-person team is constituted according to certain spiritual gifts. For example, they strongly encourage teams that are led by someone with the gift of leadership. The other two members consist of a teacher and a programmer.

Fifth, a skill-set blueprint. This includes spiritual gifts, passion, temperament, leadership role and style, along with natural gifts and talents. It is not a good idea, for example, to ask an introvert to function in the area of assimilation or gathering. They won't be comfortable in that role, and they won't be successful.

Sixth, an idea of one's disposition. What is the best temperament combination for recruiting and developing gifted, significant church-planting teams? The temperament of each team member has much to do with how successful they will be in talking with, getting to know, and eventually assimilating individuals into the core group to grow the new church. Never get to the place where a warm body that is mildly interested looks good. Poor team selections will surface six to eight months down the road, and a lot of time will have been wasted—probably including the time trying to get the ill-fitted member off the team. The number one and number two quality temperaments I want to take with me into a new work are the gift of evangelism (great gatherers) and the gift of worship leading (ability to keep what you and your gatherers bring into the new work.) The rest will come along as God raises up other leaders to join the core group. An untalented and ungifted worship leader will sink the ship. Leaders are hard to find, so if one might be used of God, pray hard and harder that they are in sync with the planter's vision.

How Do the Sponsoring Church and Lead Planter Enlist Members for a Church-Planting Team?

Pray

First and foremost, pray! Jesus said, "The harvest is abundant, but the workers are few. Therefore pray to the Lord of the harvest to send out workers into His harvest" (Matt 9:37–38). In writing about what makes for a great company, Jim Collins observed that "if you begin with 'who,' rather than 'what,' you can more easily adapt to a changing world. . . . Great vision without great people is irrelevant."[7] This most definitely applies during the first two years of a church plant, when things are changing very quickly. Ask God to send people of solid character who are committed to Christ and God's vision for the new church.

List Tasks and Define Roles Needed to Accomplish the Vision God Has Given for the Community

Simply put, know what is needed before beginning to look for someone. This step will help when it comes to praying for future team members. John Maxwell has compiled a list of "Top 20 Personal Requirements" that he looks for in poten-

---

[7] Jim Collins, *Good to Great* (New York: HarperCollins, 2001), 42.

174

tial staff members. This list could serve church planters well in putting together their leadership teams.

- Positive attitude—the ability to see people and situations in a positive way
- High energy level—strength and stamina to work hard and not wear down
- Personal warmth—a manner that draws people to them
- Integrity—trustworthiness, good solid character
- Responsible—reliable; gives no excuses
- Good self-image—one who feels good about self, others, and life
- Mental horsepower—an ability to keep learning as the job expands
- Leadership ability—a high influence over others
- Follower-ship ability—the willingness to submit, play team ball, and follow the leader
- Absence of personal problems—one's personal, family, and business life are in order
- People skills—the ability to draw people in and develop them
- Sense of humor—enjoys life and does not take self too seriously
- Resilience—ability to "bounce back" when problems arise
- Track record—past experience and success, hopefully in two or more situations
- Great desire—a hunger for growth and personal development
- Self-discipline—a willingness to "pay the price" and ability to handle success
- Creative—the ability to see solutions and fix problems
- Flexibility—unafraid of change; fluid; flows as the organization grows
- Sees "big picture"—able to look beyond personal interests and see the total picture
- Intuitive—the ability to discern and sense a situation without tangible data

Look for Ways God May Be Answering Your Prayers

Keep both eyes open for the people God brings into the lives of the sponsoring church and the lead planner. When looking for God's specific answers to our need, I have always used the "Five A's" I learned from John Maxwell. These are:

- Assessment of needs for the plant—What do we really need and not merely want?
- Assets on hand—Who are the people already in our path who are available and might fit the vision God has given?
- Ability of candidates—Who is able?
- Attitude of candidates—Who is willing?

175

- Accomplishments of candidates—Who gets the job done?[8]

Personally Invite Individuals to Join You in Your Church Planting Endeavor

I have learned over the years as a church planter that the people needed typically are the people who don't need to add anything to their schedules. They are busy people because they get things done. Since they will not look for a spot on the team, the team leader must go looking for them. They rarely volunteer to do anything, but generally they will do whatever they can do if they are personally asked or challenged.

As You Spend Time with People, Listen to Them and Observe Them in Different Ministry Situations

Over time, one learns what ministries they feel most passionate about and what ministries bring them the most fulfillment. The North American Mission Board has a booklet titled *Discovery Tools*, which is a great self-assessment aid to help bring clarity to an individual's sense of call, spiritual gifts, areas of passion, and ministry preference.

Equip and Release People for Service

Training ministry leaders every six months gives them enough tools and information to be effective, yet it does not overburden them.

Monitor Their Progress Monthly and Mentor Them as Needed

John Maxwell is correct when he states, "Mentoring is how leaders prepare the next generation of leaders for service. Without future leaders, there is no future for the church or ministry." Paul not only had a sending church, but he also had a mentor in Barnabas. Successful church planters are teachable and actively seek out a personal mentor. Ed Stetzer notes that church planters who meet as often as once a week with their mentor have a significantly larger worship attendance than those who meet monthly or less frequently.[9]

Encourage Them Often and Celebrate the Victories, Both Great and Small

If we never encourage our plant team, they will never sacrifice for significant victories when the need arises. Do not become heavy handed with them in the small things. Enjoy the victories and tell the sponsoring church of the great things God is doing in their new work!

---

[8] John C. Maxwell, *Developing the Leaders around You* (Nashville: Thomas Nelson Inc., 1995), 39.
[9] Ed Stetzer, *Planting New Churches in a Postmodern Age* (Nashville: Broadman & Holman Publisher, 2003), 93–94.

Things the Sponsoring Church Can Do to Get Ready

Here are some vital items that need to be developed while plans for the new church plant are beginning to gel.

- Put together a missions partnership committee.
- Develop an intercessory prayer team.
- Identify other partnering churches—including "entry-level" partners.
- Identify and enlist a church planter, who may even be someone in your church.
- Enlist and build a support system for the church planter and spouse.
- Survey members to identify interested individuals, and identify and enlist those felt called to participate in a new church plant.
- Contact local, state, and denominational entities.
- Start or participate in a Multiplying Church Network (MCN).
- Begin determining the responsibilities and expectations of all parties connected to the plant.
- Work on developing a weekly mentor and monthly supervisor.
- Develop the Planter-Partner Covenant.

Where Can a Mission Church Discover the Right Church Planter?

From the Present Membership

There may be someone in the mother church God has burdened with reaching people. As the church leadership begins to cast the vision for participating in a church-planting movement, do not be surprised to have laymen and laywomen step forward. In the Second Great Awakening of the eighteenth century, the Methodists grew in the American South by 300% using circuit-riding clergymen. That is great growth. But during the same period, Baptists grew by 400% through the ministries of laymen serving as farmer-preachers. A godly layman already established in a community has tremendous advantages over someone moving into the area. Besides calling out laymen from the sponsoring church, God may also burden one of the church staff members to lead a daughter congregation.

As a sponsoring church, one of the things that will help planters is to give them access to your church membership and allow them to share their vision. It is always better to be a sending church with excited members who want to participate in church-planting missions. A generous sponsoring church is so helpful to a new work because members tend to take ownership for the people they know are becoming part of the new work. It is important, however, for the planter to clear willing candidates with the sponsoring church staff, because they might know something about a particular individual who might harm the new work.

From the Local Associations and State Conventions

Over the years associational directors of missions have referred some of the best planters I have ever worked with. After the local church, the local association is a great place to look for someone who could manage a church start. State conventions and many local associations have personnel on hand who have been assigned church-planting responsibilities. These people are aware of individual church planters all over who are seeking sponsorship and ministry opportunities.

From the Forty-two Southern Baptist Colleges and Seven Seminaries

In my own denomination, the state conventions and the North American Mission Board have partnered with the seven Southern Baptist Convention seminaries in North America in creating the Nehemiah Project. Each seminary has a Nehemiah project director who oversees the identification, recruitment, development, and deployment of church-planting interns in North America. These interns usually qualify for Nehemiah project funding when appointed to an approved Nehemiah church-plant location. Campus directors also maintain information on many students who feel called to church planting but do not fulfill all the requirements of the Nehemiah program.

Several colleges and non-Southern Baptist seminaries are also involved in the Nehemiah partnership. These students have taken church planting courses developed by the North American Mission Board, and many of them have participated in the Church Planter Assessment process. Some qualify for appointment as church-planting missionaries.

Recruiting Workers from the Sending Church

Sending churches very often raise up leadership from within the church who feel called to be part of a new church. They may leave the initiating church permanently, or covenant to assist for a period of time. I have found that a minimum of eighteen months is sufficient time for a willing individual really to be used in the new work. Consider the following points in recruiting church-planting teams.

1. Prayer is the key. Pray. Now pray harder! Pray some more. Get God's word on this first.
2. Responsibility should be delegated, and it should be commensurate with spiritual maturity.
3. Offer short-term and one-time entry-level tasks for unproven people.
4. Try to plug people in according to their spiritual gifts.

5. Remember the goal of eventual indigenous leadership.
6. Communicate your expectations, philosophy of ministry, and vision to helpers.
7. In recruiting, remember that many people are more attracted by vision than by need.

Advantages of Teams from within the Sending Church

1. A ready-made core group helps the church planter know there will be assistance and accountability partners in and for the new church.
2. A ready-made core group saves time for the church planter.
3. Church-planting gifts are found among the congregations of most healthy churches, and people in these existing churches want to be used of God.
4. There is extended opportunity to do long-range training or vision casting when a core group forms early in the life of a new church.
5. Some people in the sending church may be looking for a new challenge in their Christian lives.
6. Some people in a sponsoring church may have moved far enough away that a new church in their community is appealing. Others may actually move into a community where an initiating church wants to plant.
7. For sponsor churches with a space problem, people leaving to assist the new daughter church will provide needed room in the mother church for kingdom growth.
8. Some members of larger churches feel their gifts and talents could be better used in smaller, newer congregations.
9. Some people feel called of God to remain members of the sponsor church but to use their gifts to assist in new-church development.
10. Sending church members who assist in a church plant may return to the sponsor church with new ideas, plus an infectious vision and enthusiasm.
11. Core group members from the sponsor church should be already proven, making it easier to facilitate leadership.

Challenges for Teams from within the Sending Church

1. When a lead church planter is selected from outside the church, the planter is a newcomer who must gain the respect of the group.
2. Team members may continue relating to the sending church rather than the new plant as their church home, never transferring their relationships and allegiances to the new church.

3. Sometimes an existing core group has a different vision or different core values than the church planter. In these cases it is necessary to develop a harmony of agendas.

4. Sometimes a team from the sponsor church is not the right match for the community of people the new church intends to reach.

5. Some staff and lay leaders from the sending church may resent the church plant taking "gifted" people from their areas of ministry.

6. Some team members may spend too much time talking about how things were done at the sponsor church.

7. Well developed teams from sending churches may have a difficult time including new people in friendship and leadership circles as the mission church grows.

8. Sometimes existing churches send their problem people to new churches, thinking they just need a fresh start. Actually, problem people are often an even bigger problem in smaller groups.

Recommendations Are Made Based on the Following Questions

This set of questions ought to be asked by any sponsoring church leader before he continues to develop the leadership team along with the church planter.

1. Does the potential lead church planter have a heart and passion for church planting?

2. Could the potential church planter work with a team?

3. Is this someone who could lead a church-planting effort?

4. If they are not to be the lead planter, what would be his or her role?

5. Would the potential planter follow the apostolic example and commit to planting churches again and again?

6. Is reproduction part of his vision?

7. Would the potential church planter ultimately be happier in a ministry other than church planting?

Christian Schwarz surveyed more than one thousand churches on every continent and discovered that in growing churches there were common quality characteristics. These qualities were not culture specific but rather crossed all cultural boundaries. And it was not a matter of having three or four of the characteristics; if all these qualities were present to a certain level, the church without exception grew. The thesis of the survey results is that churches grow best when they grow naturally. In other words, don't try to grow; concentrate on quality and then the quantity will come. For a church to be a healthy church, these eight qualities must be present:

Schwarz's Eight Quality Characteristics

1. It must have empowering leadership. The pastor is relationally oriented and able to empower others to do ministry in the church.
2. It is a gift-oriented ministry where people are encouraged to use their spiritual gifts. Both charismatic and noncharismatic churches were studied, so this is not a reference to ecstatic gifts, but specifically a reference to ministry gifts. People were given assistance in finding their gifts and then placed in ministries where these gifts were exercised.
3. There must be a passionate spirituality where members are on fire for God. Schwarz's study wasn't about contemporary churches with passionate spirituality and inspiring worship. Rather, the people who attended these churches had a passionate spirituality in their lives.
4. There are functional structures. Not structure bound by tradition, but organized for function. These structures were flexible and met the needs of the churches as they grew.
5. There is an inspiring worship service that is not necessarily seeker-sensitive but inspiring to the one who attends. Some of the churches in the study were traditional and some were contemporary. But the people attending these churches found the worship inspiring.
6. These churches have holistic small groups. The study showed that this was the strongest factor related to growth. And there were a variety of types of small groups found in these churches.
7. They practiced a need-oriented evangelism. This is an evangelism focusing on the needs of non-Christians. Meeting needs is seen as a venue to reaching people for Christ.
8. There is an abundance of loving, caring relationships that move beyond church meetings. It's a case of fellowship that goes well below the surface.[10]

The goal for the sponsoring church is to begin a new work that ultimately becomes a growing, thriving, fully self-supporting church. As the new work grows, it grows spiritually and corporately. There are various roles of the church planter, and sponsoring-church leaders must be aware of these various roles as they continue to develop the initial phase of the plant.[11]

The Church Starter/Initiator Role

What qualities and skills should be demonstrated by the effective church planter? A church-planter assessment will explore at least these:

---

[10] Christian A. Schwarz, *Natural Church Development* (Carol Stream, IL: ChurchSmart Resources, 1996), 22–36.

[11] Floyd Tidsworth, *Life Cycle of a New Congregation* (Nashville: Broadman, 1992), 78–81.

- The church planter exercises faith and exhibits hope and expectation.
- The church planter has a capacity for vision capacity by projecting into the future and approaching obstacles as opportunities.
- The church planter is committed to church growth.
- The church planter is personally motivated, has a desire to do well, and is committed to excellence.
- The church planter is willing to work hard and smart, and stays with the job.
- The church planter is responsive to the community and adapts the church to the character of the community.
- The church planter creates an ownership of ministry by helping people feel responsible for the growth and development of the church.
- The church planter uses people's gifts by matching them with tasks to be done.
- The church planter builds cohesiveness.
- The church planter has the spouse's cooperation, and they share the ministry vision.
- The church planter is adaptable and able to cope with abrupt and constant change.
- The church planter adapts methods to current situations.

The Founding Pastor/Developer Role

Based upon his study of forty-four young and growing churches, Tidsworth suggests that the founding pastor should be:

- Matched to the local community where a new congregation is beginning
- Experienced in the pastorate
- Prepared for the mission field by experience and training
- Willing to do most of the work in the beginning stages, but later shares ministry responsibilities
- Flexible
- Faithful and optimistic
- Patient, yet urgent about progress
- Stable enough to stay until results are evident
- Enthusiastic about the new church and has a vision for the future
- A strong leader and organizer
- Cooperative with the wider fellowship of faith but gives priority to the local field
- A self-starter
- Willing to discard ineffective methods and try others
- Able to grow personally and professionally
- Able to handle criticism and pressure

- Identified with the community or group he wants to reach
- A good manager of time and a hard worker who has a growth attitude
- Willing to involve, train, and try lay people as the work grows
- A preacher and teacher who works from a biblical base
- A good manager of money
- A builder of good relationships
- One who has a love for God and people
- Evangelistic locally but who has a world vision for sharing the gospel

The Growth Pastor/Propagator Role

All of the qualities listed above of the founding pastor also need to be evident in the growth pastor, as well as several more characteristics. The growth pastor should be one who:

- Can keep an organization going
- Leads in membership growth
- Is an outstanding preacher
- Relates well to the larger community
- Understands church financing
- Enlarges ministries of the church
- Can manage and supervise a paid staff
- Is able to lead in building expansion

Unfortunately most church planters and pastors tend to leave the new work before they ever get to the stage of leadership development. They enjoy the planter or initiator role, and they may even like the founding pastor/developer role. But the concerted effort required for success in the growth pastor/propagator role frankly is not something most people get excited about. The fact is, gifts differ. Some are initiators, others are founders, and still others are highly effective at encouraging continuing growth. Yet the really productive church planter needs to try developing the qualities for all three roles into the ministry team. Of course we must never forget God's supreme role in the process. Paul said, "I planted, Apollos watered, but God gave the growth" (1 Cor 3:6). To be successful, all of the quality characteristics of all three roles must be covered in the new church plant. Every initiating pastor and church planter should ask themselves what kind of church starter role fits their gifts and the gifts of others on the team. The planter will act as a coach raising team members up to complete specific tasks. The pastor's role is helping people to find their place in the service of ministry.

The Various Roles for the Church-Starting Team

The Sponsoring Church and New Work Leader. This is the point person in the whole church-starting endeavor.

The Lead Pastor/Planter. This is the person who shepherds the new congregation. He should be very personable and able to develop ongoing relationships. Additionally, he should be a charismatic leader who communicates energy and excitement.

The Worship Leader. This team member is a facilitator, programmer, and music specialist, one who uses all the available resources to enhance the worship experience of the new congregation. The worship leader must be talented, so much so that it is worth waiting for someone with gifts in this area rather than using someone just to fill the position. Many churches begin by using computer-generated worship songs that the congregation sings. Moving as soon as is possible to a solid and anointed worship leader will greatly improve assimilation in the new church plant.

The Recruiter-Evangelist. The entire focus for this person is to lead outreach efforts for the new work.

The Assimilation Leader. Sometimes this team member is called the small groups coach, or the base coach. Usually this is an unpaid coordinator of the assimilation process, helping people to work their way around the bases and encouraging new attendees to join small groups.

The Business and Financial Administrator is the person who manages and oversees the finances of the new work, including deputation. It is not necessary to fill this position immediately if the mother church is handling this role. But before very long, the new church will require someone in this important role.

The Discipleship Leader leads the discipling efforts of the new congregation.

The Youth Worker ministers to the youth and their families.

The Children's Ministry Leader-Recruiter. This team member establishes and directs the children's ministry of the new congregation. One of the immediate areas to develop is a preschool class. A complete children's ministry can be developed over time, but these younger children and infants need a classroom and a nursery of their own right away.

The Program Leader is an unpaid volunteer who coordinates other programs, such as finding and assigning greeters and ushers. From the very first day of the new church's public ministry, this leader needs to have other volunteers in place. It is important to make visitors welcome.

The Pastoral Care Leader. This leader organizes and maintains the pastoral care needs of the church members.

Wrapping It Up

A sponsoring church pastor or new work leader must build a team that thrives and not merely survives. Nothing is more exciting than building that church planting team and mentoring the man who will serve as the lead planter. Nothing is more exhilarating than watching God gather an effective team of individuals working toward the singular goal of launching a growing new church. That is what all this is about—kingdom expansion and ultimately God's glory. That is the end toward which all this effort is directed. The sponsoring church pastor needs to remember this when feeling, as it often happens, a bit envious of the church planter across the table in the conference room. But God blesses not only new church plants. Rich blessings come to those churches that are boldly sponsoring new works. Stay the course and watch how God will bless your leadership and your people's vision. Get ready for your own blessing and remember to give God the credit both in public and in private.

Allow the new church-leadership team to develop in a gradual and natural way, and avoid what many pastors do when presenting a new idea—scare the leadership away. Some pastors spend too much time magnifying the risk, and they scare even the boldest would-be planter away. Others minimize the rewards, and instead of talking about the wonderful joy of planting a new work, they emphasize the drudgery. Also, some pastors keep people from manifesting their spiritual gifts by being highly critical of everything they do. In this case, the team eventually will just give up and go somewhere else.

Another way an unsuspecting sponsoring church pastor can discourage people from becoming actively involved in the new work is to display a lack of confidence in the lead planter or some other team leader. When potential participants hear something like, "I wonder if you are the right planter for our work, but I'll give you a chance," this is not a high type of recommendation to become involved. If there are doubts about whether the planter is the right fit, cut bait now. An insidious way to keep others from joining the team is threatening to deny your church's full support if the new plant group doesn't do everything the way the sponsoring church pastor thinks they ought to do it. Of course planters need to listen to wise counsel, but church planting is not about always moving a new church in the same direction as an existing church. Lastly, some sponsoring church pastors spend a little too much time emphasizing the pressure of new church planting when they should be highlighting the joy of being used by God for such an exciting work.

Wait on the Lord, and when he says go, get moving. Give those who seek to be on the new church team a reality check by having the planter and sponsoring church pastor create a presentation about their vision for the new work. Include in the presentation some sobering details, such as the fact that not everyone will go on the journey, or that there will be times of loneliness, or that as the work grows there will be less time with the sponsoring church and the lead pastor because they will be focusing on new people and developing new leaders. Help these prospective team members get a clear picture that this is not a summer camp trip but something much larger. Give them a feel for where they are going and what they are getting into.

When should a new church be launched? There are a number of good reasons to wait on this. The best reason is that people are more likely to come to the first service of the new church than at any other time. Therefore the first service must be very well accomplished, everything in order, and everyone on the same page. In addition, a large group of new people coming together for the first time provides a sense of comfort to most visitors because everyone is brand new. No one is singled out. On the other hand, you don't want to wait too long. If it takes two years to build a core group of twenty to thirty people, that is probably too long. Don't lose momentum, and if there is a sociological need in the group to launch, then launch as soon as possible. Generally speaking, core preparation should last from three to nine months.

Sponsoring church workers should not be surprised if other churches in the local association are also looking for opportunities to help in a church-planting effort. Just like the church potluck, it is amazing what can happen when everyone brings a little something to the table. Welcome them and help them grow. Perhaps one day they too will be the lead sponsor of a new work. They will thank you and God will bless your church's willingness to boldly plant churches for kingdom growth.

Chapter 18

Finding Funds within the Sponsoring Church
How to Finance Your Sponsored
New Church Plant

Thcre is never a simple answer to the question of how much a new church plant will cost. This chapter will help answer many of the questions that need answering before and during preparation to sponsor another new church. Sponsoring churches should welcome the exciting opportunity to discover just how God will work in raising the funding of Christian churches. It is a blessing to rediscover that the often quoted passage of Scripture, "to whom much has been given, much is required," actually is true.

The first few years of a new church's life are vitally important because they set the tone for years to come. About 57% of the evangelical world's financial resources are found within the shores of the United States.[1] The United Kingdom has the second largest percentage—another 10%. In just two nations there is more than two-thirds of the world's Christian wealth. In a world of grinding greed and political and theological crises, people and pastors of action are needed to plant churches all over the world.

The Top Ten Signs of a Broke Church Planter
10. American Express says please, please, PLEASE, leave home without it!
9. You are considering robbing the food kitchen.
8. The long distance providers no longer call asking you to switch.

---

[1] John Hanna, "On Fundraising," *Keys to the Nations* (March 26, 1998): section 5, page 1.

7. You rob both Peter and Paul.
6. You clean your home hoping to find change.
5. Right now a lottery ticket looks like an investment.
4. Your bologna has no first name.
3. You have begun washing Styrofoam plates and plastic forks.
2. You have a lovely basket of McDonald's condiments in the middle of your kitchen table.
1. During the Lord's Supper you go back for seconds.

The initial financial support of a new church is a critical factor in its incubation stage. The early preparation phase for any plant must include this important area of support. Failure seriously to consider the work of developing resources can limit a new work or destine it to oblivion. It is obvious that new churches need money. When my wife and I were married, we had the ability to purchase everything new—if we wanted to be in debt for the rest of our lives. Thankfully we opted for a wiser approach and acquired our meager earthly possessions as we could afford them. One danger many newlyweds face is allowing debt to build up while they are filling their new homes with a lot of stuff they could have waited to buy later. Many new churches want everything new when they start, and this is where wisdom from the sponsoring church is vital. Instead of buying everything new, perhaps the new church plant could use all the extra equipment floating around in the storage closets of the mother church. Or perhaps a sponsoring Bible study class could buy the critical items needed and be a blessing to a class in the new church. Most new churches need to begin with what they have and then allow the Lord and the sponsoring church to provide the necessary resources to expand its ministry.

Too often members of existing churches assume it takes a lot of money to be a planting church. The reality is that any church, no matter the size or socioeconomic configuration, can be involved in some way in church planting. Sponsoring opportunities come in a myriad of ways.

Options When Regular Monetary Support Is Not Involved

1. No regular monetary support is required. What is required is prayer. A sponsoring church can join a church planter's intercessory prayer team and become a great blessing as they uphold the work in prayer.
2. Sponsoring church members can be Barnabus encouragers. A sponsor church can offer encouragement to the planter and his family in dozens of different ways, like writing notes of encouragement, providing support during difficult times, or having the family over for a meal.
3. The existing church can lend a genuine authenticity to the new ministry. Since a new church usually has a sponsor church, sometimes a church

with even limited financial resources can serve as the legitimizing sponsor or spokesperson for a qualified church planter. This gives the new work the authentic look of a real church doing real ministry for the Lord.

4. Many sponsor churches can offer meeting rooms in their facilities, so the new church has room to stretch out. This is especially helpful for a new ethnic church start. My home church provides the entire facility of a rather large physical plant for our Hispanic church to use free of charge. We have become a family with one common goal of reaching our community for Christ through two churches using one facility.

5. Sometimes a sponsor church can offer material resources, such as a one-time gift of Bibles, discipleship literature, sound equipment, visual projectors, chairs, and so on. The first way many new church plants get started is through this method of accepting material resources. This is an easy way for an existing church to take the adventure of new church sponsorship.

Options When Regular Monetary Support Is Involved

1. *Full sponsorship*: One church takes on the full responsibility for planting a new church. No help is needed or sought from other churches or denominational entities.

2. *Single sponsorship with supporting partners*: One church takes on the primary responsibility for planting a new church, but it also seeks financial assistance from denominational partners or other likeminded missional churches.

3. *Multiple sponsorships*: This is when several churches in a particular area join efforts as a cluster to plant new churches. They share financial support at varying levels. This option may or may not involve denominational partners.

4. *An association of cooperative churches*: Here several churches spread across the state may agree to join efforts to plant churches in strategic areas. Again, they share financial support with or without denominational partners.

5. *Ongoing adoption*: A church may choose to join an existing sponsorship arrangement by financially supporting a new church already in progress.

6. *A church-planting center*: In some cases a church or network of churches may want to establish a center for church-planter discovery, development, and deployment. These centers are raised up out of larger churches whose leaders believe they can plant exponentially more churches by working

as a mini movement that not only trains but also deploys the planters to specific target areas prepared for harvest.

Financial Resources

In addition to the right people resources, there are financial resources to consider. The type and amount of financial resources required depends upon the planter's approach and philosophy of church planting. Although the remainder of this chapter discusses financial resources, remember that people resources are just as important as, if not more important than, financial resources. Never apologize for raising support for the new church. Every Lord's Day, we do this through our tithes and offerings, which then develop resources for our existing work. We do this for our existing churches, so raising support for new mission churches should come as no surprise. Developing financial resources is a biblical concept.

How Much Will It Cost?

The cost is greater than you realize. Regardless of the type of church one plans, chances are good it will cost more than you think. Because of this, successful planters need to pay close attention to the identification of resources. No church is planted without personal sacrifice, and it has been the experience of many that one's vision always outpaces resources; so cost must be considered, and ongoing efforts to raise resources are always necessary.

Your chosen model could be the largest expense. There are many different approaches and models to church planting, but we will look at two of them, the traditional church plant and the nontraditional church plant. It is essential to have the right model to fit the target area chosen for the plant and the amount of support developed.

> *Traditional church plants*—Typically these require a meeting place and a paid church planter. Their style of ministry may or may not be traditional, but they take on a more institutional form with a very organized structure. They usually require a large amount of financial resourcing or a bivocational staff.
>
> *Nontraditional church plants*—These are usually more organic than organized. They may meet in houses, storefronts, office buildings, apartments, or club houses. They are often informal and led by either lay people or by a pastor who doesn't need a salary. They focus on multiplying and expanding through small networks. They often require very little funding, but they do require a high level of commitment.

In the planting of any church, one must begin with the end in mind. If God is leading us to an unreached people group requiring a more institutional form of church, it may be necessary to have a large amount of resources from day one. It is important to understand, however, that putting many resources into a church is no guarantee of a given outcome. Today, there is an emerging vision for planting churches requiring little, if any, revenue. These churches usually meet in homes, coffee shops, boardrooms, and apartments. By design, they stay small, but they focus on multiplying themselves through a growing network of like-minded missional lay Christian leaders. This emerging vision seems to be embraced by a young, postmodern culture and may be the antithesis of the highly organized and institutionalized megachurch.

The cost is commensurate with your launch platform. There are a variety of ways to plant a new congregation that affects the amount of financial resources needed. A general rule is the more believers you have in the core group, the less likely a new church needs to focus on a high-cost launch strategy. If believers are taught to share their faith and are actively building relationships in the unchurched community, growth can be assured through proper networking. If the planter is in a highly non-Christian context and has a traditional church-planting strategy with a small believer base, the start-up strategies will likely depend on ministry evangelism events and an effective marketing plan. Both of these approaches can be costly.

Another factor likely to impact the cost of start-up is the meeting facility and the rental cost of that facility. If the launch strategy is to attract a large group of people, it will require a meeting place able to handle the crowd. A space for two hundred to five hundred people in worship can require a sizeable amount of money. But a private home, coffee shop, or boardroom usually doesn't cost much, if anything, and opens up an entire network of new contacts and associations.

An example of a cross between the traditional and nontraditional types of church planting can be seen at Rick Duncan's church. He is the missions pastor of the Cuyahoga Valley Community Church in Cleveland, Ohio. Several years ago Rick wanted to launch a new work within its present facilities targeted towards today's twenty-somethings. Today there are two churches using a magnificent facility. The original church is still called by the original name, and the new church, which meets in the late afternoon, is called the 707 Church. Both congregations are growing and starting new churches and services to reach the Cleveland area for Christ.

The cost is contingent on ministry context. Socioeconomic factors have much to do with an individual's or church's values. What one group might see as wasteful, another considers suitable to the cost of doing business. It is true that when one's church-planting focus group represents a higher socioeconomic group, that church plant requires more financial support, because limited monetary support could spell doom right from the start. Very many factors play into this aspect of costing, so careful consideration should be given to the issue of ministry context.

The cost is dependent on one's personal skill set as a planter. Every planter is unique and will approach the task of planting based on personal spiritual gifts, heart, ability, personality, and experiences. One planter with a business background may be task-oriented due to an administrative gift. It is likely that planter will approach church planting from an organizational perspective, creating a start-up strategy similar to the launching of a new business. A highly relational church planter, on the other hand, may have a start-up strategy reflecting a more organic approach to setting up a new work.

Within various denominations are groups charged with starting churches and working with sponsoring and partnering congregations on new starts every day. These organizations often assist sponsoring churches with additional financial resources. Almost every church planting organization has as its chief goal the enabling of a new church to move towards becoming self supporting. Some conventions and organizations provide limited assistance for two or three years, but virtually no church-planting organization provides assistance much beyond this point. As I have said before, most new church plants get their initial financial support from their sponsoring church. What usually begins as a deep sense of God's conviction on the heart of the sponsoring church pastor transfers to another staff member or outside planter who is responsible to the main church for leading the new work through management, mentorship, and mutual support issues.

Most godly Christians remembered for their evangelistic hearts were able to successfully support missions by exciting people in the mother church about the worthy ministry of church planting. John Maxwell said that "people don't at first follow worthy causes. They follow worthy leaders who promote worthwhile causes."[2] There are times when a group of churches band together under their leadership to begin a new church with a clustering model. In this model, each part of the new church responsibility is divided among three to five clustering churches. It is vital that a clear line of responsibility be established so that the new church and new church planter do not fall through the cracks because everyone thinks someone else is handling that particular responsibility.

The partnering church can develop funding resources from at least six areas:

- The sponsoring church itself
- Local denominational associations
- State denominational conventions
- A core team of members of the sponsoring church who will plant the new church
- Core team members who work with the new church from the partnering church
- Individuals within the sponsoring church and new church family

---

[2] John C. Maxwell, *The 21 Irrefutable Laws of Leadership: Follow Them and People Will Follow You* (Nashville: Thomas Nelson, 1998), 146.

Pastor and church planter David Putman used to call these resources "fishing pools for funding a new church." And I have experienced in my own ministry that the greater the number of funding venues used, the sooner financial independence will come for the new church plant. Supporting the new work is an unforgettable opportunity to be involved in something wonderful God is doing. The healthy New Testament church really is a channel for money and ministry, and not a storage chamber. Consider what Scripture has to say on the theme of planning and planting:

> Keep asking, and it will be given to you. Keep searching, and you will find. Keep knocking, and the door will be opened to you. For everyone who asks receives, and the one who searches finds, and to the one who knocks, the door will be opened (Matt 7:7–8).
>
> For which of you, wanting to build a tower, doesn't first sit down and calculate the cost to see if he has enough to complete it? Otherwise, after he has laid the foundation and cannot finish it, all the onlookers will begin to make fun of him, saying, "This man started to build and wasn't able to finish" (Luke 14:28–30).
>
> In the local church at Antioch there were prophets and teachers: Barnabas, Simeon who was called Niger, Lucius the Cyrenian, Manaen, a close friend of Herod the Tetrarch, and Saul. As they were ministering to the Lord and fasting, the Holy Spirit said, "Set apart for Me Barnabas and Saul for the work that I have called them to." Then, after they had fasted, prayed, laid hands on them, they sent them off (Acts 13:1–3).

In the Luke 14:28–30 text, Jesus very clearly communicates the importance of counting the cost prior to beginning a venture. This is certainly true for church planting, which can be a costly venture requiring significant financial sources. There are two basic types of resources that exist in any church plant: people resources and financial resources.

People Resources

Three relational resources are emphasized in the New Testament pattern for church planting. The biblical pattern suggests that a church planter has a relationship with a sending church, a team, and a coach or coaches.

The sending church. The church at Antioch serves as a prime example of a sending church. The local church at Antioch was compelled by the Holy Spirit to send out both Paul and Barnabas "for the work that I have called them to." This deputation for the mission field was in partial fulfillment of their responsibility to fulfill the Great Commission. Paul and Barnabas were set aside and sent out for this work, and this clearly implies an ongoing relationship between the church planter and the sending church (see Acts 13:2–3).

The team. Paul and Barnabas were part of the team at the Antioch church, and they had an ongoing relationship with the church. This pattern began with Jesus modeling teamwork and continued throughout the New Testament. His commitment to building teams was very serious. "Then He went up the mountain and summoned those He wanted, and they came to Him. He also appointed 12—He also named them apostles—to be with Him, to send them out to preach, and to have authority to drive out demons" (Mark 3:13–15).

The coach. Although Barnabas was a team member, his relationship with Paul began as an encourager and sponsor, the two primary functions of a coach. Like Paul, church planters must be learners, and like Barnabas, church sponsors should be coaches.

What Do a Church Planter and New Church Plant Need?

There are three basic financial needs a planter has when preparing a church launch: a start-up budget, an operational budget, and salary support. It is beneficial to break down the financial needs into these three categories when it comes to raising support. For example, some people give financial support based on relationship. These individuals will most likely be drawn to give money to support the planter's salary. Other individuals like to give gifts to meet a concrete need, like a video projector. The core group and growing number of attendees will likely want to give toward the ongoing operation of the new church. Dividing gifts into manageable categories helps in organization. Here are some options working for churches sponsoring new works across the country:

Workable Options for Financing a New Work

1. Put the sponsored church within your weekly budget.
2. Use your staff minister of missions to start the new work.
3. Many mission-minded churches have found they can use their already supported staff member to get a new church up and going.
4. Have your church planter visit the mother church at least bimonthly to share the vision and successes of the new work—and then take up a special offering for them.
5. Use your churches missions efforts such as mission trips to help your sponsored church to grow.
6. Designate three percent of your weekly church general offerings to the new church plant. This would obviously be above your Cooperative Program giving and local support of associational missions.
7. Build a cluster of at least three other churches all implementing one or more of the previous ideas to support and finance the sponsored new work.

8. Build a forty-eight- or forty-nine-week budget[3] for the mother church. Give the full offering once a quarter to the new work launch. Then use the three or four additional weeks throughout the year to give the entire offering to the new plant. What a wonderful way to demonstrate God's sufficiency for both the mother church and the new church plant.

9. Develop a 5/52 New Church Sponsorship Plan, where everyone in the church gives $5.00 a week for fifty-two weeks.

A start-up budget. The start-up budget consists of those things required for launching a new church. These items would include an initial marketing strategy, worship equipment, nursery and preschool equipment, rental deposits, insurance, signs, letterhead, bulletin covers, and so forth. Some of these items will be included later in operational costs, but they are also part of the initial start-up cost.

The general operations budget. This budget consists of those reoccurring things that make up an annual budget. These items should include categories for missions, personnel, facilities, administration, and ministry. It is important to build good financial systems from day one. When establishing the first operational budget, there are a number of points to consider:

1. Establish an account in the church's name.
2. New churches should handle the finances as quickly as possible.
3. Establish financial guidelines.
4. As the planter or pastor, never handle the money.
5. Use two signatures for checks.
6. Have an outside audit conducted annually.
7. Budget with the end in mind.
8. Maintain flexibility early on.

The planter's salary support. Salary support will of course depend on the needs of the church planter and the context of ministry. It almost goes without saying that a church planter living in a high-cost area will need additional income in order to live within his ministry context. A church planter with small children will need additional income so his wife can remain at home with the children. Salary support may come from a variety of places:

1. *Becoming an intentional bivocational pastor.* Over one quarter of our Southern Baptist churches are led by bivocational ministers. Nearly thirteen thousand pastors work somewhere in corporate America during the week while ministering

---

[3] I have discovered the forty-eight- or forty-nine-week budget works well for church planters in the northern states. In the northern climate there are often weeks where severe snow storms keep the church from meeting, resulting in the usual offering being lost. I realize there are many pastors who say this will not work. But I have seen it work. There is a great deal of joy created when God's people are challenged corporately that everything brought into God's house on a particular week will go towards the launching of yet another missional church. Build a strong missional challenge and remind your congregation what a blessing it is to be able to plant a new church this way. Also, smaller churches clustering with other churches can do the same with all four churches staggering this offering and providing it in smaller amounts.

faithfully each weekend. Being bivocational opens doors to many people we simply would not be able to come into contact with otherwise. Bivocational pastors play an important role in evangelizing unreached people in North America. This subject is covered in greater detail in the next chapter.

2. *Mission organizations.* Organizations like local denominational associations or state conventions often contribute to a church planter's salary for a specific and predetermined period of time.

3. *Sponsoring and partnering churches.* Sponsoring and partnership churches are the key supporters for church planting. Some churches are able to underwrite an entire church-planting project, while in other cases a network of partners can come together to provide funding.

4. *Individuals.* In addition to congregations, individuals often want to lend financial support to church plants, especially when a personal relationship is involved.

5. *Mission-minded businesses.* A number of growing businesses desire to give a percentage of their resources directly to some type of Christian mission project.

Regardless of where the monetary resources for the church planter's salary come from, it is incumbent on the planter to develop and maintain healthy relationships with all ministry partners. In addition, it is the responsibility of the planter to be sure there are adequate resources in place before setting out on a church-planting project.

How Will I Pay for It?

The vision you engrave you must endorse. The vision God writes he underwrites. It is important that church planters not delegate the full responsibility for raising resources to anyone else, because it is ultimately the planter's responsibility. Blame cannot be put on anyone else for resources that do not materialize.

People give to people. Those most likely to support the church planter's ministry are those who have had significant relational experiences with the planters. Church planters have two primary sources for raising support: churches and their personal relationships with individuals.

Vision attracts resources. Never underestimate the power of vision because people with big resources usually are attracted to people with big visions.

Resources are in the harvest. It is important from day one to look for resources in the harvest. Developing givers from within the new church is one of the primary tasks of the church planter, and it is also a basic function of discipleship. Those who have learned to be disciples from the new ministry very often want to turn around and support the work. Jim was a new believer I discipled in a new church plant. One day Jim told me he had a vision to make God the CEO of his company. I asked how he was going to do that, and Jim had two things in mind. One was to practice biblical principles in his business. Second, he wanted to make God the highest paid executive in his company. Many new believers have a huge vision for giving back to God, if we will only be faithful to challenge and disciple them.

You have not because you ask not. We need to bring our needs before God constantly, expecting him to provide for them. And we must develop good skills at providing people the opportunity to give to God's work, along with not forgetting to invite them to do so. If we believe what we are doing is of God and is really making a difference, then asking is natural and easy.

People need a cause and an opportunity to give. People with substantial resources are often looking for a good reason to give. They have lived their entire life making good use of their resources, and now they are looking for credible ways to invest those resources to make a kingdom impact.

Resources are easier to raise prior to moving to the field. No time is better for raising resources than before moving to the church-planting field or starting the church-planting project. Avoid presuming that if you go, people will give. Experience proves that more resources can be developed before landing in the launch area, because once there, the planter instantly becomes entrenched in other aspects of promoting the new work. Many church planters fail in the work due to limited resources or resources they have been promised but never materialized once they got on the field. Whenever possible, see that resources have been raised and partnerships are firm before moving to the new church-plant location. And in working church-planting associations before moving to the field, be very sure the directors have voted to do what the leaders say they will do.

Sixteen Steps for Developing a Support Strategy[4]

Step 1	Pray first and ask God.
Step 2	Begin with the home church.
Step 3	Determine whom to approach for support.
Step 4	Record and catalog prospects.
Step 5	Mail the first prayer letter.
Step 6	Make appointments.
Step 7	Conduct the visit.
Step 8	Work with other churches around your hometown.
Step 9	Track support.
Step 10	Say thank you.
Step 11	Conduct a letter or phone strategy.
Step 12	Expand contacts.
Step 13	Cultivate support.
Step 14	Resolicit for support.

---

[4] Here are a few helpful ideas when talking about money for church planting: Build networks; talk their budget language; ask for soft needs or hard needs such as brick and mortar; remember people give to vision not to need; maybe get a job; get others involved; talk their heart language; prayerfully seek a hand up, not a hand out; always ask the sponsoring church first.

Step 15   Continue building the support base.
Step 16   Build the support base from the vision so it can be used again when planting additional churches.

Wrapping It Up

The creation of a financial plan is vital to the success of any new church, and the key to giving is a broad, dynamic vision. Church planters need to think big and cast big visions. Why? Because we have a big God who wants to accomplish big things through us. Money from the sponsoring church should never become a stumbling block when on the Lord's mission, but it is true people give more to ministries that show results. Since a new church has no track record of results, the wise church planter should develop visioning and promotional materials with identifiable results in mind. The harvest fields are full of the resources needed to plant any church.

Chapter 19

The Bivocational Alternative

After this, he left from Athens and went to Corinth, where he found a Jewish man named Aquila, a native of Pontus, who had recently come from Italy with his wife Priscilla because Claudius had ordered all the Jews to leave Rome. Paul came to them, and being of the same occupation, stayed with them and worked, for they were tentmakers by trade (Acts 18:1–3).

After publishing the popular book, *Starting a New Church: The Church Planter's Guide to Success*, Ralph Moore was asked, "If you could turn back the clock and start over in your church multiplication efforts, what would you do?" Moore responded, "I would go to a different college, get a different degree, and be a bivocational church multiplier." Bivocationalism for pastors, like church planting, is becoming more mainstream as the culture and context of Christendom in North America change.

Currently 31% of senior pastors in my own denomination serve either bivocationally or as volunteers.[1] Sadly many of the contributions of these committed servants of the Lord have been overlooked. It was refreshing to note that the book *Bivocational Church Planting* is dedicated to the sacrifice bivocational church-planting families make to the kingdom of God throughout North America.[2] Many church leaders have forgotten the tremendously important impact of bivocational pastors and church planters. We need to challenge sponsoring churches to do more through the sending out of bivocational church planting teams.

---

[1] Annual Church Profile, 2005, Executive Committee, Southern Baptist Convention.

[2] Steve Nerger and Eric Ramsey, *Bivocational Church Planters: Uniquely Wired for Kingdom Growth* (Alpharetta, GA: North American Mission Board, 2007).

Bivocational activity is accepted in our culture. Tens of millions of Americans hold more than one job. Among adults in California, for example, 12% are employed in more than one job.[3] These numbers do not include all those involved in internships, education, or volunteer jobs. Although finances are at the top of the list of reasons why people take a second job, a study by the U.S. Department of Labor showed that enjoyment and gaining experience were also two of the top four reasons.[4] In the workplace, those who hold multiple jobs are often considered hard workers and caring providers. Although 63.4% of church planters surveyed felt being fully funded was very important, only 48.9% of the pastors and 23.3% of denominational leaders viewed fully funded church planters in the same light. Is the dual career approach appropriate for the church?

I have gotten to know several employees at the coffee shop where I usually hang out. Most of them are students working their way through college, or they work there as a second job. The idea of doing just a single job is simply foreign to most young men and women anymore, and it is getting more foreign all the time. Many expect the trend towards multiple jobs, including those who intentionally hold two part-time jobs instead of one full-time position, to increase. Thus, sponsoring churches should certainly explore the bivocational alternative to a more fully funded church planting as a sound option for church multiplication.

A New Testament Model

Can you identify the names of these first-century church planters by their dual vocations? Fisherman-church planter, tentmaker-church planter, physician-church planter. Peter, Paul and Luke were all bivocational church workers, so church planting is nothing new. In the early years of my own ministry as a church planting missionary, I often served bivocationally. As a registered nurse, I was able to find employment in nursing homes and hospitals. At other times I served bivocationally in jobs ranging from gas station attendant to harvester of sugar beets. Each time my salary came from a combination of secular work, ministerial compensation, and support from individuals. The bivocational alternative allows the church to have a full staff while operating on a limited budget. This is the way much ministry will be going in the immediate future, so our churches should make local and cooperative missions a priority.

Church historian Robert Baker wrote, "In Texas . . . at the close of the Civil War in 1865, there were only three Baptist ministers in the state who were supported totally by their churches." Included in the list of bivocational ministers

---

3 The California Work and Health Survey Institute for Health Policy Studies, Monday, September 4, 2000.

4 U.S. Department of Labor, Summary 02–07, September 2002.

were Richard Furman, namesake of the highly regarded Furman University, and R. E. B. Baylor, namesake of Baylor University.[5]

The Bivocational Alternative Is Attractive for Many Reasons

1. The church-planting vocation often places the church in contact with the unchurched on a daily basis. In my first vocational church position, I served as a gas station attendant. The station employed about six people, one of whom attended my new church plant. Over a period of several months, Cindy and I witnessed and prayed for the station manager. One night during a lull in business, I had the privilege of leading Wayne to faith in Christ. The next day his wife and daughter trusted Christ. I had the privilege of baptizing the whole family a few weeks latter. If I had been in so-called full-time ministry, I never would have known Wayne or his family. One of the church growth principles is that in many situations, prolonged exposure to the Word is the best way to assure people make genuine decisions.[6] Bivocationalism allows the minister to have a prolonged relationship with those in the workplace.

2. Bivocationalism allows the church to put its resources into ministries rather than salaries. Many churches designate 30–40% of their income for staff salaries. A bivocational church planter will allow the new church to focus its resources into outreach. The danger here may be the temptation to "downsize" the budget (or downplay stewardship). The objective is not reduced giving but greater outreach. For many new churches, the savings can be used for promotion, equipment, and ministry. The return on investment of, for example, quality nursery supplies and promotional materials may result in a far greater impact than what might be gained by full-time staff in the early phases of a new church.

3. Bivocational ministry often allows the church planter to live at a higher standard of living than many fully funded strategies, which provide far less than the median family income. Impoverished pastors can be a hurdle to evangelism in some settings.

4. The bivocational approach to church planting provides legitimacy in some settings. In the past, most communities held ministers of the gospel in high esteem. Pastors and church planters who worked outside the church may have been seen as suspect or unsuccessful. But today, in many areas of the country, the church planter who works outside of the church may enjoy greater trust and acceptance from those who think the institution of the church has diminished due to greed, scandal, and seemingly endless controversy.

---

[5] Robert Baker, "The Bivocational's Contribution to Southern Baptists," in *Bivocational Ministry*, ed. Doran McCarty (Nashville: Seminary Extension, 1996), 6.

[6] Charles Brock, *Indigenous Church Planting: A Practical Journey* (Neosho, MO: Church Growth International, 1996), 161.

5. The church can consider multiple bivocational staff over one full-time staff employee. Some churches today try staffing along the lines of the Ephesians 4 model of unity and diversity. In this strategy, those who are gifted as "apostles," "prophets," "evangelists," and "pastor-teachers" serve together as a church planting team. Using the traditional fully funded church-planting strategy, few sponsoring churches could afford such a model. But when the bivocational advantage is considered, not only is this strategy feasible, it becomes realistic. In a team approach, the new church starts off in this case with four tithing families rather than one—and this is just among the staff.

Billie Kite and Ray Guilder mention some additional advantages to the bivocational alternative:

1. More laity, of necessity, become involved in the ministry of the church.
2. The bivocational pastor is not expected to be Superman.
3. The bivocational pastor is usually more in touch with the real world.
4. The bivocational pastor has more opportunities for personal witnessing.
5. Because of time constraints, it is less likely bivocational pastors will succumb to the temptation of being lazy.
6. The bivocational pastor does not have time to become involved in petty denominational squabbling.
7. The bivocational church is more apt to allow their pastor to be real.[7]

A Word to the Sponsoring Church

The pastor of an established church needs to be careful how he communicates his values. For example, in my own life, when I discussed my call to ministry with my pastor, he told me he attended a certain seminary, and sure enough, that is where I ended up. Although I do not bemoan the direction my journey has taken me, I later discovered that mine was probably not the best choice for one interested in pioneer missions. Similarly, if we speak of ministry only as full-time work, we may inadvertently shut a door that might be open for members who would like to explore the bivocational ministry alternative. Consider inviting a bivocational or tent-making pastor to share his ministry in the sponsoring church.

A pastor of a church in southern California told me he had a couple in his church who could not stop talking about their interest in church planting. After much prayer and encouragement, this church sent out the couple to assist with a new church start. Since that time, they have helped establish three church plants. As tentmakers, this couple has never received a salary for their work, but the churches they were a part of starting would likely never have gotten off the ground without their contribution of time, talent, and resources.

---

[7] Alabama Baptist Convention, State Board of Missions, "Bivocational Ministry," Billie Kite and Ray Guilder, http://www.alsbom.org/readingroom/leadercare/bivo1.html, accessed 22 May 2005.

Like bivocational pastors, bivocational church planters have available to them the same numbers of hours per week as those in full-time vocational ministry. Except that twenty to fifty of those hours will be consumed by the nonchurch-related vocation. Thus, the weekly schedule for a bivocational planter will look different from one for a full-time church planter.

Full-Time Church Planter Schedule	Bivocational Church-Planter Schedule
• Evangelism: 15 hours/50 contacts per week	• Evangelism: 3 hours /15 contacts per week
• Sermon study and preparation: 10 hours	• Sermon study and preparation: 3 hours
• Daily prayer and Bible Study: each morning	• Daily prayer and Bible Study: each morning
• Administration: 10 hours	• Administration: 2 hours
• Ministry: 15 hours	• Ministry: 3 hours
• Church attendance/small group participation: 4 hours	• Church attendance/small group participation: 3 hours

Successful bivocational ministers need to have five qualities: organization, leadership, flexibility, industriousness, and perception. The final quality, perception, relates to the leader's perception that God's Great Commission call is being fulfilled as well as having a sense of being secure in that call. This is important, because there will always be uninformed or callous people wondering why the bivocational pastor or planter doesn't get a real job![8] The sponsoring church leader can help in this regard by teaching about the biblical examples of bivocational ministry, by demonstrating an understanding of the time constraints facing bivocational church workers, and by providing affirmation in word and deed.

Full-Time to Bivocational

For the apostle Paul, the vision and call of God demanded a willingness to serve bivocationally as needed. At times Paul served as a tentmaker. At other times in his ministry, he was supported by churches and individuals. There were likely times when he received support from both sources. At all times he was faithful and obedient to the call. In my years as a church-planting missionary, I observed dozens of church planters who left the field once the two-, three-, or five-year funding commitments were fulfilled. In about half of these instances, a

---

[8] Al Fasol, "Meeting the Challenges," in *Bivocational Ministry*, ed. Doran McCarty (Nashville: Seminary Extension, 1996), 36.

small congregation of twenty to thirty members was established but was unable to support their founding pastor fully. Instead of getting a job, these pastors left the fledgling congregation to fend for themselves. Often the congregation would disband. Ed Stetzer has written that "if God has called but finances don't follow as expected, the planter can't argue that God has closed the door. Finances are not the determining factor in God's will." He goes on to write, "If God expresses a call, the planter must help make a way where there is not another way—by working at bivocational employment, at least for a period of time until the church has grown to support the pastor."[9] The sponsoring church should consider including this expectation in the early discussions with any potential fully funded church planter.

Wrapping It Up

Occasionally a new church will experience growth exceeding expectations. In these situations, the bivocational church planter may determine that either he is ready to go full-time or that the church needs to transition to a full-time pastor. A move from a bivocational staff to a full-time staff might involve a reallocation of funds from missions and ministry to salary and benefits. Providing these young congregations with best-practice examples of churches that have transitioned to a fully supported staff may ease the transition.

In *Reaching a Nation through Church Planting*, Leon Wilson tells a story about planting a church that grew to more than six hundred members, nearly three hundred in worship attendance and more than two hundred in Sunday school—all with no fully funded ministers or staff workers. Ironically, when the church called its first full-time staff minister, it experienced a decline.

Resources

LifeWay Christian Resources has more than forty articles relating to the bivocational pastor and ministry. Go to http://www.lifeway.com/ and search "bivocational."

Church Planting Village has more than fifty resources for the bivocational pastor, church planter, and planting team. Go to http://churchplantingvillage.net and search "bivocational."

Church Planter Resources Library of the North American Mission Board (www. ChurchPlantingVillage.net) provides many wonderful materials, including *Bivocational Church Planters: Uniquely Wired for Kingdom Growth* and *Seven Steps for Planting Churches: Partnering Church Edition*.

---

[9] Ed Stetzer, *Planting Missional Churches* (Nashville: Broadman & Holman, 2006), 226.

CHAPTER 20

The Denominations,
Associations, and Networking

Many people are surprised to learn that religious denominations were actually established to make unity and peace among churches possible. Without denominationalism, the Christian church would likely be divided far more geographically and even theologically than it is today.[1] Without denominations, large transdenominational events, such as a Billy Graham Crusade, would be almost impossible to pull off. In parts of the world where the state church discourages denominationalism, Christianity is almost dead while other world religions have moved in to fill the void.

Although the occasional pundit will still claim that denominationalism is dying, church planting has created a renewed relevance for many denominations. Almost twenty years ago Peter Wagner commended Southern Baptists for their investment of people and money into church planting and connected this fact to their dramatic growth while many other established denominations less interested in church planting were in decline.[2] Today many denominations have joined Southern Baptists in significant growth resulting in whole or in part from their emphasis upon church planting. These include the Assemblies of God, Evangelical Free Church of America, International Church of the Foursquare Gospel, Baptist General Conference, Church of God (Cleveland, TN), the International Pentecostal Holiness Churches, and the Presbyterian Church in America. Newer denominations such as Calvary Chapel and the Vineyard Fellowship are also aggressively promoting church planting.

---

[1] "Divided We Stand," *Christianity Today*, September 7, 1998.
[2] Peter Wagner, *Church Planting for a Greater Harvest* (Ventura, CA: Regal Books, 1990), 19.

When I was in college, nondenominational churches were considered the next big thing in American religion. But between 1990 and 2000, the number of independent, nondenominational churches in the United States declined by 7.5%.[3] During this same period, the concept of *"sponsorship in name only,"* which was commonplace twenty years ago, had been replaced by support with strong backing from a combination of denominational and sponsoring church support. Even historically, independent groups have worked together with other denominations to promote and support church planting.

Recently I spoke at a church-planting conference of a historically independent fellowship of churches. I heard the head of their church-planting initiative promote a fellowship-wide program to fund church planting and provide church-planting resources to the sponsoring and cosponsoring of new church starts. A decade ago I attended a similar meeting and the focus was upon keeping any new church five or more miles away from an existing church in the fellowship! Such welcome changes illustrate that church leaders see the importance of church planting in the fulfillment of the Great Commission. They see how denominations and fellowships of churches work together to respond to the need to plant healthy new churches.

Sponsoring churches will generally support the congregations they expect will stay within the denominational fold. But there are times churches sponsor new works across denominational lines, and sometimes churches of one or more affiliations will partner together to plant a new church. An example of this is the case of Valley Oaks Community Church in Visalia, California. First Baptist Church (American Baptist) and the Sequoia Baptist Association (Southern Baptist) came together to start a new Hispanic work in a growing community with a population of nearly one hundred thousand. One church helped recruit the church planter and provide monthly support while the other church provided the new church with a building. The transdenominational partnership allowed the new church plant to start with both a building and solid financial support.[4]

The question of dual alignment—churches that claim membership in more than one denomination—is becoming a heated and debated issue in some regions of the country. But why? While working as a church-planting missionary, it was not uncommon for me to work with a church affiliated with both the Southern Baptist Convention and the National Baptist Convention, USA. After all, dual alignment was commonplace in early Baptist history. John Bunyan, the great Baptist preacher and writer, ministered at a church aligned with both the Baptist Union

---

[3] *Congregations and Membership in the United States 2000.* Copyright © 2002, Association of Statisticians of American Religious Bodies (ASARB). Published by Glenmary Research Center, 1312 Fifth Ave., North, Nashville, TN 37208. Accessed March 17, 2005, http://www.thearda.com/

[4] Valley Oaks Community Church disbanded in 2004 after nine years of ministry. The church experienced growth during the first three years, followed by six years of decline. According to a letter from one of the denominational leaders involved, the failure was due to a lack of evangelism on the part of the leadership and, consequently, the church. The building reverted back to First Baptist Church as per the original sponsoring agreement.

and the Free Church. Today his former Bedford, England, church is aligned three ways.

In church planting, the question of denominational affiliation is often assumed by the sponsoring church. The church planter or planting team, however, may not be operating under this assumption. According to a major study by the North American Mission Board, between 1990 and 1999, 368 Southern Baptist church plants changed affiliation at some period between being reported as a new start and constituting as a church.[5]

Keeping Them in the Fold

The first key to keeping new plants in the fold is to provide your church planters with your network. Most pastors and church leaders have developed good working and personal relationships with a small number of denominational leaders. Wise sponsoring church leaders will not hold onto their networks, but rather openly share their circle of friends and associates with the church planter. Tim Sanders writes, "Immediately think, how can my network help?"[6] This is great advice for pastors who have been programmed to play the cards close to the vest regarding their contacts. This is a "give and it shall be given" mind-set, and it will help keep new plants in the fold.

The next key is to involve the church planter and team leaders in healthy denominational meetings and activities. As a young pastor, I vividly recall my first associational meeting. The pastor asked me to serve as our vacation Bible school director and suggested I attend an associational VBS training event. This event exposed me to the truth that we can do together what we cannot do alone. Our one church could never have come up with the amount of teaching and evangelism ideas we learned that day. I left my first denominational meeting believing that my denomination truly had something to offer.

During the eleven-year period I served in California as a church-planting missionary, I frequently brought church planters and team members to a weekly breakfast sponsored by the local Baptist association for area ministers. The fellowship, prayer, networking, and learning that took place in ninety minutes were incredible. Over the years I have observed pastors lead their church out of their denomination only to return almost solely on the strength of this weekly fellowship meeting. They missed the fellowship and networking that this denominational meeting is able to provide.

I have a pastor friend who led his church to sponsor a new work being planted by someone new to the denomination. For the next two years, David brought Marc, the church planter, to the state convention meetings, the state evangelism

---

[5] Richie C. Stanley, *A Study of Church-type Missions Removed from Southern Baptist Convention Rolls During the 1990s,* from the Executive Summary, North American Mission Board, July 2001.

[6] Tim Sanders, *Love Is the Killer App: How to Win Business and Influence Friends* (New York: Three Rivers Press, 2003), 132.

conference, and other denominational gatherings. Needless to say, Marc is now active in serving Christ through both the association and the state convention of that denomination.

Networking

One benefit of denominational affiliation is the networks they provide. Many church planters are also networking outside their denomination, because helpful networks exist for all sorts—seeker-sensitive churches, house churches, purpose-driven churches, and others. Groups such as the Willow Creek Association link churches along the lines of a shared philosophy for ministry. They claim more than 10,500 member churches in thirty-five countries. Although denominational affiliation is not required, a vast majority of WCA member churches are also denominationally affiliated. Their Web site claims members from 90 denominations, and their online application includes 110 different denominations. To join, churches must submit a statement of faith affirming a "historical orthodox understanding of biblical Christianity," and pay an annual membership fee. Members can access extensive online resources and receive discounts as well as membership benefits, such as a monthly CD containing a sixty-minute audio journal for leaders.

The Purpose Driven Church movement is an affinity group similar to the Willow Creek Association. Currently Purpose Driven conferences are offered for Pentecostal/charismatic churches, children's ministries, youth ministries, worship leaders, small groups, new churches, and churches in recovery. Most PD resources can be purchased. As with the Willow Creek model, PD churches are affinity based, sharing a common approach to ministry that is purpose based. Their Web site claims that more than three hundred thousand church leaders speaking twenty-two languages have been trained in the Purpose Driven model.

Denominational structures provide opportunities for those with apostolic and prophetic callings. Often denominational positions are the only outlet for such leadership gifts as church-planting missionaries, catalytic church planters, directors of missions, regional or area missionaries, and district coordinators.

Resources

Not surprisingly, more than 50% of those participating in sponsoring church surveys say the first place they would turn for church resources is the denominational entity. Fewer than 20% said they would first seek out a fellow pastor or another local church. The Internet, with all of its resources, came in at 12.5%.

Of course denominations provide far more than money. For many church planters, however, the denomination is a major source of income. A few years ago the average was nearly $10,000 per year to church plants from state and national sources among Southern Baptist church planters. Although this number changes from year to year, depending on the resources available, it is also dependent upon the strategy, because some church plants are far more resource intensive than others.

Out of Sight, Out of Mind

A self-proclaimed church planter showed up at an associational meeting for the first time. After the meeting he asked to meet with me and the associational missionary. After sharing his vision to plant a new church, he brought the conversation around to money. Although he had a detailed plan, it had been developed around a mistaken notion that the association and state convention would completely fund the work. As we attempted to share the process for approving a new work, it was evident he was dismayed that the association and state convention did not have a million-dollar fund for church planting stashed away in a safe. We encouraged him to begin at the point of relationship, and we also shared the importance of having a sponsoring church. We invited him back to the next meeting and closed with prayer. Over time the church planter developed relationships with several local church leaders and eventually planted a church with state and associational funding supplementing the strategy but not underwriting it. If the planter had not heeded our encouragement to become a regular at the weekly fellowship, I am positive his church would never have launched, nor would a penny of state or associational funding have gone his way.

Sponsoring churches will do well to remember the theme of this story—out of sight, out of mind—before asking for money from denominational sources. Before asking the denomination to support a church plant, invest time in building good denominational relationships. It might only take a few phone calls to say hello and to introduce yourself, but the return on the investment of time is often great.

Part 6

The Route to Spin-off Success:
Putting the Rubber to the Road

It is vital that the sponsoring church get expectations down on paper early. Good communication is the key to good relationships. The partnering church appoints a new-work assistance team to work with the mission congregation's new-work navigation team, and it is the responsibility of the two teams to develop and maintain good communication at all times.

CHAPTER 21

The Sponsoring Church Agreement

Covenants have a historical and practical place in Christian ministry. One of the greatest benefits to having a written agreement is that it clarifies the roles and commitments of each party. Rather than copying what others have done, church leaders will benefit from contextualizing the partnering church covenants with the new works.[1]

There are many ways to approach the development of a sponsoring church covenant agreement. One way is to use the workable agreement others have already done. The appeal to this approach is that it takes only a few minutes and does not require much personal contact between the partnering church and the church-planting team. One church planter noted that in fifteen years of ministry, he saw several sponsoring church agreements where the forms had been photocopied so many times that they were almost illegible. The only contextualization applied to the sponsoring church covenant agreements was the changing of names. A liability to using the template method of copying another's covenant is that it often reveals differences in philosophy or ideology that might not have otherwise arisen. When such conflicts occur, however, they help the parties decide whether or not the partnership is a truly viable option.

One advantage to constructing an individually contextualized covenant between the sponsoring church and the church planter is that the time spent developing the document strengthens relationships among the leaders of both the established church and the new one. As with the other methods, this one also has some liabilities. The primary disadvantage is that it takes more time and creative effort than

---

[1] This Multiplying Church Network Unit: Developing a Partnering Covenant is available at www. ChurchPlantingVillage.net under the equipping icon.

other approaches. Even so, the time spent on covenant development will be well spent because it is critical to the future direction of any new work.

Another thing that is critical is for the sponsoring church to get expectations down on paper early. Good communication is the key to good relationships. The partnering church appoints a new-work assistance team to work with the mission congregation's new-work navigation team, and it is the responsibility of the two teams to develop and maintain good communication at all times.

In reality, the mission congregation is the church. It is simply the church meeting in a different place. It is the church extended. The mission congregation shall be governed by the constitution of the partnering church in all matters that pertain to it.

Covenant for Success

Covenants are renewable collaborative agreements intended to define accountability and clarify performance targets in fulfilling a certain job description. Consider the need to engage, empower, and release the church planter in the written agreement.

Engage: Does the covenant engage the spirit and passion of the church planter? To work, engagement needs to attract, hold, and induce the planter to participate at all costs.

Empower: Does the church planter have the authority to act? Empowerment is the delegated personal authority to act in the accomplishment of the mission. It is also delegated personal authority given to planters of churches to fulfill their Christian calling and use their God-given gifts.

Release: Does the church planter have the freedom to act? Release is the permission for a delegated individual to exercise their best judgment in the accomplishment of the mission. It allows for innovative, creative thinking, risk taking, and even potential failure. Too many covenants are overly constrictive in design and represent command and control rather than engage, empower, and release.

A church covenant defines necessary relationships and is an objective document used to make decisions relating to membership. Since the covenant is a statement defining the relationships into which new members are received, it also becomes a clear statement for church discipline. Churches may adopt four different kinds of documents:

1. A statement of faith providing a biblical and spiritual foundation
2. A constitution defining an organizational structure
3. Articles of incorporation to provide legal protection in certain situations
4. A covenant defining the relational character of the church body

Christians voluntarily associate together by nature of covenant and thereby constitute a New Testament church. The section on the church in The Baptist Faith and Message begins with this statement:

> A New Testament church of the Lord Jesus Christ is a local body of baptized believers who are associated by covenant in the faith and fellowship of the gospel, observing the two ordinances of Christ, committed to His teachings, exercising the gifts, rights, and privileges invested in them by His Word, and seeking to extend the gospel to the ends of the earth.

Covenant describes believers' connectedness with each other. A body of people becomes a church in a covenant relationship under the headship of Christ and the presence of the Holy Spirit. Churches affiliated with my own denomination are covenantal in nature. People comprise a body of Christ by coming together in a covenant relationship that is clearly identified, articulated, and affirmed. It is at the point of covenanting together that a church formalizes its existence. When a body of people understands that they are the church of the Lord Jesus Christ, they then begin intentionally to define their covenant with God and with each other. A covenant based on the various "one another" passages in the New Testament would show the relationship Christians should have in their commitment to each other to be the church.

Drafting a Sponsoring Church Covenant Agreement

Prepare a rough draft of a covenant for a new work and organize it with the sponsoring church and new church work in mind. To help in this preparation, divide into small groups and discuss the elements of the covenant that should be included, and why they are warranted. A new congregation should take the following four steps toward adopting a covenant:

Step one is to develop sensitivity to the Lord's leadership. There comes a time when the Lord "births" his church. At that point, the covenanting process should begin.

Step two is to lead the congregation in a study of Scripture, concentrating on the "one another" passages. Examine the New Testament for characteristics of Christians' relationships to each other in a local church.

Step three is to identify the relational elements that are indispensable in the church and to structure them into the covenant document.

Step four is to secure unanimous and personal agreement by every church member.

It is always a good idea to have a covenanting service because this should be a significant event in the life of a new church. It is not a goal to achieve. Rather, it is an outward expression of a church's internal awareness of its status before God and its spiritual birth as a local expression of the body of Christ. A church should celebrate its covenant often.

. . . And Now a Word to Our Sponsors

1. No church planting partners sponsor a new work correctly 100% of the time. But the sponsoring church gets better at it each time they choose to start a new work.
2. Just as babies survive with weak parents, new churches can also survive a weak sponsoring church. In fact, many missions are begun by sponsoring churches with fewer than fifty people.
3. Weak babies can grow to be beautifully strong adults.
4. Jesus Christ is the head or authority of the new work.
5. Sponsoring a new work helps the sponsor church by forcing it to work outside of its own programs—and at times its own comfort zones—where God can really lead. An outward vision does wonders for existing churches, even revitalizing them.
6. A sponsoring church allows people to serve God in ways they never thought possible.
7. This is leadership development that will strike blows for the kingdom of God forever.
8. Church-planting partners assist the sponsoring church because people who are inactive, with no activity or little activity, can now be put to work with the chance to be rejuvenated in their faith by assisting a new church ministry. Pastors are continually expected to bring bigger numbers into the worship services. But the missional pastor has the desire for each of the saints to find their unique place of service. When they find this place through church planting, the sponsoring team really becomes their shepherd.
9. It is not easy to say, but some members of the congregation need to leave the sponsoring church, such as disgruntled individuals or families. There are some people for whom the church has become too large. If they feel more comfortable in a smaller setting, they should be encouraged to find one. Some people are just sitting in the pews with no direction in ministry. Maybe they should leave the church and find one where they can be more fruitful in service. Then there are those who live far away from the church and can offer only very limited participation as passive worshippers. Finally, those who have perhaps too much of the pioneering spirit often cause grief in an existing congregation. They might be encouraged to work with the new church plant.
10. The home church can multiply itself by enlarging the kingdom of God through church plants. When this happens, the church's investments

215

multiply as well. Commissioning twenty people to a new-work core group can multiply five times in the course of a year or two in a church plant.

11. Help and guidance are available, and no one has to walk this unknown path alone.

12. Church-planting missionaries all over the nation can serve as starting strategists, and they desire to assist if given the opportunity.

13. If your church starts as a clustering church participator, it will enjoy all the success of the mission church by simply giving to it whatever it has to offer, whether large or small. This is biblical Christianity, sharing the joys and heartaches with each other as well as the responsibilities. People at the mother church will have a new baby to take care of in the family of God.

14. Church planting is like having a baby. If you wait until you can afford to do it, then you probably will never do it. There will always be a price to pay, but along with that comes a measure of faith helping us depend totally on God.

15. Do not be afraid of failure. It can happen, and it does happen—even to the best of them. But being afraid to follow the voice of our Lord into the unknown path of church planting is worse than trying and failing.

16. Starting new churches is a biblical necessity. After all, someone started every church now in existence, and someone has to keep adding to the work.

CHAPTER 22

How a Sponsor Church Coaches and Supervises the Church-Planting Team

As a sponsoring church pastor, perhaps the greatest gift that can be given to the new church plant is a gift of willingness to mentor them and help them grow where they may have a need. It was reported that Walt Disney said there were three types of people in the world. There are the well poisoners, who discourage others by stomping on their creativity and always reminding them what they cannot do. Then there are the lawn mowers. These are the people with good intentions, but in reality they are self-absorbed, mowing their own lawns and never helping others. He said the third type are the life enhancers, those who reach out to enrich the lives of others. They lift up, enhance, and seek to inspire others. They want the best for other people and want to see them reach their potential. Partnering churches and partnering church pastors are truly life enhancers when it comes to the coaching and mentoring of the church-planting team.

Once the sponsoring church has crossed the critical milepost of calling a church planter, it is now time to help with the task of planting a healthy New Testament church. Of course the day-to-day hands-on work will be done by the church planter and his team. But a very important role will be played by the mentoring team launching this new work. It is important for the lead pastor to make his schedule open to the planter on a weekly basis. Schedule a specific time each week for about forty-five minutes to an hour where he can call or drop by for hands-on mentoring. Take him to lunch several times a year, or invite him to attend a particular training event with you for a week. Give him some assignments to help him grow and further develop, and hold him accountable in his development as a preacher, communicator, and evangelist. Investing such time will bring many dividends and ensure you do not waste God's resources on a failed plant.

Remember that coaching or mentoring is "a relational experience through which one person empowers another by sharing God-given resources."[1] Seven important characteristics should characterize most mentors:

1. The innate ability to see potential in others
2. The freedom of heart and mind to be flexible in dealing with diversity in people and circumstances
3. The wisdom and patience to permit a leader to develop
4. Perspective and vision to help the protégé see down the road
5. The temperament and ability to encourage and empower without sacrificing truth and reality
6. An uncanny sense of timing and sensitivity to the Holy Spirit's leading
7. An awareness of resource networks to which the protégé can be directed[2]

Providing your time as a mentor is a powerful statement to the planter and your own church leadership. Mentoring and coaching were vital during biblical times, and they are still critical to the success of a new church plant. The Church Planting Group of the North American Mission Board has designed many tools to assist with the journey of coaching the church planter. The Bible is full of examples of mentors, but my favorite in the line of mentors are the Pauline mentors, the initiators of this great movement we know as "the churches," which began during Paul's missionary journeys. Remember, it all started with Barnabas, who coached Paul and John Mark. Then Paul mentored or coached young Timothy and Titus. Within the same framework Aquila and Priscilla mentored Apollos.[3]

Why Do You Need to Become the New-Work Coach?

The performance of new church leaders who are trained, coached, and taught how to develop a detailed church-planting plan makes all the difference in the world. Compared to other new church plants, where the leader is sent out on his own with no such support, national studies done over the last ten years reveal that church planters following no specific training track and developing no plan have only a 30% chance for the church to be functioning and viable five years later. On the other hand, church planters who are trained, coached, and taught to develop a planting plan, have an 89% chance for the church to be functioning and viable five years later. The sponsoring church pastor can quickly see why it is so important

---

[1] Tom Jones, *Church Planting from the Ground Up* (Joplin, MO: College Press Publishing Co., 2004), 171.

[2] Ibid., 171–72.

[3] Howard & William Hendricks, *As Iron Sharpens Iron* (Chicago: Moody, 1995), 181.

to train and coach the planter personally. Helping with the new plant planning by coaching the church planter is perhaps the most critical element facing a sponsoring pastor.

Most coaching experiences are dynamic in nature, and so is the church-planting coaching experience. There are five cycles or seasons in the coaching life that the sponsoring and planting teams will go through.

The Courtship Phase

The courtship phase is where most sponsoring church pastors begin with the new church planter, and this usually is in the initial phase of working together. During this phase the sponsoring pastor and the church planter are very close and there is little if any friction between the two. Because of this, it is easy to become lax in one's responsibilities toward establishing clear expectations. Don't make this mistake. In fact, much attention should be given toward expectations at this phase, so that if and when the waters get a little rough later on, it is still clear what is expected upfront.

One thing to be clear about is that the courtship is a short-lived cycle that will last only until the first standoff or difficulty. When the planter and partnering leadership do not see eye to eye, the romance has pretty much come to a close. Do not sweat this. It is natural and should never be allowed to derail the vision and commitment towards sponsoring the new work. During this courtship or romance phase, there is the need to communicate the game plan continually. The strong sponsoring church coach will work from a game plan and should have one not only for each individual on the new work team, but a plan for the development of the whole team over the course of the current and upcoming phases of the five cycles. Once the plan has been drawn, the sponsoring church pastor can communicate it to the planter. From that point on, the planting team is led from the plan on an almost continual basis.

Bear Bryant effectively communicated his game plan to the University of Alabama football team. He recognized there are five specific things a coach should do and that the players need to know:

- Tell them what you expect of them. This lets them know how they fit into the game plan so they know what they should try to do.
- Give them an opportunity to perform, to be a part of the game plan, to carry out the vision.
- Let them know how they're getting along. This gives them the opportunity to learn, improve, and increase their contribution.
- Instruct and empower them when they need it, which will give them the means to learn, improve, and increase their contribution.

- Reward them according to their contribution, and offer them incentive for their effort.[4]

The sponsoring team coach must take responsibility for establishing and communicating clear expectations, and this needs to begin in the courtship phase. The key to productivity is the continuing exchange of information between the sponsoring church coach and the new work planter. When there is interactive communication, this empowers everyone to succeed.

The Clashing Phase

The second phase in the coaching life comes when one or both of the planning parties no longer fully trust the other. This is a hard cycle to work through, and it is the spot where many sponsoring church leaders and church planters walk away. Don't let that happen. Seven things a partnering church sponsor can do to lessen this possibility are:

- Work hard so the planting team sees your true heart for the new work. Let them see your deep desire to help them win at the task of church planting and fulfilling the Great Commission.
- The sponsoring church should model the behavior the church plant should exhibit. Remind them they are an extension of the mother church and have the same privileges as well. Resource the planting team each time you are together. Fit into their world and begin the development of trust and loyalty.
- Let your word be trustworthy, and do not allow what is going on in the sponsoring church to be avenues for abuse of authority, forcefulness, or control. When things get tough, don't bring the church planter and his team into it. Keep quiet. The planter has enough to bother about, so don't add to the load already being carried. Be a cheerleader and the plant's biggest supporter.
- As the sponsoring church leader, show some patience with the planting team by allowing them the ability to make discerning decisions on your behalf. Do not force the team to call the mother church every time they need to make a crucial decision.
- Constantly display the heart of a servant. Remember that the planter and planting team carry the heavy load and high demands of beginning a successful new work. In this process, some things will go awry. Display a redemptive spirit so that when this happens you will draw the planter closer because he realizes you want to help him become successful.
- Remind the planting team that the collective IQ is better than one man's ideas. When you meet with the planter or planning team, expect them

---

[4] John C. Maxwell, *Developing the Leaders Around You* (Nashville: Thomas Nelson, 1995), 154–55.

all to be engaged in the discussion. They should feel free to offer ideas and suggestions about the work they do, and not be forced to listen to the sponsoring church leadership exclusively.

- Finish the task. It is the bottom of the ninth, and the bases are loaded. You are tied, and there is a full count. Swing at the ball, take it deep, run the bases, and then celebrate. The planting team and the partnering church must step up into the batter's box, take authority, and carry out the planting plan. God has put us all in a certain place in the batting order, and the victory belongs to him.

The level of any clashing and resistance will depend on the temperament and teachableness of the planter. The clashing phase is hard to stave off when the planter believes he has more expertise than the one coaching him. Sometimes that is true. But the sponsoring church pastor has many resources available that can be used with the planter such that staying informed and leading the planter is not as hard as it once was. Many effective church planters have shared their materials with us via the North American Mission Board's Church Planting Village Web site. Many of the resources needed to share with the planter and planting team are right at our finger tips—just a few easy clicks away. As a sponsoring church pastor, every time I was with the new-work planter, I would give materials and resources helpful to the planter at the stage they were in. Then I would allow them the ability to make it their own or not. That way, they could lead their new-work team and I could lead them.

The Coolness or Resentment Phase

The coolness phase depends usually on how well things are going. Not many coaching relationships are able to avoid the resentment phase entirely, unless the partnering church takes a "whatever" view of the new work, which is never advised. So there will be some skirmish, but be sure as a coach not to burn any bridges. Keep the relationship vital and seek health in all cases. There will be times as the lead pastor of the sponsoring church when you will need to allow the planter to grow a little bit; for example, when he is resentful of how blessed you and your church have become. He will get over it, and working harder is one way to get over it fast.

Once when I was a church planter I had a supervisor who was not only lazy but noticeably resentful about our new church's growth, as well as having to take up his time to do supervision. I needed a leader to train me and take me to the next level, and this person was not willing or able. I became resentful that it was not available. In hindsight, it would have been better to ask for a long-distance coach and not to have allowed this to continue. As the pastor of the sponsoring church, be careful how you share the blessings the mother church is experiencing. You don't want the new-work planter to focus on your growth and blessing and fail to see his own.

221

In the area of constructive criticism, there are some important things to know when assisting a church planter. Criticism is usually well received when it is kept constructive and offered in order to elevate and challenge. If you don't offer good suggestions and constructive criticism, it will sour the experience for all. Most forms of criticism fall into three forms. The first is a constructive form of criticism best offered in oral from and not in writing. The second is implied criticism, which is more easily misunderstood no matter what the situation. The third form of criticism is sarcastic criticism that not only hurts the planter but the sponsor as well. Wise is the coach who places a higher emphasis on the other individual than he does himself. Keep in mind that correction is always the goal, not destruction. If the clashing or resentment phase appears, there are some helpful things to do. Actively seek to repair the relationship. Reflect on your differences and work them out. Refresh your mutual commitment to plant and sponsor a healthy church. Revitalize your friendship through time together. Refuel your passion through prayer. Rethink your strategy and move forward.

The Confirmation Phase

Many partnering churches feel relief when the turbulence has settled down. Optimism and glimmers of hope give both the planter and the partner church growth excitement. Usually this happens as the corner is turned and the planter begins to see that success is just a few steps away. These are heady days for both the sponsoring church and the new work planter. Stories about the new work are fun again, and the sponsoring church revels in the successes they are feeling through the church planting vision of their pastor and church leaders. The planter is energized and the work takes on renewed purpose and excitement. These are the good days with confirmation that God is at work in the new plant. The result is the high prize for the hard work of planting a new church.

Yet during this positive time of confirmation, it is easy to lose focus and for goals to become cloudy. A clear list of what has been done and what still needs to be accomplished must be developed. It is imperative during this phase to process ideas, practice creativity, and set clear priorities so that the sponsoring and the partnering church can finish the task. This is also a good time to focus on the gifts of the planter and team to determine if other gift-sets need to be added to the mix.

The Compensation Phase

When my wife and I (like I did the hard part) went to the hospital to have our first child, she went through twenty-one hours of intensive, painful labor before we had our son Drew. It was hard on her, and I felt inadequate to help. All I could do for most of the time was just sit there next to her and hold her hand. But then! Drew was born into this world and all of the pain Cheryl felt was gone as she looked down and smiled at our newborn boy. All the pain and the tears and the twenty-one hours of labor were worth it. As the sponsoring church and the new-work team will discover, there comes the compensation phase where everyone knows that the entire struggle was worth it, and now there is great joy and excitement. The joy of sponsoring a new church work does not come by substitution of one place for another, but by the transformation of a place that was in darkness and now is a lighthouse.

The same baby causing the pain now causes the joy. Pain was not replaced by joy, but rather the sorrow was transformed into joy. And that is how it is when planting new churches. There are times of pain and times of sorrow, and finally there are times of joy and success. God takes the seemingly impossible situation of starting a new church, adds the miracle of his grace, and transforms days of trial into days of triumph. The task of planting a new church for the glory of God is awesome. It is never easy, but it can be done successfully.

Qualifications for a Sponsoring Church Coach

The coach for the new church plant should be chosen by the sponsoring church. Of course there should be some degree of input from the lead planter, but in the final analysis the sponsoring church should make the final decision on who will be the coach for the new work. If the new church plant is far away, the sponsoring church ought to make all arrangements for an honorarium to be paid to the coach and to care for the travel expenses and such. Securing a qualified coach to mentor the planter and planting team will put the new work light years ahead of the ones where sponsoring churches just let the planter drift alone.

If there is only one church sponsor of the new work, the sponsoring church might want to consider budgeting for the planter to return to the mother church at least monthly. When the sponsoring church pastor is vitally involved in the new work, and when the church-plant pastor is vitally involved in the established work, things are better aligned to the mission both churches have in mind. There will be fewer disconnects, and productivity is enhanced.

Avoid pitfalls such as autocratic dictatorship in coaching, sloppy supervision and follow through, weak decision making from the sponsoring church leadership, and poor communication to the planter and his team, as well as the sponsoring church committees and membership. If a coach cannot be secured with the sponsoring church underwriting this component, then the church planter ought to secure such a coach and include it as part of his new work budget. Here are a few characteristics that would be necessary in a coach for the new church plant:

- The new work coach must have a deep-seated passion for the church plant being started, and for the individuals making up the church-planting team.

- The new work coach must be able to grow to love the planter and his family and all members of the new-work team's family. Displaying genuine care for the planter and church-planting team will keep the bonds strong and communication freely open. Caring about the plant alone is not enough, however, as the new work coach must care for the individual members of the team also.

- The new work coach must have evangelism as a primary interest and be able to coach the church-planting team in effective ways to do evangelism and personal witnessing. Many church planters have not been properly trained in how to draw the net and lead others to faith in Christ. Relationship building is a wonderful thing, but it is just "hanging out" together if it does not lead to evangelization. Having a coach who is a soul winner is vital to the new work planter.

- The new work coach should be a good listener. Offering ideas and suggestions will come later, but first learn what is happening in the church planter's life. That way, guidance and expertise that will really help are right where they are. Diagnosing the needs of the new work team comes after first hearing what is going on in the work and in the lives of the team members. James 1:19 is a really good verse for coaching: "My dearly loved brothers, understand this: everyone must be quick to hear, slow to speak, and slow to anger." Coaches are those who have learned to talk less and listen more and to keep their personal feelings and agendas in check while helping others discover what God wants to do in and through them. Proverbs 18:13 says that "the one who gives an answer before he listens—this is foolishness and disgrace for him." The ability to listen well enough to ask effective questions is perhaps the single most important key to good coaching by the sponsoring church pastor. The primary purpose of good questioning is to gather information, increase awareness, focus priorities, and promote action. Construct your questions so they are clear and encourage full self-disclosure, not just one- or two-word responses.

- The new work coach must have some level of experience in the planting of New Testament churches. A completely inexperienced individual cannot coach the church planter. If such a person wants to be a coach but is not quite up to speed, have someone co-coach alongside in order that both the coaches and the planter can stretch.

- The new work coach needs to be able to deliver the medicine when it is needed. Delay can cause the sick to get sicker. I hate cough medicine, but when I am really sick and coughing, taking it helps me get better and back on the road again. In the same way, the new work coach must be able to give guidance when it is needed and in a way that it is willingly received. Always criticizing, scolding, and giving heavy-handed coaching advice usually creates a huge and often irreparable disconnect with the planter and new work team.

- The new work coach will make this coaching partnership a long-term commitment, perhaps as long as three years. Several church-planting gurus suggest twelve to eighteen months, but for anyone who has been planting very long, it is only at the end of eighteen months that the new work is just getting moving. Quit now and you walk away from the plant when the fun begins. With a shorter commitment, the sponsoring church never gets to experience the fun side of planting, only the hard side. Spend the time. It will be worth it.

Coaching is basically hands-on. It is the process of helping the church planter and the new church succeed. There are many ways to coach. There are times to act as the highly intentional coach. Then there are times to act as an active coach making suggestions and giving guidance. There are those times to become the passive coach, allowing the planter to take more and more of the total leadership reins. Good coaches exhibit certain distinct qualities, including objectivity, compassion, the ability to challenge others, encouragement, motivation, listening, strategic planning, and love of celebration over victories. These characteristics enable the planter to stay and not run for the hills during the growth experience. Sometimes the coach from the sponsoring church will act as a mentor, and at other times they act solely as a coach, motivating the planting team to put forth their best effort. And there are times the coach from the sponsoring church acts as the sponsor only and gives assistance, encouragement, and hope. Good coaching will involve all of these activities.

Coaching is distinct from supervising or giving advisory wisdom. Coaches have the greatest potential to influence positively or negatively the planter they coach. Not only is coaching a proven way of developing success in many areas of life; it is also a proven way of encouraging success in ministry.[5] Coaching is a relational process whereby a leader helps another leader discern and carry out God's purposes with the Holy Spirit's help.

How does one choose the new work planter and begin coaching? John C. Maxwell provides five thought-provoking suggestions on coaching others:

1. Select people whose philosophy of life is similar to yours.
2. Choose people with potential you genuinely believe in.
3. Select people whose lives you can positively impact.
4. Match the man to the mountain.
5. Start when the time is right.[6]

---

[5] Steven L. Ogne and Thomas P. Nebel, *Empowering Leaders through Coaching* (Church Smart Resources: Somis, California, 1995). An excellent audiotape discussing the unique paradigm of coaching. Anyone undertaking the task of coaching a new-work team should consider obtaining this. Further information and materials can be obtained by contacting CRM ChurchSmart at 1-888-253-4CRM.

[6] John C. Maxwell, *Developing the Leaders around You* (Nashville: Thomas Nelson, 1995), 202.

So What Do I Do Now As the Sponsoring Church Coach?

Here are some practical guidelines for coaching your new church work planter and team:

- The partnering church pastor should set coaching appointments on at least a biweekly basis during the start-up stage. Once the work launches, perhaps this could be moved back to once a month, unless the coach and the planter both mutually agree to continue meeting biweekly. Some pastors continue to meet because they have grown together as ministry partners. Each scheduled meeting should be not less than one hour and probably not more than two-and-one-half hours. If a physical meeting is not possible due to special circumstances, then it should be done over the phone as soon as possible.
- The partnering church pastor should seek to meet with both the planter and his wife. This will be an encouragement for the spouse.
- The partnering church pastor should make his schedule available between coaching meetings, via e-mail or phone conversations, should the need to contact him arise.
- The partnering church pastor must be actively praying for the planter and the new-work team on a regular basis.
- The partnering church pastor should listen to concerns from both the spouse and planter. Allow them time to blow the pressure off with someone they trust.
- The partnering church pastor should help with brainstorming times with either the planter or the planting team. This is a great way to answer the challenges that the new-work team faces on a daily basis.
- The partnering church pastor should ask probing questions to find out the strengths and weaknesses of the plant at each meeting. This will allow him to assess the health of the work at each stage.
- The partnering church pastor should be able to point out potholes and potential pitfalls so the planters will be aware of potential problems and warning signs.
- The partnering church pastor should allow the new-work planter to develop and carry out an effective time line for the plant.
- The partnering church pastor should conclude each coaching time with a list of critical paths or tasks to be completed before you meet again. Then at the next meeting, after a time of reconnecting and prayer, review the things that were accomplished. Accountability is always a key for the coaching relationship to be complete.
- The partnering church pastor should work with his leaders within the sponsoring church to discover other ways they can work with the new-work team. Bible teachers, outreach leaders, deacons, various staff, and

the general congregation should all be given opportunities to participate in the partnering church's new work through projects and care.

• The partnering church pastor and those who are leading the new work from within the partnering church should receive some training in various coaching and mentoring skills. Contact the Church Planting Group at the North American Mission Board for further assistance.

Gary Rohrmayer has a wonderful Web site for those finding themselves coaching and mentoring church planters. I love his list of rules for coaches, and I share rule number three here. Gary says, "I will ask 10 Questions for every recommendation or directive I make in a coaching appointment."[7] He further offers six ideas on how we can grow in the skill of asking good questions:

1. Recognize "bad" questions before you ask them.
2. Discover the anatomy of good coaching questions.
3. Learn how to turn statements into questions.
4. Be a collector of good questions.
5. Don't be afraid of silence.
6. Be creative in developing your coaching questions.[8]

Developing Solid Holy Spirit-Led Strategic Thinking for the New Work

There are two types of people in life: those who divide people and things into groups, and those who do not. As one of those persons who do, I offer some thoughts on strategic thinking when led by the power of the Holy Spirit.

Some sponsoring church leaders leap without thinking, which usually displays a lack of careful planning and preparation. Some think without leaping. These are the individuals who love to go to meetings but never seem to get around to the implementation of the plans. There is a third group of partnering church leaders—those who love to plan strategically and implement aggressively. May their number increase.

When one plans strategically, it will surely bring about results. This is a process not to be avoided or rushed through. Failure to plan strategically can hurt the new work. There are at least five things strategic thinking does.

1. Strategic thinking crystallizes the working plan.
2. Strategic thinking increases ownership by all of those involved.
3. Strategic thinking builds confidence.

---

[7] For more resources and a fuller explanation go to: www.yourjourney.org. Gary Rohrmayer is an excellent coach and a wealth of vital resources in the area of coaching the church-planting team. Gary and Greg Kappas have developed a useful manual on coaching titled: *Top 25 Questions for Planting a Healthy Church.*

[8] Ibid.

4. Strategic thinking ensures productivity.
5. Strategic thinking maximizes results.

The strategic thinking and planning team should have at least some members

- who are visionaries (the dreamers)
- who are conceptual thinkers (the designers)
- who are strategists (the developers and implementers)
- who are influencers (the motivator of others)

Sponsoring church pastors really are pioneers who venture out into unexplored territories. They guide those whom God has placed into their care, often taking them to unfamiliar destinations and moving them into areas of strength. As a sponsoring church planting coach, the pastor's main job is to move others forward, to get them going someplace, and to help them reach their fullest potential. There are both advantages and disadvantages when the partnering church pastor or a member of the partnering church leadership becomes the coach.

Advantages When a Partnering Church Pastor Becomes the Coach

- The partnering church pastor would best understand what is going on in the new work start.
- The partnering church pastor knows the sponsoring church perhaps better than any one else.
- The partnering church pastor's enthusiasm for the new work will be greater if he is involved in the hands-on nature of the new work.

When the partnering church pastor is aware of what is going on in the new work he can better inspire the rest of the sponsoring church with the joys of starting a new work.

Disadvantages When a Partnering Church Pastor Becomes the Coach

If the partnering church pastor has never been involved in church planting, he may not understand various issues involved in the launching of a new work.

The partnering church pastor may feel he is already overloaded and overwhelmed. It is important that the pastor take the needed time to consider carefully whether his schedule will allow for the coaching and mentoring of the new-work team.

A Quick Primer on Coaching[9]

1. *Remember to limit your advice giving.* The coach's role is to help the planter discover God's direction. Advising him on what to do without giving him an opportunity to explore the possibilities limits the planter's ability to hear and obey God on his own. Don't short circuit what God is doing in the church planter by sharing advice too early in the process.

2. *Release the planter to "share his heart."* Allow the new work planter the freedom to explore problems and solutions without interruptions. Do not feel pressured to fill a lull in the conversation. The planter may be about to share a breakthrough thought and trying to find the right words to express it. Only ask questions to keep the planter on track, and to help clarify a goal, value, problem, strategy, need, idea, situation, or priority.

3. *Help the planter brainstorm options and then evaluate those options for wise implementation.* Help the new work leader look at each option from as many angles as possible to see what will really work and what will not.

4. *Think "circular."* Circular thinking takes things as they come, as opposed to "linear" thinking, which sees life, growth, and success as a logical progression from A to B to C to D, and soon. "Just in time" (learning as we reach it) is the most effective way for new-work planters to discover answers to their challenges.

5. *Clarify worthy goals.* Help your church planter set goals worth striving for. The great artist Michelangelo said, "The greatest danger for most of us is not that our aim is too high and we miss it, but that it is too low and we hit it."

6. *Listen tentatively and actively.* It takes discipline to really listen to what people are saying and to hear their hearts. Most of us tend to stop listening because we think we know what the person is going to say next. Ask pertinent questions and listen to learn from your new-work planter.

7. *Help the planter navigate the roadblocks and potholes.* A good coach will help the church planter accept the reality and legitimacy of a barrier and discover the reason for it. When this happens, both parties often find that the barrier disappears or they discover a way around it, over it, or under it.

8. *Always have an agenda for coaching sessions.* A good coach prepares for each meeting time with the planter by reviewing past sessions, the goals the planter has set, progress toward those goals, obstacles that have been encountered, and actions they have agreed to take. From this review, the coach should draw up an agenda to follow up on in each of these areas

---

[9] Steven L. Ogne and Thomas P. Nebel, *Empowering Leaders through Coaching* (Somis, CA: Church Smart Resources, 1995). An excellent audiotape discussing the unique paradigm of coaching.

and check on progress. He should also prayerfully seek insight from the Lord as to areas that need to be addressed. Most importantly, the agenda should always allow ample time for the planter to bring up issues of importance to him or her.

9. *Never be afraid to say, "I don't know."* The coach's role is to help the new-work planter discover answers to his questions, not to supply all the answers to him. Know the valuable resources and point planters in the right direction so they can explore the possibilities for addressing their problems or needs themselves.

10. *Help the new-work planter look at the big picture.* Challenge the church planter to look beyond immediate needs to the long-range fulfillment of the vision God has given. Help your planter seek lasting solutions, not just short-term Band-Aids.

11. *Never, ever give legal or investment advice, even if you have "been there" and know what you are talking about.* Refer the new-work planter to the state director of missions and the local association director of missions for help.

12. *Remember, it is not about you but about them.* This relationship is about the church planter and the church plant. Any time you talk for more than thirty seconds at a time about yourself, you risk undermining the value of your role as a coach.

A Sample Coaching Meeting Agenda for the Sponsoring Church Supervisor

- ❏ *Begin with prayer. (Prayerful Preparing)*
  - Planter's family, new work, sponsoring church (Relate)
- ❏ *Explore how the planter is doing. (Focused Listening)*
  - What are you excited about right now?
    - † How would you describe your morale this month?
    - † What have you done for fun this month?
  - How can I pray for you?
- ❏ *Review notes from last meeting. (Reflection)*
- ❏ *What assignments have you completed? (Strategic Questioning)*
  - What goals are you working on?
  - What steps are you taking to achieve your goals?
  - What are the obstacles you are facing right now?
  - What needs to be changed at this time?
- ❏ *What are your major projects for the next few weeks? (Refocus)*
- ❏ *What are the priorities you have for the next few months? (Review)*
- ❏ *Ask about the general direction of the plant.*
  - How would you describe the current direction of the church plant?
  - What are you doing, and what are your immediate goals and projects?
  - What are your team members doing?
- ❏ *Review what has been done in the area of assimilation and evangelism.*
  - How have you used your personal testimony and witness since the last meeting?
- ❏ *Ask the planter what resources are needed at this time. (Resource)*
  - Equipping and training?
  - New staff?
  - Funds?
  - Volunteers?
- ❏ *Clearly delineate what assignments are being made for completion by the next scheduled meeting.*
  - What could you do in the next forty-eight hours that will help you meet your goals and make them a reality?
- ❏ *Give clear steps towards achieving assignments.*
- ❏ *Review each other's schedules; set date, time, and place for next meeting.*

Close the time with both of you praying. Make sure you pray for the planter's prayer requests offered at the beginning of the meeting and anything else that came out during the session.

Now that the meeting is over, transition from coach to friend. Take him to lunch, have some fun, and pick up the tab!

CHAPTER 23

The Top Ten Mistakes
Sponsoring Churches Make

Even under the best of circumstances, there are some pitfalls sponsoring churches should know about when planting churches. Here are the top ten mistakes sponsoring churches make in church planting. Why do most of our failed new churches fail? Why is bad church leadership perpetuated? It is because most of us who lead have not been formally trained and we have not had good role models. So we lead as we were led: we wing it. No sponsoring church does everything 100% right, just as no church planter does all things wrong. No matter what the mess, God can take the mess and turn it into a message for his glory.

How often do we face overwhelming situations that appear impossible? For many, sponsoring and planting new churches represent the impossible. But remember, in those times of need, our confidence comes from Jesus. Our first instinct may be perhaps to back away from the work due to fear. But that's exactly when we need to look to Jesus, "the source and perfecter of our faith" (Heb. 12:2).

Mistake Number Ten: Inadequately assessing
the church planter's core abilities

The first and often the most crucial mistake the host or sponsoring church makes is inadequately assessing the church planter's core abilities, or even not assessing the planter at all. The chief reason new works fail is due to poor planter selection.

Maybe the person is a frustrated pastor or a pastor of a dying church. Maybe the church planter is placed where his spiritual gifts just do not fit the target area. Many sponsoring church pastors will grab someone right out of their fellowship and thrust them into the role of a church planter, only to discover later that it was the worst thing they could have done for everyone. These swift and uninformed decisions are most dangerous because they are almost always surrounded by feelings rather than facts.

Lack of assessment of a church planter is tantamount to hiring someone based on how they look or whom they know. It fails to go below the surface. Assessing church planters helps sponsoring churches know how the planter measures in the most crucial characteristics found in successful church starters. Every sponsoring church needs to be sure that the planter they have selected is vetted and approved by leaders of the denomination's church planting group. Never settle for "he's a great guy; we don't need to assess him." It will save resources and keep us good stewards to be sure the planter has the much needed competencies for starting new churches. Most potential church planters struggle at one point or another with the question whether they would be effective in this type of work. Actually this question should receive strong consideration because one may have spiritual gifts of which they are not fully aware—gifts that are especially suited to effectively starting a new church.

Communities across America need high-caliber church planters. It takes a special leader to plant a successful church, one that grows quantitatively and qualitatively. Efficient church planters are special not because they are better than other people, but because of their unique giftedness. Church planters have an utterly significant ministry, for they are concerned with building God's kingdom on Earth, and we know that church planting is the most effective method of fulfilling the Great Commission. We need unique persons to start churches in all North American communities. Selecting high-caliber church planters reflects good stewardship, something that is often thought of in terms of how we handle our financial resources. Stewardship certainly applies to money, but considering only money is a narrow perspective. A broader view of stewardship includes the management of human resources.

Within the body of Christ, members should be strategically deployed where they can make their greatest contributions. Unfortunately we in the church are often guilty of poor stewardship—deploying people in areas of ministry for which they are unsuited. When this happens, everyone loses. Misplaced church planters become frustrated and disillusioned, and they may drop out of ministry altogether by questioning their suitability for any type of pastoral assignment. It is common for members of the church-plant team to experience psychological and spiritual setbacks. But when some give up on the church, potential converts in the harvest never get reached. Selecting high-caliber church planters is the most important decision in planting churches.[1]

What if the selected church planter does not have the personality type to be the leader? We all know God uses all types of people for all types of ministry, but personality types for church planters really are important. Without question, many different personality types are needed to create an effective church-planting staff, but there are certain types of individual personalities that are better suited for the lead planter's position. There are four personality types that surface as the most helpful for the task of church planting. They are (D) dominant personalities, who are task and leadership driven; (I) influencing personalities, who are people driven and relationship driven; (S) steady personalities, who are relational and group-cohesiveness driven; and (C) compliant personalities, who are detail driven and quality-control driven. Using the Personal Profile System, Paul Williams and Rick Rusaw surveyed sixty-six lead church planters from independent Christian churches and discovered that churches planted by lead planters with . . .

---

[1] Charles Ridley conducted a study of church planters in the United States and Canada. His subjects in the study represented thirteen Protestant denominations. Based upon his research and subsequent field testing, as originally documented in his book, *How to Select Church Planters* (Pasadena: Fuller Evangelistic Association, 1988), he developed a list of thirteen prominent performance dimensions. For over a decade, these dimensions have been used to select church planters. Here is his list of dimensions and their definitions as used by the North American Mission Board.

1. *Visionizing Capacity* is the ability to project a vision into the future, persuasively sell it to other people, and bring the vision into reality.
2. *Intrinsically Motivated* by approaching ministry as a self-starter and committing to excellence through long and hard work.
3. *Creates Ownership of Ministry* by instilling in the people a sense of personal responsibility for the growth and success of ministry and the training of leaders who reproduce leaders.
4. *Reaches the Unchurched and Lost* with the ability to develop rapport, break through barriers, and encourage unchurched people to examine themselves and commit to a saving knowledge of Jesus Christ.
5. *Spousal Cooperation* by creating a workable partnership that agrees on ministry priorities, each partner's role and involvement in ministry, and the integration of ministry with family life.
6. *Effectively Builds Relationships* and takes the initiative in getting to know people and deepening relationships as a basis for more effective ministry.
7. *Committed to Church Growth* by valuing church growth as a method for building more and better disciples while striving to achieve numerical growth within the context of spiritual and relational growth.
8. *Responsiveness to the Community* by adapting the ministry to the culture and needs of the local residents.
9. *Uses the Giftedness of Others* by equipping and releasing people to do ministry according to their spiritual gifts.
10. *Flexible and Adaptable* with the ability to adjust to change and ambiguity, to shift priorities when necessary, and to handle multiple tasks at once.
11. *Builds Group Cohesiveness* and enables the group to work collaboratively toward a common goal while skillfully handling divisive elements.
12. *Demonstrates Resilience*, the ability to sustain oneself emotionally and physically through setbacks, losses, disappointments, and failures.
13. *Exercises Faith* and demonstrates how one's convictions are translated into personal and ministry decisions.

High "D" Dominant personalities averaged 181 after 5.2 years
High "I" Influencing personalities averaged 174 after 3.6 years
High "S" Steady personalities averaged 77 after 6.3 years
High "C" Compliant personalities averaged 71 after 4.3 years

Based on this research and more than twenty years of church-planting experience, it's fair for me to say that barring unusual circumstances, lead planters should always be high "I's" (influencing personality), high "D's" (dominant personality), or a combination of both.[2]

Mistake Number Nine: Trying to clone the mother church

It is a serious mistake not differentiating the new church plant from the established sponsoring church. While it is very complimentary to have your membership want to clone another replica of their church, it is unwise unless the sponsoring church is doing a nearby satellite clone with the same staff and preacher serving both places. It is all about church planting, and nothing about cloning.

O'Charleys is one of my favorite restaurants. There are three items on the menu I tend to rotate ordering, depending on my diet and just how good I have been that week. One of those items is the bar-b-que chipotle salmon. When I am ready for this, I can practically taste the fish even before the order arrives at the table. You can imagine my disappointment recently when I went to another restaurant and ordered the same thing. Their version was a bar-b-que with minimal chipotle salmon. It was there if you hunted for it, but I wanted to taste the chipotle salmon in every bite. I prefer getting what I expect.

I think all of us really do want to get what we expect, although there are a few exceptions to this idea. Think about trademarks, service marks, and registered brand names. I say I have Formica countertops at home, when in reality I have a facsimile of the brand name Formica. We have cloned the word *Formica*, so that when we want countertops we ask for the brand. When it is my turn to clean out the cat's litter pan, I ask for Kitty Litter. I am also getting a facsimile, since there are many brands of cat litter and I am not sure which one my wife has purchased. When I make photocopies of papers for my classes, I do not use a Xerox machine but a photocopier. I have allergies and I often ask for a box of Kleenex. My best friend works for Kimberly Clark (the company that makes these facial tissues), and we know that most Americans refer to facial tissue by the brand name of Kleenex. When I ask for a Kleenex, I seldom get what I expect. Don't misunderstand, I get a facial tissue, but it is seldom a Kleenex. It is one of those specific brands that have become the generic designation for a product—like Kitty Litter or Xerox or Formica. None of these trademarked items are the only ones available in their product line, but they are the most recognizable of these brands.

---

[2] The complete study can be obtained GYCM, P.O. Box 9, East Islip, NY 11730.

Partnering church planting is something of the same thing, sort of the "Kleenex" of church sponsoring. When a church pastor is challenged to consider sponsoring a church, most often this is assumed to mean partnering church planting. Partnering church planting is an important sponsoring model, but it is not the only model.[3] Partnering church planting happens when one local church initiates and leads the planting of a new reproducing and multiplying church. The sponsoring church takes on the primary responsibility for discovering a planter, delivering the funding dollars, and developing the new plant ministry. In this example the sponsored church becomes an extension of the partnering church into its area.

A mistake many partnering churches make is cloning a church plant instead of sponsoring one. Leaders of the sponsoring church want another congregation like itself but meeting somewhere else. They use the exact preaching style, teaching style, music style, ministry composition, and evangelism methodologies. The partnering church dictates all the new work does. When that happens, there is no freedom for the new church to become its own unique self. Unless doing a satellite plant, cloning exact replicas must be avoided. The sponsored work will be like the sponsoring church, to be sure, but it should not be the sponsoring church. It will have its own unique style and substance, and it might even become a new church many in the sponsoring congregation would not enjoy attending. The point in partnering church planting is to reach people the sponsor may not influence effectively. It is important the new work differentiate itself from the sponsoring church.

Another mistake for many sponsoring churches and new church planters is to adopt a philosophy and strategy of ministry that have not been personally experienced. Another way to say this is, stay with what you know. If you are experienced starting traditional works, then stick to that. If you are experienced working in blended style churches, stay with that. Do not let the yearnings to do it differently derail you before you even get started. All over North America church after church has tried to replicate either Saddleback or Willow Creek, and yet to this day it has never happened. How many churches have tried to follow John Maxwell's leadership from his church in San Diego only to find out that it was not reproducible? Build on your values, not someone else's. The most successful sponsoring church pastors are those who take a realistic inventory of what they have done well in their past ministries, and then put those principles into practice in the new church launch.

Mistake Number Eight: Inadequate funding and support

I love this little ditty I found years ago:

> Two guys were shipwrecked on a desert island. The first guy is freaking out with worry. He says: "It's bleak, man; I mean, this is really bad.

---

[3] Tom Cheyney, "It's About Planting Not Cloning" first appeared as an article written for the Church Planting Village. The Village is a huge Web site for church planters and those who work with them worldwide. Check out the Village at: www.ChurchPlantingVillage.net

We have no food and we have no water. We're going to die." The second guy is peaceful, at ease, and completely tranquil enjoying the peacefulness and serenity. He cozies up under the shade of a palm tree to catch some Zs. This is driving the first guy nuts, so he turns and says: "How can you sit there so relaxed? Are you clueless as to what is actually going on? We have no water. We have no food. We have no shelter. We have no help, and we have no hope. We are going to die. We're going to die!" The second guy says: "But you don't understand. I make $100,000 a week." He leans back with his hands folded behind his head and attempts to go back to sleep. The first guy now is ticked off, and he says, "What difference does that make? Who cares how much you make? What good does your money do us out here and right now? You don't get it! We have no food. We have no water. We have no shelter. We are going to die. We're going to die." The second guy interrupts, "No sir! You are not getting it, for you see I make $100,000 a week, and I tithe to my new church regularly. My pastor WILL find me!'"

This story is far fetched, but there is a tiny morsel of truth there. Asking people for money is both the most difficult and the most important part of growing a new church. The ability to raise or develop significant resources for the cause of church planting from within the sponsoring church is imperative. Most church planters do not work hard at raising support. They rest on the partnering church until the new work gets going. But if the sponsoring church is really interested in becoming a sending church, they will need to develop a financial base for launching the new work. Before most denominations had a missions agency, we all started churches with little or no resources. Local churches would do it themselves as a call to kingdom missions. Today, however, there are various ways to develop funding for a new church plant.

Mistake Number Seven: Premature launch and birth of new work

Far too many churches are launched prematurely. Usually this stems from a lack of preparation on the part of both the sponsoring church and the new church plant. Some think they are in the *Field of Dreams* movie in church planting: if you begin the work, they will come. But church sponsors and planters who rush into a premature launch have a much-better-than-average chance of failing. Something I have learned from years of church-planting experience is that a premature launch always shows up in the postmortem exam. Care should be given towards not pushing the planter to launch too quickly. Wise sponsoring church pastors might want to consider bringing the planting team into the staff meetings for nine months or so, in order to meet and pray daily and to seek the advice from other staff before they are sent to the field.

Starting a church plant at just the right time is an art, not a science. I always say, "It is ministry, not brain surgery!" The usual window of time required is between twenty-four weeks and fifteen months. The optimum time is nine months to a year. Once a core group has been developed, it will take great wisdom not to launch too early, especially when your new-church membership is chomping at the bit to get going. Caution should be displayed at this point since an early launch could hurt the future growth potential of the new work. I always encourage the planters I work with across the country to develop eighty-five adults within the committed core group before the launch, and that generally takes around twelve months. Take a look at these eleven consequences of a premature launch.[4]

1. A premature launch will waste a lot of everyone's energy. You will find yourselves always regrouping. You will find yourselves always repositioning. You will see your church always experiencing a re-opening of sorts because you will keep starting over. You could lose some of the core group membership, as well as needed momentum!

2. Most premature launches display a lackluster look to potential new members. More often than not, it says to them that you don't have your act together and that you're just winging it trying to keep your head above water. Additionally, it is possible your credibility will be questioned because you appear so haphazard.

3. A premature launch is a waste of kingdom resources, kingdom money, kingdom timeliness, and kingdom power.

4. Launching prematurely might cost many of the core group members due to a big build-up and a fizzle at the church start.

5. If a new plant is launched prematurely, the necessary momentum will be strained if not entirely lost.

6. A premature launch runs the risk of making the new church vision fuzzy and unclear, resulting in always playing catch-up.

7. If a sponsoring church launches a new plant prematurely, this usually requires constant and major revisions of the church-planting plan.

8. Launching too quickly might bring about an unclear launch strategy. The strategy will become useless because the destination remains unclear and the worthiness of the journey comes into question.

9. A premature launch might mean the new church will lose the opportunity to grow. Never rush to launch because a person or a committee suggests it. If God suggests you launch right away, he will provide the way every

---

[4] Tom Cheyney, "Eleven Consequences of a Premature Launch" appeared as a brief bulleted sidebar written for the Church Planting Village. The Village is a huge Web site for church planters and those who work with them worldwide. Check out the Village at: www.ChurchPlantingVillage.net . An amplified teaching on the subject first appeared at: www.PlanterDude.com.

time. On the other hand, if you have not launched in two or three years, you are not planting a church but a Sunday school class.

10. If one launches prematurely, the new church might find itself lacking spiritual discerners or advisors. These discerners are vital in assisting to discern the will of God.

11. A premature launch might blur the ability to clearly see God's activity because we are doing our own thing and not his.

Mistake Number Six: The three-week-slide syndrome[5]

The three-week-slide syndrome is the loss of momentum that often happens immediately after a planned church launch, and it is usually due to a lack of continual assimilation, evangelism, and development of leaders. This happens as the result of spending so much time getting ready to begin the new church, and not enough time gathering. Too many sponsoring churches are part of the challenge at this point because some of the members helping the new plant require too much time from the plant team. This is time that should be given towards continual development and gathering.

Mistake Number Five: Conflict of values and agenda

Many new church plants have been derailed or even destroyed by a conflict of values and personal agendas from the sponsoring church and church-planting team. The sponsoring church leadership must keep everyone operating from the same play book, and not let things develop in a new work that is in conflict with the direction they should be going. It is hard to kill bad things once they have infested the tiny new work. One of the ways to avoid these conflicts is to develop a clear covenant that delineates the parameters and defines who is going to do what.

Why do you need a covenant? Church planters who fail to develop a covenant with their sponsoring church are allowing the mother church to unintentionally set them up for difficulty. A wise church planter will use the opportunity of a covenant to face expectations and relational concerns that need to be dealt with in advance. These boundaries will keep communication lines open and relationships growing. Done correctly, a covenant can be the most advantageous tool for all parties involved in the church-starting process. It is a naïve mind-set to think we'll all get along so we don't need to worry. A church covenant defines relation-

---

[5] Further information regarding the three-week-slide syndrome of a new church can be obtained by attending a *Starting High Impact Churches: Developing the Tools for Launching Large* conference with Tom Cheyney and Rodney Harrison. For information contact Tom at tcheyney@namb.net for conference information.

ships and is an objective document that can be used to make decisions relating to membership and everything else.

A new congregation should take the following steps toward adopting a covenant:

- Step 1: Develop sensitivity to the Lord's leadership. There comes a time when the Lord "births" his church. At that point the covenanting process should begin.
- Step 2: Lead the congregation in a study of Scripture. Concentrate on the "one another" passages. Examine the New Testament for characteristics of Christians' relationships to each other in a local church.
- Step 3: Identify the relational elements that are indispensable in the church and structure these elements into a document.
- Step 4: Secure unanimous and personal agreement by every church member. This is important because the covenant is a statement defining the relationships into which new members are received.

A covenanting service should be a significant event in the life of a new church. It is not a goal to achieve but an outward expression of awareness of status before God and its spiritual birth as a local expression of the body of Christ. A church should celebrate its covenant often.

Mistake Number Four: Family health of planter and planting team

The church planter and church-planting team's family health and personal issues must be addressed by the sponsoring church at the initiation of the launch. Strong, healthy families are an asset to effective ministry, but effective ministry does not guarantee the existence of a healthy family. Alarming statistics reveal that divorce occurs more often in church families than in families outside the church. The number of divorces occurring among ministers' families is high too. Ministers and their families are too often scarred by the effects of pressures placed upon them. While no one can live a stress-free existence on Earth, learning to cope with the challenges of life for the minister's family can help keep God's servants from experiencing burnout, depression, or failing marriages. Help the planting team learn how to schedule its time for their families before someone else plans their time for them.

Another mistake sponsoring church leaders make is failing to affirm and praise the church-planting team privately and publicly. Everyone thrives on affirmation and praise. We wildly underestimate the power of the tiniest personal touch of kindness. Learn to read the varying levels of affirmation your planting team needs.

Mistake Number Three: Lack of leadership development

Having qualified, committed leaders when launching a new church plant is an absolute necessity. The leadership of the sponsoring church should do everything possible to assure the new plant has individuals capable of developing other leaders. This usually starts with someone training the planter and then moves on from there. The new church vision needs to be owned by the entire plant congregation, not just the church-planting leadership team. In my personal experience, I never achieved success until a sponsoring church pastor poured his life into me and taught me how to become a leader others would want to follow.

When the new work does have qualified, committed leadership, the sponsoring church needs to relax and let go. Overmanaging a new launch is one of the great cardinal sins of church planting.

Mistake Number Two: Preaching and worship

Sometimes it takes quite a while for new churches to become proficient in their planning for worship and preaching. But the leadership needs to get connected fast to find out which preaching and worship models are going to work for the new group of people to whom they will be ministering. They can't just fall back on what they did in the former church. Help the planter work hard to develop at preaching and worship. Send him to a homiletics conference, or buy a subscription to a preaching magazine or journal.

Mistake Number One: Forgetting to focus early on the spiritual dynamics

Any church, regardless of size, will get flat and stay flat without intentionally focusing early on the spiritual dynamic. This means that prayer is vital and must be continual. It is about Jesus, not a popular technique. In seeker-focused churches this is a battle from the start because many are overly cautious about deeper spiritual matters. No prayer in any case should become the norm. Instead, keep God before the people and help focus the new work towards prayer. Never should the sponsoring church take prayer or spiritual warfare lightly. To get God's perspective, the church planter and the church-planting team must spend time in fasting and prayer. Christians are involved in a spiritual battle, and we are in the line of fire. There will be wounded, so the new church plant needs to adopt a plan to deal with the wounded. We must gird our loins with truth, wear the breastplate of righteousness, shod our feet with the gospel of grace, take the shield of faith, wear the helmet of salvation, and take the sword of the Spirit. It is time we quit struggling against flesh and blood and dealt with the real enemy. We have only one

241

weapon, and it is not preaching, teaching, singing, or organizing. It is the Word of God. Our prayers contribute to the kingdom of God and thereby work to destroy the kingdom of Satan. But where there is no prayer, there is no warfare. Where there is no warfare, there is no spiritual reality. Where there is no spiritual reality, there is no victory. Where there is no victory, there is nothing glorifying to God. Jesus said, "I have glorified You on the earth by completing the work You gave Me to do" (John 17:4). Like Christ, we are to glorify the Father, but if we don't enter into the fray of spiritual warfare, we will never fulfill God's plan for our lives.

You have either heard it before or you have said it yourself at one time or another in the development of a new church plant: "I'm just too busy to pray right now. . . . there's so much to do." Excessive work load is never a viable excuse for not taking the time to address God. One of the grave dangers in church ministry generally, and certainly in church starting particularly, is the neglect of prayer. Usually there is so much to do, and no one seems on hand to help in the work. But busy as we are, we are never too busy to pray. The most important thing we can do is bathe all that we do in prayer. God's protection and direction need to be sought throughout one's entire ministry.

Church planting is God's work for God's church, and the very first step we take in planting is earnestly to seek God in prayer. Jesus never did anything in his ministry that he did not consider before the Father in prayer. He said, "When you lift up the Son of Man, then you will know that I am He, and that I do nothing on My own" (John 8:28).

Here is an action plan to remind us to keep the church plant bathed in prayer:

1. Pray and ask God to raise up intercessors for you, your family, and your ministry.
2. Make a list of possible intercessors you could ask to become prayer warriors on your behalf.
3. Invite them to join the larger team. It is advisable to have at least ten to twenty strong intercessors, as well as to have an inner core of three colleagues you can contact at any time. Add others as the new church grows.
4. Clarify and covenant upon prayer commitments and maintain either weekly or monthly contact.
5. Pray for your intercessors, at least weekly, and ask God to protect them. A great example is how the apostle Paul prayed for the various churches in Scripture.
6. Renew covenant prayer partners yearly.

Wrapping It Up

There is a great cost to church planting, and both the church planter and the sponsoring church need to realize this. It is not easy to plant churches, but it is highly rewarding. If it were easy, we would see more churches displaying such a kingdom mentality instead of the opposite. We must be willing as sponsoring churches and church planters to work hard and be willing to stick it out. Even in the midst of a serious challenge, it is vital that the sponsoring church pastor remain positive and upbeat. Otherwise the planter is doomed. I have a friend who says I'm the most positive person he knows. Even when I'm down, he claims, no one would ever know really because I'm so positive! What he forgets is that I am a church planter first, and a sponsoring pastor second. And with a church planter, there is no room for grumbling and groaning.

Jesus paid the ultimate price through his suffering and death on the cross. Kingdom work and faithful church planting never come cheaply. Whatever the cost, reaching lost men and women must be seen as the will of the Master and the call to arms of his church. The compensation will come in the Master's words: "Well done, good and faithful servant."

CHAPTER 24

The Top Twenty Mistakes
Church Planters Make

We need to beware of some harrowing pitfalls in the field of church planting. Every church planting specialist has their own list of top mistakes made by planters. With a little tongue in cheek, I present my list of twenty serious mistakes church planters make, which are the top twenty reasons new churches fail.

Mistake Number Twenty: Relying solely on the advice of experts

There is a temptation of listening to successful church planters and trying to model their admonishments and accomplishments. Remember, however, that their plant and their situation are not your church plant and your situation. Your plant is your vision and not theirs. Their role is to help keep your feet firmly placed on the ground and to help you make sound judgments. Let God be your true sponsor and final authority.

Mistake Number Nineteen: No assessment of any kind of the church planter

Communities across America need high-caliber church planters. There are various personality traits that go into making a great church-planting team, and there are certain personality types one wants to see in a lead church planter. The DISC

Personal Profile System identifies four basic personalities, and it has been shown that successful lead planters possessing a personality of either a high D (task and leadership driven) or a high I (people and relationship driven) give the church a greater chance for growth.[1] Members of the body of Christ should be strategically deployed where they can make their greatest contributions, and this is never more true than when selecting church planters.

Mistake Number Eighteen: Ignoring spiritual warfare

As mentioned earlier when looking at the top ten mistakes sponsoring churches make, church planters and planting teams cannot take spiritual warfare too lightly. It is real, and we are all on the firing line. This requires much time in fasting and prayer for the church-planting team. Our weapon against the enemy is the Bible. If we don't use the Sword and enter into the warfare of prayer, we will never fulfill God's plan for our lives.

Mistake Number Seventeen: No planning on the part of the planter

The critical ingredient in almost every successful church start is ample planning on the part of the church planter. Church planters need a vision, values, and a mission to accomplish the church plant. What is this new church going to look like? What will make this church different? What is God asking this new church to do? Planning plays a major role in a church start, and these questions and others must be considered to plant healthy reproducing churches.

Mistake Number Sixteen: No covenant agreement with the sponsoring church

Church planters who fail to develop a covenant agreement with their sponsoring churches are setting themselves up for difficulty. There are boundaries that must be agreed upon to keep the communication lines open and to keep relationships growing. Those boundaries are spelled out in the covenant agreement, which is an objective document defining relationships and responsibilities.

---

[1] The complete study can be obtained for $20 by writing GYCM, P.O. Box 9, East Islip, NY 11730. Make check payable to GYCM. Mark your memo "Performax."

Mistake Number Fifteen: Failure to match
target and match strategy

All church planters need to better define their target area and match their strategy to the location. There are often many subgroups within a given community, so how does the planter know which group to reach? He or she needs to isolate and define the distinct communities within the target area, to know which are churched and which would be more responsive. Then the planter should examine those communities with the greatest need and determine which best matches their giftedness. The largest population is not always the right choice. The planter will need to choose the target prayerfully and understand that God could change things in any way at any time. There are two ways to determine where to plant the church and who the target group will be. There is the "undefined target approach" that is used by many church planters, and there is the "targeted approach." Having a target can actually save years of frustration and anxiety. Every church will develop a target group even if it is unintentional. A church develops a character over a period of years, and the people they attract will usually be of a particular culture. The result is an established target group. Establishing a target group enables one to reach more people and experience much less frustration. Planters experience enough frustration even when everything is done correctly. No need to add any more to the list.

A church attempting to reach everyone will be frustrated at every turn. Jesus had a particular target group that he focused on while he walked the earth and trained his disciples. It was the nation of Israel. "Jesus sent out these 12 after giving them instructions: 'Don't take the road leading to other nations, and don't enter any Samaritan town. Instead, go to the lost sheep of the house of Israel" (Matt 10:5–6).

Useful Resources for Compiling Target Research. It is imperative the church planter does a thorough job of researching the target community. The goal should be to become the most informed expert on the community and to understand better than anyone what makes it tick. This research can begin with some concentrated study from various resources, such as the few suggested below, but should always be verified through on-site observation and knowledge.

SCAN US/ACORN/PRISM—This can be obtained from your state convention or the North American Mission Board. It provides both the demographics and psychographics for any area you request.

U.S. Census Data—Census data can be obtained from the Internet by logging on to the Web site www.census.gov.

Public Utilities—Public utilities can tell you how many "hook-ups" have been made in a given period of time as well as existing subscribers. Potential growth rates can often be determined from this data.

Chambers of Commerce—A visit to the chamber of commerce can provide insights in many ways.

City or County Planning Commissions—These planning commissions can provide present data and projected information, and a visit to these offices will prove very fruitful.

School Boards—The county school board district can provide a wealth of information.

Real Estate Firms—Real estate professionals often have the latest information on a community. They know the type of people moving into a specific community. It is often very fruitful to stop in to the model homes sales offices of new subdivisions for an informal visit. They can give you printed materials showing the exact number of homes to be built, the time frame for build-out, the price ranges, and possibly the ethnic make-up of those moving there.

Local or State Universities—Very sophisticated data can be obtained from colleges and universities, and often it will be the most reliable data at your disposal. There may be a cost, but it will be minimal.

Public Libraries—Access their files to pull up newspaper articles relating to growth and other changes in the community.

Religious Information—The Yellow Pages are probably the best resource to discover the churches already existing in your target community, and phone calls to the churches of interest will produce much religious information.

Mistake Number Fourteen: Failing to adjust to what God seems to be doing

One of the key mistakes many successful church planters make is taking their pile of ministry toys, trinkets, and tools from one place to another, expecting God to use them exactly as he did before. When that happens, that simple failure to adjust to what God seems to be doing can thwart the growth of any new work.

There is a high degree of learning that goes into successfully planting a healthy New Testament church. It is never wise to simply copy the latest model that has become the current rage in church planting. Go ahead and listen to the podcasts, read the books, and wear their t-shirts. That does not make you just like them. The most triumphant church planters are those taking account of what they have done really well in their past, and then implementing those same ideas in the new church setting. This is not done in exactly the same way, but with an eye on the local horizon and what God is doing in that locale.

Mistake Number Thirteen: Not having the ability to see the time line clearly

Many church planters fail to see the time line of a church plant clearly. They either wait too long to bring on church staff, or they rush into it, failing to allow God to raise up leaders out of the harvest. Rushing into the new work and bringing staff along with you is certainly not matching the gifts of the individual to any actual immediate need. Hiring one's best friend cannot help. Having grown up together or attended seminary together is not a good enough reason to bring someone on board, unless that person can add something of value to the mix. I have a friend who did just that. After twenty-one years of a wonderful friendship, a new church work began and my friend was the church planter. He hired a personal friend and the new plant began to explode because the staffer was not adding to the ministry. In fact, he was causing people to leave because his abilities were not sufficient for the task of growing the work. Hindsight is always twenty-twenty, but my friend wishes he had listened to me seven years ago when he saddled his church with someone who just could not cut it in an ever-growing ministry.

It is wise starting with what you can afford over that which you hope you can eventually afford. Most business people know this, and frankly most church planters do not. Adding staff should only come after growth has taken place and the work is becoming prosperous. I believe in multistaff church plants, but I am beginning to think that most churches should start with no more than two staff members. That's big enough to create synergy, but small enough to become self-supporting in a reasonable amount of time. If more staff members are required, they can always be hired as funds allow.

Church planters also fail to see the time line clearly when they lease office space too hastily. Most church planters tend to overestimate their need for a large office for midweek activities. I believe there is a need for a permanent midweek presence in the community, but church planters have confessed that the activities they thought warranted extra space could just as easily have been accomplished in private homes If you really need an office, get the smallest office space you can get by with, but negotiate a lease that can be renewed two months after your first public service. At that point you should have a good idea of the attendance and giving potential of the new congregation, and if more breathing space is needed, things can expand then. If not, you won't be strapped for cash.

Mistake Number Twelve: No plan for the other six days of the week

It is important to model community in your new work, and one of the best ways is to have a strategic plan for connecting with present core group members, worship attendees, and potential membership prospects. People need to be connected to each other and to God during the week. Community happens by developing and orienting attendees to the mission of the new church, by helping them plug into the work of the church, and by equipping them to connect to the ministry and the community.

Modeling community can also be done by inviting new people to your home, and by encouraging your core leadership group to practice hospitality. Create social opportunities and make it easy to connect. Remember that people matter to God, and it is vital to develop a plan to connect with others outside the regular ministry flow. Church planting is primarily a mission to unchurched people, not primarily a gathering of the faithful, so it is imperative to understand and accept secular people.

Mistake Number Eleven: Fear of not talking about money until it's urgent

Sooner than later, if you are going to be successful as a church planter, you must learn how to unashamedly ask for money. We all realize it takes money to conduct ministry and grow a church plant. And even once a church plant is up and running, it will still take money. When new ministries are added, they will need even more money. Asking people for money is both the most difficult and the most important part of growing a new church. One rule has been proven over and over again: church-planting organizations and sponsoring mother churches tend to be a lot more confident about their ability to raise needed funds than their past track record justifies. If the organization has enough money saved to pay a pastor's salary for one year, or has historically received a monthly income comparable to the monthly salary needs, I would jump at the chance if God was in it. If not, you'd better be convinced of your personal ability to raise money. You may find yourself doing it more than you expected. Remember, most church-planting organizations are run by volunteers with limited time.

If a church planter has never learned the blessing of tithing, it will always be hard to ask others for resources. If he is not displaying a sacrificial heart through his own regular giving, don't expect others to follow a good example. Additionally God will not provide those extra, unplanned contributions unless he sees a heart willingly giving towards the work.

Mistake Number Ten: Not differentiating the new church plant from the established sponsoring church

Too many new churches act like older churches with everything they need. It is important to differentiate the church plant from the sponsoring church because in most cases the new plant will not be able to do what the established church can do. It will get there, but meanwhile act your age and allow God to lead you as the church you are. This is an issue of development and it takes time. And don't try cloning the sponsoring church because that would just stall the new ministry.

Mistake Number Nine: Formalizing leadership too quickly

We usually develop leadership qualities in two ways. First, we learn by making a lot of mistakes on our own. Second, we learn from other peoples' mistakes. Church planters would be wise in their new work not to formalize the leadership structure too quickly because this could well be a learning experience of the first kind. I have seen planters rush out and immediately select deacons, only to find out later that a few really were not God's selection. It is true, however, that church planters say the quicker they formalize their leadership in the first two years of operation, the quicker the church grows.

In the early phase of a church plant, decision making needs to rest primarily in the hands of one person—the lead church planter. A good rule of thumb is that a new church should not have a formal deacon body until they are well under way towards becoming fully self-supporting. In the interim period between the initiation of the church plant and self-support status, the local association, state convention, or more importantly, the mother church can substitute as the official deacon body and provide accountability to the staff.

Planning informal home groups for Sunday school and other occasions usually works well for most plants. Too often I have seen church planters start classes only to be forced to make a transition. Maybe their rented building was sold out from under them. It could be anything.

A collapse of formalized leadership can be disastrous. One of the biggest examples of a failure in formalized leadership is found in Numbers 13:1–14, when the appointed spies returned after scouting out Canaan. Moses wanted the men to answer one simple question: "Is the land good or bad?" These men were with Joshua and Caleb, and they were actually selected leaders from among the people, one from each of the ancestral tribes. What happened? There are six major leadership blunders we can learn from this account:

1. Often by formalizing leadership too quickly, those selected will misunderstand their task.

Numbers 13:17–20 indicates that the scouts were not selected to see if they could take the land, but rather how they were to go into the land and what to look for while there. A common mistake made by new church leaders is that they over analyze their task.

250

2. Often by formalizing leadership too quickly one builds on their weaknesses instead of their strengths.

When the tribal leaders of Israel saw the land, they saw that it was good and bad, but they made the mistake of allowing their focus to be drawn to their inadequacies. Good church-planting leaders will not draw attention to the weaknesses and allow the facts to obscure the truth.

3. Often by formalizing leadership too quickly it is easy to fail to recognize God-developed potential for the task.

The Lord seeks people of faith to give leadership to his new works. Such stuff was obviously lacking in the hearts of these ten spies. In fact, they actually went so far as to refer to themselves as grasshoppers and erroneously declared that it would be the way their enemies would see them also (Num 13:33). We learn from Rahab that the people of Canaan were actually terrified of the people of Israel once they heard of God's intervention on their behalf (Josh 2:8–11). Too bad Israel's leaders didn't have the same confidence in God's power as their enemies did.

4. Often by formalizing leadership too quickly we fail to understand the infectious consequence of a negative testimony!

Numbers 14:1 describes the mass hysteria that occurred after Israel heard the evaluation of the scouts and refused to enter Canaan. There was no rejoicing in the streets that day, no excitement or expectancy of great and new things in the Lord. There was only the sound of a frightened and rebellious people.

5. Often by formalizing leadership too quickly, we fail to let God work his mighty power in drawing key leaders to the new church plant.

The ten plagues of Egypt and the deliverance through the Red Sea should have been fresh in the minds of the Israelites, yet they seem to have forgotten what God did for them in an impossible situation.

6. Don't be afraid to use the leadership of new believers, just don't formalize them too quickly.

A couple of the scouts, Joshua and Caleb, did become great leaders, and Moses was not afraid to use them. But their leadership was not formalized right away.

Mistake Number Eight: Once the project is moving forward, failing to refocus on the real target

Remember that the new work exists to reach lost and unchurched people. After the launch, don't stop gathering them and moving them out of the mix. Keep gathering. Keep sowing, and God will find you faithful. A common mistake is to emphasize the "core group" even after the launch.

Mistake Number Seven: No connection with unchurched people

Don't say, "We are going to evangelize later." Any new church start without evangelism as a core ingredient is at best sheep stealing and, at worst, dead weight. Remember that evangelism and church starting are two sides of the same coin, and they need each other to continue. Sponsoring churches need to model effective evangelism and encourage new church starters in this area because church planting is the most effective method of evangelism in the world today. Today many new and existing churches teach that relationship building is evangelism. It is not! Evangelism is going out into the highways and byways and telling others about the glorious good news of Jesus Christ. I am alarmed at the high number of new churches that do not teach their people how to share God's plan of salvation on a regular basis. Some of these churches are growing, but think how much they would be growing if they actually committed themselves to being evangelistic churches.

Mistake Number Six: A premature public launch

There are lots of pros and cons about having a core group before going public, but the overwhelming evidence suggests that to grow beyond two hundred congregants, there should be eighty-five people committed to the new church launch before going public. The norm within my denomination after four years (among those who survive) is ninety-six. The point here is not to launch the plant prematurely. Develop those individuals committed to your church before going public, and allow them to provide workers, givers, and a relational structure in which to weave newcomers.[2]

I've seen it happen many times in the past when the lead planter is wound up about starting a healthy new church. He goes across the country raising support and telling potential supporters how many people will come to their first service.

---

[2] The exceptions to this rule seem to be new churches that have permanent Sunday morning worship facilities such as warehouses or strip malls, or new churches that have large subsidies for massive advertising throughout the first year.

The planter gets to the field and starts recruiting people to join this exciting voyage. He says to potential church members, "You're not going to believe how many people are going to show up our first day." Well, the first day comes and the church planter is correct. A large number of people actually do show up, sometimes one hundred, two hundred, or even three hundred. Is there a problem? The problem is the planter has been telling everyone that 350 are going to show up. The people who support this new church are frustrated, the core group is disenchanted, and the staff is disillusioned. What could very well be an extraordinary turnout is somehow diminished by unmet or unrealistic expectations. Resist the lure to make people think this church plant must be larger than everybody else's church plant in order to be a success! Attempt to have the largest first service possible, give it everything you've got, but communicate to people that you will be quite content to work with whomever and however many people God brings your way. Celebrate. Jump up and down. God is planting a seed in a place where there was only darkness before.

Mistake Number Five: The recruiting ceases after the launch day "grand opening"

Many church planters move out of the gathering role and into the pastoring role shortly after the launch opening. All the effort up to this point has been directed towards gathering people and building new relationships toward beginning the new work. But at this point many church planters move from chief gatherer to pastor. Far too many planters spend the majority of their time on those who are coming through the door, rather than those who are not yet in the door. This is all wrong. As church planters, the most important thing we will do during the first three years of the present plant will be gathering, gathering, and more gathering. And for significant growth thereafter, only four things will bring high dividends: gathering, evangelism, preaching, and leading. The rest can all be done by others.

Mistake Number Four: Not sharing the ministry with the laity

Church starters are by nature self-starters. Unfortunately that usually means they are sometimes oblivious to the need to delegate, especially early in the process. They spread themselves too thin, afraid to delegate effectively, not wanting to say "no" to requests, or being tied to the office phone and procrastinating. The sign of a strong leader is how well he or she delegates. Strong planters recognize that delegation achieves two important goals at the same time. It frees the church planter to focus on the significant parts of their calling and responsibility, and it enables additional staff (volunteer or paid) to develop their own skills and ministry competencies. If church planters do not learn how to pass other work along, they will waste the time the Lord has given them for ministry. Do you have the time needed to complete the day-to-day tasks of your ministry responsibilities? If not, delegate the things that are keeping you from accomplishing your assignments.

Not only is it wise thinking to involve the laity according to their giftedness, it's a practical help to the new church planter. A sponsoring church can help a new church plant by providing a few capable people to help assist in the beginning stages of the new work, and by staying on top of who is assisting in the work being done. This helps free the planter to emphasize ministry expansion. Smart delegation also gives the staff the gift of learning by doing, taking risks, and becoming comfortable with the consequences of their own growing ministry performance.

Mistake Number Three: No support network

The most common complaint of new church starters is that they feel so all alone, so isolated in their work. To that end, our denomination and local entities have worked diligently to provide a nurturing, encouraging support network for the new work starter. This includes a mentor, a church-planting network (a support group of peers), a partnering church, and a sponsoring church. Church planters need to know of the continuing prayer, love, support, and encouragement coming from others. It makes a world of difference to them. When there is someone to talk with, it makes those alone times bearable. Remember also that much of a solid support network is developed by the planter taking the initiative. It does not just happen; one needs to work on making it happen!

Mistake Number Two: No prayer, little prayer, or impotent prayer

One of the grave dangers in church ministry, including church planting, is the neglect of prayer. We simply must keep our church plant bathed in prayer, as was explored in the previous chapter.

Mistake Number One: No commitment to the call

When I went through new planter orientation, I heard one of the most stirring speeches I ever heard about starting new plants and remaining committed to the new church planting call. It was delivered by the individual who led the orientation. It stirred my soul. A few months later, when this individual left for warmer climates, those words felt hollow.

In my estimation, the primary and main reason church starters fail is a lack of discernment and commitment concerning the call of church planting. Satan is very wise in his ways, and he tries to make us second guess the Lord's calling on our lives. Some Christians never go into church planting simply because they cannot discern the call of God on their lives. For others, it is more a matter of creature comfort and not necessarily a desire to glorify God through church planting. Obedience and commitment to God's call on our lives are primary. If the Lord does call one into church planting, that person will never be the same. God's calling is what keeps us at the task when the ways are hard and the results are slow.

The last thing so dangerous to do is to view church planting as a romantic journey. It is anything but. Sometimes there is the romance of a new church start, or the appeal of a brand new congregation free of the troubles and turmoil of past churches. But there will come days when only the conviction that God has called us here to start a church will keep us from leaving. Some planters have the astonishing notion that if the new plant doesn't work out, they can always go back home to minister. They are planning their departure the day they begin the plant! Remember that our call and the gifts God gives us to do the work of the ministry are from God and God alone. He called, and He will enable. He is your resource in every time of need, and He is more than sufficient.

Part 7

Selling the Idea for Becoming
a Sponsoring Church

*We ourselves don't make the church grow or repro-
duce, any more than pulling on a stalk of corn would
make it grow. Paul plants, Apollos waters, God gives
the growth. We sow, water, weed, fertilize and fence the
crop, but rely on the church's own God-given potential
to reproduce. An obedient, Spirit-filled church has to
reproduce at home or abroad. It's her very nature; she
is the body of the risen, life-giving Son of God.*
— *George Patterson*

CHAPTER 25

Promoting the Set Free
and Inner City Method
to Your Church

Today the major cities of the United States are exploding with population growth. Each day thousands of new people saturate the cities at different levels. Most of us are aware of the immigration of people from Mexico, Central and South America, and so on. The number of new Asian and eastern European immigrants is rising dramatically as well. The immigration issue is one of the major ones facing our country.

At another level is the growing popularity of moving back into the inner cities by the young professionals. Developers are remodeling old buildings into condos and lofts for the Yuppie urban migration. The down-and-out population in the city is also growing rapidly. There are more homeless people on the streets today in our major cities than ever before, and about half of them are families. A large percentage is single women with children. Many of our lower income families are one paycheck away from the poverty level, one paycheck away from homelessness and life on the city streets.

Most church-planting strategies gravitate to the suburbs as it is popular to sponsor churches in the new housing developments. At any given time, there are around twenty thousand houses under construction where I live in southern California. I could spend all of my time developing strategies and recruiting church starters for these fast developing communities. Under the radar screen of most Christians, however, exists the underbelly of the city where one finds broken lives and battered people. They are beaten down by drugs, alcohol, crime and despair. They live in fear and defeat, crushed by the cycle of constant destructive and dysfunctional behavior to the second and third generation! They have been ignored by our society. They have been judged and condemned by our society as useless throwaways. Sadly they have even been judged and condemned by many Christians.

Some Christians think that if these people really wanted help, they would clean themselves up and come to church. But do those comments arise from the heart of God? What we hear from the heart of God is: "Come to Me, all of you who are weary and burdened, and I will give you rest. All of you, take up My yoke and learn from Me, because I am gentle and humble in heart, and you will find rest for yourselves. For My yoke is easy and My burden is light" (Matt 11:28–30).

What is Christ's church going to do with the poor of the inner cities? What is the church going to do with the poor families who are trying hard to keep their kids and not lose custody to the state? What is the church going to do with those families sleeping in their cars at night, or even worse, sleeping on the streets in our downtown areas? What is the church going to do with the dysfunctional and mentally ill people who have been abandoned on the streets of our downtown cities? What is the church going to do?

The truth is that the church does not know what to do with the poor in our cities. When people do not look like us, smell like us, act like us, and function at a normal level in society, we tend to leave them to their own affairs. That is why so many churches and denominations have left the inner city. As they followed their members to the suburbs, they simply forgot the people they left behind. Many think if we can just distance ourselves from the poor, we can ignore them and not feel guilty about it.

But that doesn't wash. Christians know we should share with those less fortunate than ourselves. We know that God wants us to minister to the poor, the homeless, and the hurting families of the inner city. Many believers have good intentions about getting out of their comfort zones to minister to the poor, but they allow fear to control them. An outreach team from a large church not too far from downtown Los Angeles is a good example. The church felt a concern for the homeless on the streets, but they were afraid. So they did the best they could. They made food baskets, drove down to the homeless area, rolled down their car windows a little way, and then handed the baskets out the window before driving away as fast as they could. At least they were trying, even though they were afraid they might get too close and too involved with the street people.

God in his wonderful grace always seems to raise up a group of godly soldiers who are willing to plant their lives among the poor as a living sacrifice in order to touch the hearts of hurting people. Today God has raised up the Set Free Church movement to go to the inner cities of America. They need support and encouragement from the whole body of Christ so they don't go alone.

William Carey was the founder of modern world missions. He was willing to go to India and lay down his life to reach the people there with the gospel. As he spoke to the sending board, he challenged them with these words: "I will go. I will go deep into the darkness. But, as I go, I need for you to hold the ropes." He was referring to the "ropes" of prayer, support, and encouragement. The Set Free Church movement needs a support team of Christians and churches to hold the ropes as they go deeper into the world of hurting people and broken lives.

Why Should Our Church Sponsor Inner City Ministry?

I escorted a mission team from St. Vincent in the Caribbean so that they could sing and preach at Set Free Church of Skid Row in downtown Los Angeles. St. Vincent is a small island in the Caribbean, which is a poor country compared to the United States. After walking the streets of Skid Row, where thousands of homeless people live, the team broke down and cried as they attempted to sing for a worship service. Their hearts were broken over the shattered lives they saw on those streets. How can this happen in the richest country in the world? How can this possibly be?

If the church in America has a good answer to that question, I would like to hear it. The only answer I can think of is human sin. The sin of the people on the streets as well as in the mansions has destroyed hope and purpose in many lives. Sin is a tough taskmaster and has no mercy for those who yield to it. On the streets today, drugs like crack cocaine control souls and bodies, and so do alcohol and crime. Individual sin is one of the main reasons thousands of people live (or just barely exist) without hope out on the streets of our inner cities. But there is also collective sin.

Homelessness, drug addiction, crime, and violence on the streets of our major cities can be seen as the results of the sin of our government. The government has taken over the benevolent ministry of the local church by setting up the multiple social service system we have in America today. That seemed like a good idea in the era of the Great Depression, when so many needed government assistance. But the system has gotten so big that the individual gets lost in the numbers game. The hurting person becomes just another cog in the system. It is a sin for the system to be so big and ineffective that thousands have to sleep on the streets of our cities every night.

God has raised up Christ's church to minister to the poor and needy in our generation. Let us go back to the calling that Jesus had on his life. As he stood up in the synagogue on the Sabbath day in Nazareth, he read from the prophet Isaiah: "The Spirit of the Lord is on Me, because He has anointed Me to preach good news to the poor. He has sent Me to proclaim freedom to the captives and recovery of sight to the blind, to set free the oppressed, to proclaim the year of the Lord's favor" (Luke 4:18–19). That was the reason Jesus came to this earth, and this is now the calling he has passed on to his church. In the upper room, Jesus told the disciples, "Peace to you! As the Father has sent Me, I also send you" (John 20:21).

Drive through the streets of your downtown area, and as you pass by the row of cardboard boxes and sleeping bags filled with homeless people, instead of locking your doors and looking the other way, try seeing them as Jesus does. When Jesus saw the crowds, "He felt compassion for them, because they were weary and worn out, like sheep without a shepherd" (Matt 9:36).

The church needs to overcome the sins of indifference and neglect. It is time we stepped up and got involved in inner-city ministry to the poor and needy.

Why Should Your Church Sponsor a Set Free Church or Ministry in the Inner City?

Homelessness

A few years ago, the Set Free Church in Skid Row of Los Angeles was ministering in Hollywood. They would give coffee away every morning and food baskets every Thursday morning. They would conduct a worship service and serve a hot meal on Thursday nights. As they ministered there, they came across a man in his mid-forties (who looked like he was sixty-five). His street name was "Hollywood," and he had been a great drummer in his youth. He came to California to become a star. But while pursuing stardom, he got hooked on heroin. When I first saw him he weighed about eighty pounds, had not showered in six months, and was sleeping under a bush in a park in Hollywood. Set Free tried to help him by inviting him to go to their Discipleship Ranch, where he could kick the drug habit, get a shower and warm clothes, and sleep in a bed in a safe environment. The best that he would ever let us do for him was give him a warm coat and a sleeping bag so he could be warm at night. He soon slipped back into the dark alleys of Hollywood and to his all-consuming heroin habit. There are hundreds of people like "Hollywood" on the streets of your city. Why should your church sponsor a Set Free ministry? Because people deserve and should have a safe place to live.

The Set Free Church movement exists to minister to people like "Hollywood" and to help provide safe places for people to live. Your church could help support the Discipleship Ranches that Set Free has around the country. Or, it could do this along with several other churches. We could help with money for food or with providing bunk beds with linens and blankets. What if several churches could rent a home in the city to house those who have completed the Ranch phase and are coming back to the inner city to minister and live?

When people think about the homeless, many think of Joe Wine-O, falling asleep in the gutter every night holding a cheap bottle of muscatel in a paper bag. But things have changed. Today women and children make up half of the homeless people in any given city. That should not be so. James 1:27 tells us that "pure and undefiled religion before our God and Father is this: to look after orphans and widows in their distress and to keep oneself unstained by the world."

As the church, we need to put James 1:27 into practice. This can happen by working with Set Free to provide homes for women with children, or rent a large house with several bedrooms. Set Free provides lots of bunk beds to take care of

needy people. The ministry will give women job training so they can find employment and help support the cost of the house with program fees. What a blessing
to see the smiles on faces of those who have slept cold, wet, and hungry on the
streets, but now have a safe and secure place to put the pieces together toward
becoming a productive citizen again. What a joy it is to watch children play and
have fun in a safe place, and to watch broken lives renew and change.

Food

The Set Free ministry desires to give people of the inner cities the Bread of Life,
who is Jesus. To do that in a credible way they must give people actual bread or
food to feed their bodies before they can feed their souls. Some years ago Robert
Martinez was passing out bread at a new Set Free Church in San Bernardino,
California. Victor Alverado, who had been out on the streets for seven years doing
drugs, came by for food. Robert gave him bread and shared Jesus with him. Victor
got mad and cussed him out. But Victor kept coming back for bread every day,
and soon he confessed that he was a backslidden Christian who needed to get right
with God. He tried to run away from God, but he could not! He started putting his
life back together and remarried the wife he divorced while he was doing drugs
and living on the streets. Later God called Victor to preach. Now he is the pastor
of the Set Free Church of Sun City, California. He came for bread, but he got the
Bread of Life, and he is now sharing that same spiritual nourishment while passing out bread and food to needy people in Riverside County.

Any church can help Set Free congregations and other inner-city ministries by
partnering with them in various food ministries. Some church members are not
quite ready to do street witnessing in the inner city, but that does not disqualify
them from ministry to the poor. They can give food away and feel safe in doing it.
By giving food with grace, the hardest of hearts can be touched and changed by
the Spirit of God and become open to the gospel message. As one person offers
them food, another ministers to their physical needs, and another shares the message of Jesus Christ and the plan of salvation.

I took Alan Balabat, pastor of Cornerstone Church in Diamond Bar, California,
to a church starter meeting. On the way I dropped some clothes off at the Set Free
Church at Skid Row in Los Angeles. Alan met pastor Ron Thomas, heard his testimony, and saw what they were doing in ministry. As we continued to the church-
starters' meeting, Alan told me he wanted his church to partner with Set Free. He
said, "This is where Jesus would be. This is where we need to be." Alan went to
his church leaders and shared his new concern and passion for inner-city ministry.
He took some of them to Skid Row, and they also got excited. Some of the new
believers in the church worked for a restaurant chain in southern California, and
they shared the needs of the poor in Los Angeles with their bosses. They worked
out an agreement to provide the food to feed the needy at Thanksgiving time. On
November 22, 2006, the police blocked off the street next to where Set Free meets,

and three thousand people were fed a full meal. People from the church distributed the food while people from other churches shared the gospel. That day more than fifty people accepted Christ. As food filled their stomachs and the gospel filled their souls, everyone was blessed. This is just one example of a wonderful partnership between a local church and the Set Free ministry. Cornerstone Church continues to partner with Set Free by distributing food, teaching Bible classes, and providing clothes. Through this partnership many have been blessed and ushered into the kingdom, and there is no reason other churches can't do the same thing in other cities.

Clothes

It will surprise no one that as people live on the streets they get cold, and their worn-out clothes get dirty. They get sick and weary from living in these conditions. In the typical closet of the average Christian family there are enough extra clothes to warm many homeless people. Christians need to start sharing what they have with the poor and needy in the inner cities, and our churches should be partnering with inner-city ministries by sharing your clothes with them.

I used to be a pastor in Pomona, California. Our church decided to feed the poor on the Sunday before Christmas. We advertised, we gathered up food and had the tables ready. One homeless couple came early to the church for the meal. They were invited to come to the worship service and that morning, as the invitation to accept Christ was extended, they came forward and gave their hearts and lives to Jesus. They stayed for the meal and got fed. To our delight, one of the brand new couples in our church took them home with them and allowed them to take a shower and get cleaned up. Then they pulled clothes out of their closets, which they gave to the couple. They did what should be natural for Christians to do—give from our own things to those in need. I have heard some Christians say, "I don't have enough clothes for myself. Why should I give to the homeless?" If you have more than one set of clothes, more than one pair of shoes, you have more than the people in the streets have. The book of James challenges the church with these words: "If a brother or sister is without clothes and lacks daily food, and one of you says to them, 'Go in peace, keep warm, and eat well,' but you don't give them what the body needs, what good is it?" (2:15–16).

Why Should Your Church Help Minister to the Poor in the Inner City?

God has also called his church to minister to the spiritual needs of all people, including people in the inner city. It is great to help meet the needs of the inner city, such as seeing a hungry person fed. To clothe a person who was walking around in ragged and dirty clothes is exciting. To hear from women with children who lived in an abandoned car know they are going to a safe and warm house thrills one's soul. The church is called to do all this when ministering in the streets. But we are not to stop there. We can't stop until we also share the gospel of the Good News of Jesus Christ.

Why should our churches care about helping minister to the poor in the inner city? Because the greatest experience in human life is to know Christ, to know God loves us and has forgiven us, to know he has written our names in heaven in the Lamb's Book of Life, and to know that he will never leave or forsake us. The greatest privilege a Christian can have is to share the Good News of Jesus with another person and to have the blessing of seeing them give their heart and life to the Lord. That is what it is all about! That is what Set Free and many other inner-city ministries are doing very effectively today. Our churches need to partner with them in that task. As I have walked alongside Set Free workers for the past decade, I have seen more than fifteen thousand souls come into the kingdom of God through outreach ministries and evangelistic work. That sets my heart on fire afresh and keeps me going back to the inner cities.

The Rising Tide Church brought forty members to Skid Row in Los Angeles to do street evangelism and conduct the Saturday evening service. The Rising Tide Church is a new fellowship meeting in private homes in the Mission Viejo area. After the service the team walked and shared with the street people who had come to the service. Mike and I spoke with Daniel, a "crack head" who was sleeping in his truck a block away from the Set Free Church. As we shared the gospel with Daniel, he prayed with us to accept Christ into his life. Mike got so excited about Daniel's decision that he showed up the next morning for Sunday worship and watched as Daniel made his public profession of faith by walking down the aisle at the church. Mike spent time discipling Daniel. Mike still comes to help witness and disciple the men on Skid Row. As I understand Scripture and God's master plan of the ages, every Christian should get excited about sharing their faith with others and helping new believers grow in Christ. Working or partnering with others who work in the inner city is thrilling.

Why should your church help with the urban ministry in your inner city? Because it is the Christian thing to do, and because God called the church to do it. More than any other reason, the church should give to and love the poor into the kingdom because it honors God. We all need to remember that we have an audience of only One, and so our first priority should be to please the heavenly Father and to bring glory to the King of kings. "The one who oppresses the poor insults their Maker, but one who is kind to the needy honors Him" (Prov 14:31).

How Do We Get Our Churches to Be Spin-off Churches in the Inner City?

The dire needs of the people of the inner city should be presented to the local churches in that city because Christians need to understand the real issues that hundreds of hurting and hopeless people face every day. Issues like the overwhelming control that drugs have over body and soul, or the utter despair that hunger, homelessness, and disease bring to the human essence. We need to know what it means to live homeless in the streets. But we need to know more than that, more than mere facts. With just the facts in hand about the inner-city condition, our members will feel helpless to solve the problems.

The facts can be overwhelming, but we serve a God who is bigger than all the problems, bigger than all the hopelessness, and bigger than all our abilities combined. In today's world, we are constantly being bombarded by the negative effects of illegal drugs. What we see on TV, read in the newspaper, and hear on the radio is real, and we see the words "no hope" written all over it. The problem is that we are only hearing the negative stories. Have Christians gotten to the point of denying that God can change people and things?

Many of us have come to believe that a drug addict can never change, that a gang member can never be redeemed, and that homeless people can never be transformed. Instead of trying to reach out to the inner city to minister to these people, we head the opposite direction and fall back into our comfort zones. But God is calling us to leave our comfort zones and go to the places Jesus would go and love the people Jesus would love.

How do we get our churches to be spin-off churches in the inner city? The potential sponsoring church must be challenged to present the gospel to everyone. With an emphasis on *every* one. The truth of 2 Peter 3:9 needs to be presented from our pulpits and Sunday school classes: "The Lord does not delay His promise, as some understand delay, but is patient with you, not wanting any to perish, but all to come to repentance." Sin does not need to control one's life. God can overcome any and all sin. Nothing is impossible to overcome by the power of the resurrected Christ. A series of sermons or Sunday school lessons can be prepared and presented in the potential sponsoring church about how God changed lives in the Bible and still changes lives today. In both the Old Testament and the New Testament, God took care of the poor and needy. If God could take care of their physical and spiritual needs in the past, he can certainly do it today. As the church, we must believe that "Jesus Christ is the same yesterday, today, and forever" (Heb. 13:8), and that he will continue touching, ministering, and transforming the poor and outcasts of society.

Demonstrate the Victories

Study the victories found in the Bible, and it will be a real blessing as your church digs into the Word. As they become aware of what God has done in the Bible and read stories of victories being won today, the sponsoring church needs to be challenged to go the next step toward sponsoring inner-city work. Ask Set Free pastors, or leaders of other inner-city ministries, to share in the church service. As the brethren hear testimonies of people from your inner city and see how far God has brought them, the hearts of some will get ready to sponsor an inner-city ministry.

One such testimony is from Pastor Dirk Patterson, who grew up in Compton, California, with the highest rate of murders of any city in Los Angeles County. He was a third-generation gang member, so he grew up in the gang scene, running the streets and living hard. He saw many of his relatives and friends gunned down in gang fights, drive-by shootings, and retaliations. In fact, Dirk was shot three times himself. He was doing drugs and selling them at the same time. But he had something most other street thugs lack. He had a praying mother and grandmother who lifted him up to the Lord every day.

Dirk came to Set Free for help. He gave his life to Christ, went to the Discipleship Ranch, and God started changing him. He met his wife Beatrice while she was at the Women's Discipleship Ranch. She had been working the streets of Los Angeles and Pomona for years. She met Christ at the Set Free Church of Pomona, California. They fell in love, and God has changed their lives together. God called Dirk to be a pastor. He went to the Set Free pastor's school and felt led by God to go back home to Compton to reach out to the gangs. Dirk Patterson is now the pastor of the Set Free Church of Compton. As he or someone of a similar background stands before your congregation and shares his testimony, they will know without any doubt that victories can still be won today on the streets of our inner cities.

If the membership will be in prayer and sensitive to the Spirit of God, they will be touched and challenged. And as the transformed lives of people off the streets stand before the church, average Christian people will get more excited about sponsoring a work in the city. Set Free has also made some excellent videos/CDs about their ministries that can be shown as spots in the morning or evening worship service. As people watch the Thanksgiving service at Set Free Church on Skid Row in Los Angeles, where three thousand people are being fed a hot meal, and as they observe volunteers passing out meals, distributing booklets of the Gospel of John, or sharing one-on-one about Jesus, they will be touched and challenged to find a place for themselves in this kind of ministry. The will see that ordinary people, just like themselves, can do volunteer work in the inner city. When enough people step up, the prospective sponsoring church can commit to stepping up to the plate to sponsor a Set Free Church or similar urban ministry in your own city.

Victories Need to Be Observed and Experienced

We need to have a personal experience of what God is doing in our inner cities. We will never understand what actually is happening until we touch, feel, and taste what is going on among those who were beaten down but now live victoriously in Christ.

The best way to get a pastor or other Christian leader excited about sponsoring a Set Free Church in the city is to get them on-site and involved in the daily ministry. I received a phone call from Howard Waller, the minister of missions at Bear Valley Church in Lakewood, Colorado. He heard about Set Free and saw the need for such a ministry in the inner city of Denver. I told him about what God was doing and that he needed to come and see for himself. While in southern California, he and his wife visited the Set Free Church in Yuciapa. Then I took them to Riverside to an outreach at an apartment complex. They ate a "Set Free steak," better known as a hot dog, watched the band perform, listened to the testimonies and a simple gospel message, and saw several people give their lives to Jesus that night. They told me that same thing could happen in Denver. So Howard went back to Denver to tell his church what God was doing in the inner city. Because he saw it firsthand, felt it, and experienced God's Spirit working, the leaders got excited and were all for it. Today there is a strong Set Free Church in Denver because Howard experienced it on site and got involved. The point is that church leadership needs to encounter inner-city ministry in a personal way.

As potential church sponsoring pastors and leaders come to experience the heartbeat of the inner-city ministry movement, they can pass the excitement on to others in the church. As the church members experience inner-city ministry firsthand by going on the streets with the Set Free pastors, they will be encouraged and set on fire for evangelism. As the excitement spreads through the congregation, others will volunteer in other ways to help minister in the inner city.

Valley Baptist Church of Bakersfield, California, was challenged to help sponsor the Set Free Church of Bakersfield. Pastor Mike Salazar started the Set Free Church about two years before and was on his own. The pastoral staff at Valley Baptist visited Salazar's plant and saw what Set Free was attempting to do in the inner city. They felt the heartbeat of the ministry and challenged their church to get involved. At first they sent the men's ministry team down to Set Free to go witnessing. As they went out in the streets of Bakersfield, they saw the zeal and enthusiasm that the ex-cons, ex-gang members and ex-drug addicts of Set Free had in sharing their faith—with anyone and everyone. The men from Valley Baptist got excited. They took that excitement back with them to their church, and then more men started giving their time and talents to help Set Free expand and grow.

Over the years there has developed a bond between the two churches as they have done ministry side by side. The communication and trust between the two groups is strong, and they work together as a team to reach Bakersfield for Christ. Today the two congregations have come together to remodel an old warehouse in downtown Bakersfield to be used jointly by both churches. On certain nights of the week, the college ministry of Valley Baptist uses it as a coffee house ministry to young adults. The rest of the week Set Free uses the building to minister to hurting people in their inner-city community, including using the two-hundred-seat auditorium for worship on Sunday mornings. Through this significant partnership hundreds have come into the kingdom of God. Each church has been a blessing to the other. That is what partnering is all about.

Chapter 26

Three Questions and One Incredible Challenge to Churches Planting Churches

Perhaps the greatest passage in Scripture challenging the people of God is found in Numbers 13, when the scouts reported back to Moses about entering Canaan. After the twelve returned and after ten of them reported the Israelites should not try taking possession of the land, Caleb spoke up and stilled the crowd.

> Then Caleb quieted the people in the presence of Moses and said, "We must go up and take possession of the land because we can certainly conquer it!" But the men who had gone up with him responded, "We can't go up against the people because they are stronger than we are!" So they gave a negative report to the Israelites about the land they had scouted: "The land we passed through to explore is one that devours its inhabitants, and all the people we saw in it are men of great size. We even saw the Nephilim there." (The offspring of Anak were descended from the Nephilim.) "To ourselves we seemed like grasshoppers, and we must have seemed the same to them" (13:30–33).

Moses appointed one leader from each of the tribes of Israel so that everybody could be properly represented. After all the years of wilderness wandering, and after coming up out of bondage in Egypt and crossing the wilderness of Zin, the Israelites came to the edge of the Promised Land and looked over into Jordan. The men appointed by Moses thought it was a marvelous land. But the majority of the scouting team lacked a sustaining faith in what the Lord was able to do, and refused to enter the Promised Land. The people started complaining about Moses and Aaron. Only Caleb and Joshua disagreed with the report. They said it could be done and should be done.

The report of Caleb and Joshua is the word we need to hear today when the topic turns to churches planting other churches. There is still a tremendous need to sponsor and plant new churches all over this land. Never in our nation's history has there been a greater need for established churches to partner together for the cause of Christ to plant healthy New Testament churches.

After the scouts incited the community by giving a false report, there was the usual murmuring around the Israelite camp. Everyone was upset! They were divided between the popular report (let's do nothing right now) and the unpopular report (God is able to do this, so let's get going). The majority of those gathered to hear the account even threatened to take away the leadership of Moses. And because of this, God said the children of Israel would not be allowed to enter the Promised Land. God said they should go back into the wilderness and wander around for another forty years, until that generation died off and a new generation was in place and ready to see God's glory rain down once more upon them as God's people. It has always intrigued me that the other ten men of the twelve scouts died in the fourteenth chapter of Numbers of a plague before the Lord. The Lord had his word about negativism. When God tells us to move forward, we better move forward toward sponsoring and planting new churches. We need to go into areas all over this great land, plant new churches, and ensure there is a vital, worshipping group of believers within easy reach of every man, woman, and child in the world.[1] Our local communities of Bible-believing churches can do it, and all of us who call on the name of the Lord can play a part.

We might think we're not called to plant churches. But that is just not true. It is always the will of God to have people worship in spirit and in truth. Whatever ministry we have or do, we must understand that church planting is not for us but for God. We do it because God wants a people to worship him.[2] God has been good to us. He has blessed us beyond all imagination. Most Christians have not heard about this, but we have just completed the most amazing and miraculous feat within our time. For the first time since we began recording the number of church plants, we have seen God bless us as his people by planting just short of five churches a day in the United States. Seventeen hundred eighty-one Bible-believing, evangelical churches were planted in the year 2004. That is 4.9 new churches planted each day. The sponsoring and planting of these new spirit-filled churches is a blessing for all of us in the kingdom.

God has given us so many blessings, and in the midst of it all, he has given us a vision of a new land. There are still hundreds of thousands of new churches that need to be sponsored and planted all across North America while there is still time. The Lord didn't make us a people to be overly satisfied with our own

---

[1] Patrick Johnstone, "Covering the Globe," in *Perspectives on the World Christian Movement: A Reader*, ed. Ralph W. Winter and Steven C. Hawthorne (Pasadena, CA: William Carey Library, 1999), 546.

[2] Floyd McClung, "Apostolic Passion," in *Perspectives on the World Christian Movement*, 186.

successes. He did not design us to stand around, put our thumbs in the pie, and say, "What good boys we are." God made us for a tremendous purpose!

This is what God says to us: "I have known only you out of all the clans of the earth" (Amos 3:2). Of all the people on Earth, God still knows us. For every privilege, however, there comes a responsibility. We are coming to a place where we have got to make some hard decisions about how the Lord would have us be a part of his next great movement. This movement has to do with building the kingdom and reaching our nation and the world for Christ. In this book I have suggested the best way to do this is through the sponsoring and planting of new churches. As we close, I would like to ask my readers three questions in relation to church planting.

What Do You See?

In light of where you are in the ongoing mission plan of Christ's church, do you see God, or do you see the giants all over this land? In every circumstance a pastor and the church leadership have to make decisions about what they see. We could talk about how bad it is or how bad it is going to be. As to planting and funding new church works, it is getting harder and harder to do anything anywhere. The cost for being a missional church is high, and it will escalate even more. These escalating prices will drive us all against the wall of defeatism if we are not centrally focused on the will of God to reach this land for Jesus' sake. But God is able, and he has never run out of resources for his kingdom and the expansion of godly multiplying churches to reach the lost of this land.

We are tempted to say, "We can't do that. We better back up and hold off sponsoring or planting that new work for now. We better turn inward and just take care of our own." Every time the children of Israel got to a place where there was a hard decision to make, they had to decide whether to go forward or backward. When they went to God and sought his face, the answer was always, "Go forward! You can do it! I'll be there in the hard times and in the easy times." God never once said, "Turn around and go back!" And I believe if we sought his face now, he would never say, "Hold off sponsoring and planting that church for now."

Our plans should begin with a divine sense of God within our hearts, a sense that we should consider the vast need for sponsoring new churches across this land. The sales manager of the copy-machine company met with the salesmen. Sales of their machines were not going well. The manager put up a very large poster containing a black dot down in the lower corner. The salesmen all pointed to the little black dot. Then the sales manager said, "That's the problem. Your focus is all wrong. Our sales are down. We are not moving any of our copier products. At the same time, I am sure each of you would like a bigger pay check. Before you is an opportunity to see potential, and what do you see? You see the black dot. Realize that there is enough room on this poster to write up a sales contract. This blank poster represents an incredible opportunity, and yet all you can see is the problem with it."

What do you see? Do you see the black dot? Or can you see the opportunity to stretch for God's glory? Do you have church members who are just like the sales team? There are some people within almost every church who say we can't do everything we set out to accomplish by becoming a spin-off church. Yet God is calling us as mission-minded churches to dig down deep and stretch ourselves for his glory!

We are living in a day of great opportunity and, as we look around at the opposition, we could call ourselves grasshoppers. Yes, the economic forecast is bad when it comes to starting new churches, and it will get worse. But have you ever tried to plant a church in a good economic year? The prophets of gloom and doom will always say, "We can't make it. There is going to be a down surge." Has the Lord God ever gone out of business because the financial markets have gone up or down? The negative prophets can make the sons of Anak seem so big. God, however, did not bring us to this place simply to rest out on the grassy plains and look on while others do what God has called us to do.

Do you see the sons of Anak, or do you see the Lord God Almighty? Do you see the sons of Anak, or the Lord God who brought us out of bondage? Do you see the sons of Anak, or the God who took us to the Holy Mountain? Do you see the sons of Anak, or the God who went with us in the wilderness of Zin? Do you see the God of all history, or do you see the sons of Anak, who make us feel like grasshoppers?

We may feel like grasshoppers before all the forces that swirl around. And if we look at the giants against us, we will begin to feel so small. Remember though, God has made us a church-planting people and he has brought us safely this far.

The apostle Paul talked about the power of the resurrection. He did not debate all of the theories; he simply talked about the power of the resurrection. The tomb was empty. That is our power! The power that rolled away the stone is the power that goes against the sons of Anak and the power that goes with us when we plant new churches. Do we see God, or do we see giants?

Whom Do You Follow?

Do you follow the mob or do you follow Moses? We are not number crunchers. We are supposed to give a vision for how the people of the church ought to be used by God in reaching this nation for Christ. As Christian leaders, we can accomplish this vision best by sponsoring new churches. As spin-off pastors and leaders, we need to rally all of our energies, our resources, our people, and our organizations to accomplish the vision that God has given us. That's what a leader does.

Pastors try many things to keep their congregants happy. But to please the Lord, we need to remain focused on missionary causes through the sponsoring and planting of new churches. A true missionary-sending church has a leadership that says, "There is a land out there to be conquered in Jesus' name. Come on. Let's get going, for God's glory by God's power." It is our task to run ahead and present the body of Christ a missionary vision for where they are going and how they will get there. The pulpit is the tool God has given missional pastors for doing just that. We should be proclaiming from those pulpits a ministry of planting new churches through existing churches.

Where Are You Going?

Where are you going? Are you going into the Promised Land, or back into the wilderness? The wilderness is a sorrowful place to be. I do not want to see North American churches turning back into the wilderness. There are older countries of the world with magnificent cathedrals that did not accept the challenge of taking the mission of God. They were turned back into the wilderness, and now they are empty and used only as museums. On the other hand, missionary churches of all shapes and sizes that have taken the evangelism challenge are growing. What if God removed our candlestick right now because we were not the people he wanted us to be? What if he turned to somebody else and gave our missionary blessings and heritage away? What if he turned another way to plant new churches and sponsor new works? What a wilderness we would experience.

What will church historians say about the twenty-first-century church? Will they talk about what a strong church we were early in our history, and how we ceased being the missionary sending agency we once were? Will they say we squandered our chance to change the world? Will they talk about us being pulled apart in a thousand different directions? Will they talk about our replacing the concern for missions with secular how-to-discover-yourself manuals? When they eventually do look at our contribution, I pray the historians will say this of us: "This generation saw the missionary challenge of sponsoring and planting new churches all over the world and took it! Their evangelistic outreach and renewed soul-winning fervor saved the local church and took it on to the heights God intended. This was the finest hour in the life of the evangelical movement as they planted and sponsored new churches at a rate never before imagined."

That would be one incredible challenge, wouldn't it? Our efforts could be part of the last Great Awakening just before Jesus returns in glory to lead his people home. The decision is ours.

Wrapping It Up

I ask again the three questions I asked before.

1. What do you see?
   Do you see the giants, or do you see God?
2. Whom do you follow?
   Do you follow the mob or Moses?
3. Where are you going?
   Back into the wilderness, or into the Promised Land?

Afterword

When I planted my first church, I did not know much. For that matter, I could not find many resources to help me figure out what to do next. I knew I needed help but did not know where to go to find it.

A decade later I wrote *Planting New Churches in a Postmodern Age,* and its second edition, *Planting Missional Churches,* to provide church planters with the knowledge and skills built from my research and personal experience. But, there have been some missing things that I, and many others who have written on church planting, have not developed—that is, a focus on church-planting churches. In other words, not much has been written on how churches can and should plant churches.

In *Spin-off Churches,* my friends provide us with a tool that develops what it means to be a church-planting church. For that I am grateful. And I believe that many churches across North America will be as well.

The book you are holding is a key tool to help sponsoring churches plant new congregations. My hope is that it will help thousands of existing congregations to be challenged by God and to meet the demands of the Great Commission. I believe it will help them step out in faith to multiply their impact through church planting. Rod Harrison, Tom Cheyney, and Don Overstreet are men who have spent more than 60 combined years planting churches and equipping sponsoring churches—and they are worth listening to.

I can attest to the benefit of a great sponsor and to the challenge of an ill-equipped sponsoring strategy. If I had to start over again, one of the things that I would do is to challenge my sponsoring churches to read this book. I believe it would have helped us all avoid some of the common problems in sponsor/church plant relationships. We are always more effective when we learn lessons from those who have gone before us.

Spin-off Churches is filled with insights and tools to help readers count the costs, communicate effectively with the church planting leadership, and address doubters. These issues are especially critical when dealing with finances and cross-cultural issues, which are often like hidden landmines in the church planting process.

The authors ask a question we must all ask: "Can the Great Commission be fulfilled without the planting of new churches?" Others will benefit from this historical journey of sponsoring churches through the ages. It is encouraging to realize that the growth experienced by the early church continues in many places today.

I know these men as friends. I actually was Rod's boss at one point, served in the office next door to Tom, and have had many dollars taken from my budget by Don to help fund church planters. They are good men, and they bring a good message.

The authors have brought their tools of experience to the task. Now is the time to put these tools to use. When we sponsor a new church, we are not the first ones to discover the adventure. People and churches have been starting churches for two thousand years, and you are now ready to embark on a journey with a guide filled with knowledge from lessons learned along the way.

Rod, Tom, and Don have provided a great service to the church—practical insights from people who have been there and speak from experience. They help pastors and church leaders to count the cost and not to be afraid to start a biblically faithful and contextually relevant church. This book is a gift to the church that will help its planters to think biblically, missiologically, and experientially about church planting.

I still remember when we planted our two daughter churches in Erie, Pennsylvania. We sent out about 20% of our new church, a significant amount of our budget, and a lot of our energy. We planted two churches on one day—and over 500 people came to the two new churches on that day. God blessed and we celebrated our "twins," or two new churches. It was good and God was honored, but I know we would have avoided much heartache and many mistakes if we had had a book like *Spin-off Churches*.

I hope you will learn from these men. Their passion, knowledge, and ideas will help you multiply churches for the name and fame of Jesus.

Ed Stetzer, Ph.D.
Author, *Planting Missional Churches*
www.newchurches.com

Bibliography

Books

Allen, Roland. *The Compulsion of the Spirit.* Grand Rapids: William B. Eerdmans. 1983.

_____. *Missionary Methods: St. Paul's or Ours?* Grand Rapids: William B. Eerdmans, 1962.

Blackaby, Henry, and Claude King. *Experiencing God.* Nashville: Lifeway, 1990.

Britt, David T. *Concepts of Church Growth in the Southern Baptist Convention.* Atlanta: Home Mission Board of the Southern Baptist Convention, 1980.

Brock, Charles. *Indigenous Church Planting: A Practical Journey.* Neosho, MO: Church Growth International, 1994.

Bruce, F. F. *Commentary on the Book of Acts.* Grand Rapids: Wm. B. Eerdmans, 1984.

_____. *The Book of Acts.* The New International Commentary on the New Testament. Gordon D. Fee, gen. ed. Grand Rapids: Wm. B. Eerdmans, 1984.

DuBose, Francis Marquis. *God Who Sends: A Fresh Quest for Biblical Mission.* Nashville: Broadman, 1983.

_____. *How Churches Grow in an Urban World.* Nashville: Broadman, 1978.

Engelmann, Charles Frank. "Developing an Associational Strategy for Establishing Church-Type Missions in an Exurban Setting." D.Min project, Golden Gate Baptist Theological Seminary, 1979.

Foster, Charles R. *Embracing Diversity: Leadership in Multicultural Congregations.* New York: The Alban Institute, 1997.

Freudenberg, Ben. *The Family Friendly Church.* Loveland, CO: Group, 1998.

George, Carl F. *Prepare Your Church for the Future.* Grand Rapids: Fleming H. Revell, 1992.

_____. *The Coming Church Revolution: Empowering Leaders for the Future.* Grand Rapids: Fleming H. Revell, 1996.

Getz, Gene A. *The Apostles: Becoming Unified through Diversity.* Nashville: Broadman & Holman, 1998.

_____, and Roy B. Zuck. *Adult Education in the Church,* 5th ed. Chicago: Moody, 1976.

Hesselbein, Frances, Marshall Goldsmith, and Richard Beckhard, eds. *The Leader of the Future.* San Francisco: Jossey-Bass, 1996.

Hunter, George G., III. *Church for the Unchurched.* Nashville: Abingdon, 1996.

Jung, Shannon, Pegge Boehm, Deborah Cronin, and C. Dean Freudenberger, eds. *Rural Ministry: The Shape of the Renewal to Come.* Nashville: Abingdon, 1998.

Kouzes, James M., and Barry Z. Posner. *The Leadership Challenge.* San Francisco: Jossey-Bass, 1995.

Lewis, Larry L. *The Church Planter's Handbook.* Nashville: Broadman, 1992.

Logan, Robert, and Steven Ogne. *The Church Planters Toolkit.* Alta Loma, CA: CRM, 1996.

Looney, Floyd. *13 Golden Years: History of California Southern Baptists.* Fresno, CA: The Southern Baptist General Convention of California, 1954.

Matin, Glen, and Gary McIntosh. *Creating Community.* Nashville: Broadman & Holman, 1997.

McGavran, Donald A. *Understanding Church Growth,* 3rd ed. Grand Rapids: William B. Eerdmans, 1990.

Mounce, Robert H. *Romans.* The New American Commentary, vol. 27. Ray E. Clendenen, gen. ed. Nashville: Broadman & Holman, 1995.

Nee, Watchman. *The Normal Christian Life.* Revised edition. Washington, D.C.: International Student, 1969.

Overstreet, Don. *Sent Out: The Apostolic Move of God at the Beginning of the New Millennium.* Riverside, CA: Overstreet, 2000.

Rainer, Thom. *The Book of Church Growth.* Nashville: Broadman & Holman, 1993.

_____. *Bridger.* Nashville: Broadman & Holman, 1998.

_____. *Effective Evangelistic Churches.* Nashville: Broadman & Holman, 1996.

_____. *High Expectations.* Nashville: Lifeway, 1999.

Romo, Oscar. *American Mosaic: Church Planting in Ethnic America.* Nashville: Broadman, 1993.

Schaller, Lyle E., ed. *One Church, Many Congregations.* Nashville: Abingdon, 1999.

_____. *44 Questions for Church Planters.* Nashville: Abingdon, 1991.

Schwarz, Christian A. *Natural Church Development.* U.S.A. edition. Carol Stream, IL: ChurchSmart Resources, 1996.

Shelley, Marshall, ed. *Growing Your Church through Evangelism and Outreach.* Nashville: Random House, Inc., 1996.

Shenk, David W., and Ervin R. Stutzman. *Creating Communities of the Kingdom: New Testament Models of Church Planting.* Scottdale, PA: Herald, 1988.

Starr, Timothy. *Church Planting: Always in Season.* Cap-de-la-Madeleine, Quebec: Publications Chretiennes Inc., 1987.

Tidsworth, Floyd. *Life Cycle of a New Congregation.* Nashville: Broadman, 1994.

Tinsley, William C. *Breaking the Mold: Church Planting in the 21st Century.* Dallas: Creative Church Consultations, Inc. 1996.

Towns, Elmer L. *Getting a Church Started.* Nashville: Impact, 1975.

Wagner, C. Peter, *The Healthy Church.* Ventura, CA: Regal, 1996.

_____. *Strategies for Church Growth.* Ventura, CA: Regal, 1987.

_____, with Win Arn and Elmer Towns. *Church Growth: State of the Art.* Ventura, CA: Regal, 1984.

Warren, Rick. *The Purpose Driven Church.* Grand Rapids: Zondervan, 1995.

Wilson, A.N. *Paul: The Mind of the Apostle.* New York: W. W. Norton & Company, 1997.

Periodicals

Reccord, Bob. "Bob Reccord on Partnering." *On Mission*, March-April 1999, 26–28.

Scoggins, Dick. "Seven Phases of Church Planting Phase and Activity List." EMQ, April 1997, 161–165.

Manuals

The Church and the Legal Explosion. West Des Moines, IA: Preferred Risk Mutual Insurance

Company, 1994.

Greer, Thomas E. *Business and Legal Traps for Church Planters to Avoid.* Mission Viejo, CA: Saddleback Valley Community Church, 1995.

Guide for Planting Congregations. Atlanta: New Church Extension Division, Home Mission Board, SBC, 1995.

Multiplying Church Networks. Brentwood, TN: Home Mission Board, SBC, April 1997, 25–26.

Pamphlets

The Cornerstone. Commercial Marketing Department Series. West Des Moines, IA: Preferred Risk Mutual Insurance Company, 1995.

1998 North American Mission Board Ministry Report. Alpharetta, GA: North American Mission Board, 1999.

On Mission Prayer Map. Alpharetta, GA: North American Mission Board, 1999.

Planting New Congregations Sunday. Alpharetta, GA: Church Planting Group, North American Mission Board, 1999.

Electronic Media

California Government. California Information Homepage. www.california.gov, 4 March 1999.

Calvary Chapel Church Planting Homepage. Calvary Church Planting. www.calvarychapel.com/ cccpm/, size 3K, 5 March 1999.

Church Planting Guidelines. The Mother/Daughter Model. Database online. Available at www. victoryint.org/ planting/htm1, size 4K, 5 March 1999.

Scan/U.S. 1998 SBC Data Consortium CD. Nashville: The Sunday School Board, BC, 1999.

Appendix 1: Are You Ready to Sponsor Yet?

1. Are you able to clearly share and discuss your conviction that God wants your church to be a spin-off church?

2. How do you view the statement, "Existing churches planting new churches is the most effective way to reach unchurched people for Christ"?

3. How have you prepared the congregation to sponsor or help plant a new church?

4. Have you and your church mission council prepared a strategic plan for sponsoring a new church? If so, do you review and update it annually?

5. Do you have effective communication strategies in place to develop an increasing commitment to church planting in the hearts of all your people?

6. Have you worked with the local association or state convention of your denomination to begin seeking and assessing a qualified church planter?

7. Does your church have a genuine commitment to generate resources, especially financial, for sponsoring a new church?

8. Do your church and staff have a working relationship with a qualified church-planting specialist or consultant?

9. Do you and your church have a commitment to use only assessed and trained church planters?

10. How has your church planned to provide quality weekly coaching for the church planter during the first two years?

11. How will you connect your church-planting team with a support system in the designated target area?

Appendix 2: Sponsoring Church Agreement Resources

Sample 1: The Sponsoring/Partnering Covenant Worksheet

Instructions: Please respond to each of the questions using a 1-to-5 scale, with 1 meaning the respondent believes the Church Plant is responsible and 5 meaning the respondent believes the Sponsoring Church is responsible. A 3 would indicate shared responsibility. The sponsoring church and the church-planting leadership should each complete this form and use it to promote communication and expectations when developing a sponsoring covenant.

Examples:

The person completing this form feels the selection of the church planter is the mission's responsibility only. He or she would circle 1.

1. (Sample) The selection of the church planter	①2 3 4 5

However, if the person completing this form feels the selection of the church planter is the responsibility of the sponsoring church, with some input from the mission congregation, he or she would circle 4.

1. (Sample) The selection of the church planter	1 2 3 ④ 5

Please complete the following. If a question is not applicable, do not circle any number in that answer section.

    1 = Church Plant or Planter   5 = Sponsoring Church

1. The selection of the church planter?   1 2 3 4 5

2. Who should decide on supervision issues for the church planter?   1 2 3 4 5

3. Who will select the meeting place and times?   1 2 3 4 5

4. To which group are the mission church members accountable?   1 2 3 4 5

5. Who is responsible for the financial needs of the new work?   1 2 3 4 5

6. Which group is responsible for handling the money of the new work?   1 2 3 4 5

7. Who will determine polity for the new work, such as baptisms, Lord's Supper, and receiving new members?   1 2 3 4 5

8. Who will take care of tax and legal issues?   1 2 3 4 5

9. Who will determine the name of the new work?   1 2 3 4 5

10. Who will take care of the Annual Church Profile or other annual reports?   1 2 3 4 5

11. Who is responsible for the development of goals and action plans for the new work?   1 2 3 4 5

12. Who is responsible for the selection of volunteer leaders and workers for the new work?   1 2 3 4 5

13. Will the church planter be considered a staff member of the new work, the sponsoring church, or both?   1 2 3 4 5

14. Who should determine when the new work should constitute as a church?   1 2 3 4 5

15. Who is responsible for sending in monthly Cooperative Program and Associational giving?   1 2 3 4 5

Sample 2: A Contextualized Sponsoring Church Worksheet

To assist in developing the partnering church/new church covenant, please have the pastor or other appropriate person complete this worksheet. Please share this information with other appropriate leaders in the sponsoring church, the new church, and denomination.

1. Does the sponsoring church have a missions committee? ☐ Yes ☐ No If yes, what is the role of the committee in relationship to the new work?

2. Whom will the church planter report to in the partnering church?
   Name _____
   Title _____
   Phone _____ E-mail _____
   Address_____

3. How long will this covenant be in effect?
   ☐ One year
   ☐ One year, renewable annually
   ☐ Two years
   ☐ Three years
   ☐ Five years
   ☐ Other (Specify)

4. Can the sponsoring church provide liability insurance for the new work?
   ☐ Yes ☐ No
   If yes, what are the name and contact number of your insurance company?
   _____

5. What is the projected financial support, if any, that the partnering church is prepared to provide per month during the first year?
   $_____
   Is this amount to be available beyond the first year? ☐ Yes ☐ No
   ☐ To be determined

6. What other benefits (such as use of a copier, phones, office, etc.) can the sponsoring church provide the new work? Please be specific.
   _____

7. What does the sponsoring or partnering church expect of the church planter and the new work that is not addressed above?
   Name: _____ Date: _____
       Sponsoring Church Pastor or Moderator
   Name: _____ Date: _____
       Church Planter

Sample 3: A Traditional Sponsoring Church Agreement

This covenant has been adopted by the members of First Baptist Church, Anytown, FL, and the members of First Baptist Church's new work, church-plant name, Anytown, FL. The provisions of this covenant shall serve as the administrative, doctrinal, and logistical guide between the sponsoring church and the new work until such time as amended by mutual consent, or until such time as the new work becomes an organized sister Baptist church.

The ongoing administration of this covenant is assigned to the missions committee, First Baptist Church, Anytown, FL, and elected representatives of the new work, including the new work pastor.

The following provisions are expressly addressed as part of this covenant and shall be observed as herein agreed:

Membership

A. Members of the church-plant name, hereafter referred to as the "new work," shall be considered to be members of First Baptist Church, Anytown, FL, hereafter referred to as "the sponsoring church."

B. Members may be received by the new work at any regular service. When received by the new work, their names are submitted to the sponsoring church secretary to be added to the church membership rolls.

281

C. When members of the new work are removed or transferred, a written notification will be sent to the sponsoring church secretary.

D. People received into membership by the new work must meet the essential membership requirements of the sponsoring church, with the exception that membership orientation will be given by the new work pastor.

Pastor

A. The new work pastor will be recommended by the new work and called jointly by the sponsoring church and the new work.

B. Dismissal of the new work pastor requires joint action by the new work and the sponsoring church.

C. The new work pastor must subscribe to the articles contained in the Baptist Faith and Message.

D. The new work pastor will be a full member of the church council and will be expected to attend council meetings.

E. Guest preachers or interim pastors must be approved by the sponsoring church in advance, unless they are ordained Southern Baptist ministers.

F. The new work pastor will be authorized to perform all of the routine pastoral ministries to the new work congregation, including, but not restricted to, serving the Lord's Supper, baptizing candidates for membership, and conducting weddings and funerals.

Other New Work Officers and Ministers

A. The new work is encouraged to elect members to perform the routine duties of treasurer, secretary, Sunday school director, Women's Missionary Union (WMU) director, and Brotherhood director for the new work.

B. The new work is authorized to recommend the calling or ordination of deacons to the sponsoring church. Deacons will not be called or ordained without approval of the sponsoring church. Deacons who are members of the new work will function as deacons for the new work when approved by the sponsoring church. The chairman of the new work's deacon body shall be designated as a member of the deacon body of the sponsoring church and expected to attend meetings of the sponsoring church's deacon body.

Doctrines

The pastor and members of the new work must be in agreement with the doctrines contained in the Baptist Faith and Message and with the expressed doctrinal position of the sponsoring church as contained in the articles of faith of the sponsoring church.

Use of Church Property

The new work will be assigned the following space for their use on the days and hours indicated.

A.   The main auditorium or sanctuary may be used each Sunday morning from 9:00 a.m. to 10:30 a.m., on a regular basis. All other usage of the main auditorium or sanctuary, or other space not assigned to the new work by this covenant, will be prearranged with the pastor of the sponsoring church at least two days in advance.

B.   Rooms 6, 9, 11, and 14 are assigned to the new work for regular use at all times, until a mutually agreed upon change is made.

C.   Keys to the rooms assigned the new work will be issued to the new work pastor and are restricted to his use.

D.   Care, clean up, and maintenance of rooms assigned the new work are the responsibility of the new work. It is expected that the new work congregation will maintain the rooms assigned to its use in the same general condition as other church property.

E.   There will be times when the sponsoring church will need to use the rooms assigned the new work. Arrangements will be made with the new work pastor at least two days in advance.

F.   Other articles of sponsoring church property or equipment may be used by the new work when authorized by the pastor of the sponsoring church at least two days in advance.

G.   The new work will not be expected to pay a rental fee for the use of buildings or equipment belonging to the sponsoring church. However, the new work will be expected to pay a percentage of utilities and general maintenance expenses, the amount to be agreed upon by the sponsoring church and the new work. The amount will be reviewed every six months and mutually agreed upon.

New Work Finances

A.   The new work will collect, bank, and manage its own finances in a separate account.

B.   The new work will not incur any financial indebtedness without the approval of the sponsoring church.

C.   The new work is responsible to pay the new work pastor a salary and allowances. The new work is also responsible for all of its operating expenses.

D.   The new work will elect a treasurer who will be assigned the administrative duty of maintaining an accurate record of all income, expenses, and bank accounts.

E. The new work will submit a monthly financial report to the sponsoring church. This report must include income, new work giving, expenses paid, expenses awaiting payment, and bank balances. The report will be submitted in writing at the sponsoring church business meeting.

Joint Activities and Services

A. In the interest of developing a good relationship between the sponsoring church and the new work, it is desirable to have joint worship services and other fellowship activities periodically.
B. As an ongoing practice, it is agreed that the new work congregation will attend the evening service of the sponsoring church on the last Sunday evening of each month. The new work pastor will participate in the service program.
C. Other joint services or fellowship activities will be arranged by mutual agreement, at least thirty days in advance.

Relationships and Communications

The new work pastor and congregation are encouraged to develop close communications and relationships with other Southern Baptists, both within the sponsoring church family and through other Southern Baptist Convention (SBC) agencies. The relationships are to be fostered within the normally accepted communication channels that are available to Southern Baptist churches.

When the New Work Becomes a Church

A. The goal and desire of the sponsoring church and the new work are for the new work to grow and constitute into a sister Baptist church as rapidly as possible.
B. The decision to constitute itself into a Baptist church rests entirely with the new work after consultation with the sponsoring church.

Sample 4: A Traditional Sponsoring Church Agreement

A. Relationships

1. The mission congregation and the partnering church shall agree on the person to be called as pastor of the mission congregation.
2. A committee of five—three members from the mission congregation and two members from the partnering church—shall be elected as a pulpit committee.
3. The prospective pastor shall be asked to speak before both congregations and be voted on by both.

4. The mission-congregation pastor shall move his church membership to the partnering church.

5. The mission-congregation pastor and the partnering-church pastor shall agree on evangelists to invite for mission-congregation revivals.

B. Church Membership

Mission-congregation members can be received according to membership provisions of the partnering church's constitution. After accepting a candidate's request for church membership, the mission congregation shall submit the candidate's name to the partnering church for vote and baptism or to obtain a church letter.

C. Business

1. Any ordinary business items related to the mission congregation's work may be transacted by the mission congregation. Business items that directly involve the partnering church should be represented to the partnering-church clerk one week prior to the church's monthly business meeting. In no case will the mission congregation become indebted without the partnering church's approval.

2. The mission congregation shall submit a written report of all mission-congregation business, attendance, and growth at the partnering church's monthly business meeting.

3. The mission congregation shall be in contact with the partnering CMD council on matters of business and meet with the council as needed for reports and other communication.

4. The mission congregation may observe the ordinances of the church upon approval of the partnering church.

D. Tithes and Offerings

1. All tithes and offerings shall be kept by a treasurer, elected by the mission congregation, and approved by the partnering church. The treasurer shall take a monthly report of all receipts and expenditures.

2. The mission congregation shall support world missions through the Cooperative Program.

3. The mission congregation shall designate a percentage to associational missions.

E. General

1. The mission congregation shall use the Bible as the basis of its teachings.

2. The mission congregation shall use Southern Baptist program materials.

3. When the partnering church and/or the mission congregation determine that the mission congregation is strong enough to organize into a New Testament church, they should express this to the New Work Assistance Team. In business session, the NWAT should recommend, for church and

mission congregation action, that the mission congregation constitute as a church.

4. The partnering church shall do all in its power to enable the mission congregation to be the church God intends it to be. Prayer for the mission congregation is essential. The church shall be available for spiritual guidance, counsel, and assistance in visitation. The mission congregation shall pray for, love, respect, and cooperate with the partnering church for the mutual blessings of both.

Partnering Church Name _____

Partnering Church Approval Date _____

Signed_____

(pastor/moderator/clerk)

Mission Congregation Name _____

Mission Congregation Approval Date _____

Signed _____

(pastor/moderator/clerk)

Sample 5: Church Planting Agreement

The following agreement is between _____ and the _____ Church.

The Church Planter Agrees to:

1. Maintain personal character and be consistent with the principles of Scripture regarding the character and conduct of an elder (see 1 Timothy and Titus).

2. Maintain a whole-hearted commitment to the Statement of Faith _____Church.

3. Strive for the following spiritual dynamics of the new congregation:
Conversion Growth Rate. The church will strive towards a minimum of an annual 25% conversion growth rate. This will be evaluated every six months. If the 25% Conversion growth is not realized, the church planter will consult with the mentor and the church-planting committee for help in facilitating ministry adjustments.
Core Group Development. The core group will be trained in personal evangelism and discipleship. This group will support the core values that are agreed upon three months before launch.
Example. Since people do what they see more than what they are told, the pastor(s) will set the example in disciple making, beginning with personal evangelism. Pastors should share about their personal efforts in soul winning and discipling with the emerging congregation.

4. Raise $ _____ per month of support, which is the remainder of the funds necessary for his salary in the start of the new church. The planter commits to focus on this fundraising need until it is 100% raised before beginning work in the start up of the church. In addition, the planter is free to raise additional funds that can be used to provide for start-up expenses in the new church.

5. Secure an adequate policy of health insurance from the first day of employment for both the planter and family. This policy must be approved by _____ before beginning coverage unless the policy is currently in force.

6. Work full time in this ministry with the goal to start a church that will become self-supporting within a three-year period.

7. Maintain a commitment to work in the church plant for a period of at least three years, even through periods of discouragement or fatigue.

8. Plan a church-planting church that has a goal to mother another church within a period of three to five years from launch. Then continue to mother churches throughout its life span.

9. Develop a mentoring and accountability relationship for supervision and support acceptable to the _____ committee/board.

10. Organize the new church in a manner consistent with the membership requirements of _____ (fellowship of churches) and bring the new church into affiliation with both local and national associations upon incorporation.

11. Submit monthly reports to _____ in the manner requested to establish accountability with _____.

12. Include _____ in the new church mission budget beginning the month when the new church has its first public worship service. Missions support to _____shall begin at 5% of the offerings of the church. When the church expands its missions program, we strongly recommend that first priority be given to missionaries of our own family of churches.

13. Attend the _____ annual meetings, seminars and other appropriate meetings in attempts to build associational relationships and spotlight church-planting efforts.

14. Teach the new church about the _____ denominational family and relationships (on Sunday morning, in new members classes, missions committees, boards) and offer the church opportunities to be involved in the activities of our fellowship.

15. Do not enter any mortgage or other continuous financial commitments as a church without the approval of _____.

16. Provide liability insurance coverage for the new church from the time of incorporation. Until that time, the church will be covered under the _____ policy. The planter must notify the insurance agent

when public services begin so coverage can be accurate and billed appropriately.

17. The principles of *The Dynamic Daughter Church Planting Handbook* will be followed and the vision/plan/time line will provide the framework for ministry process accountability during the development of the church.

Mother Church and Its Church-Planting Committee Agree to:

1. Support the church plant with $ _____ per month for the first year, $ _____ per month for the second year, and $ _____ per month for the third year. This money will go toward helping to provide a salary of $ _____ per month and benefits of $ _____ per month for the church planter. The first priority in the benefits support is to provide adequate health insurance for the planter and family.

2. Oversee the receipting and distribution of contributions toward the support of the church planter according to the _____ financial policies.

3. Oversee the administration of all new church operating funds until the new church is able to take this responsibility. This includes receiving of offerings, disbursing church funds, accounting, and reporting to the new congregation.

4. Provide a mentoring relationship for the purpose of encouragement and guidance on a personal level.

5. Support the planter and the new church in as many other ways as possible. Anything the _____ church can do to help the new church planter will be considered high priority by the church-planting committee.

6. Provide sick leave. The pastor shall be allowed a maximum of twelve (12) sick days per year.

7. Provide vacation time. During each calendar year, the pastor shall be allowed four (4) weeks of paid vacation, which includes no more than four (4) Sunday absences. Vacation time must be approved and scheduled with the church planting mentor and is contingent upon approval.

8. Allow conference time. The pastor shall be allowed to attend up to two (2) applicable conferences or workshops per year that aid in the enhancement of his ministry. Any such conference must be approved by _____. Financial assistance is contingent on funds available in the new church.

9. Provide accountability. The new church and its pastor will be allowed to develop its own plans for leadership training, church growth, building plans, etc., and submit them to _____ who will intervene as necessary for the effective development of the new church.

288

10. Provide the following additional resources from the mother and partner churches:

_____

_____

_____

_____

Arbitration Clause:

The Pastor and _____ agree to resolve any disputes with each other in private or within the church in conformity to Matthew 5:22–24; Matthew 18:15–20; and 1 Corinthians 6:1–8. Therefore, they agree that any controversy or claim arising out of this relationship that cannot be resolved within sixty days, shall be resolved through mediation or, as a last resort, through legally binding arbitration carried out by the Center for Conflict Resolution (626-585-9729) or other equivalent Christian organization.

Term

This agreement shall take effect on _____ and shall remain in effect for three years or until superseded by an updated agreement or terminated according to the provisions of the termination clause of this agreement.

Termination

This working agreement shall be continuous for a period of three years or until dissolved by either party with a written statement giving a three-week notice. Shorter notice is acceptable if by mutual consent of the pastor and the

_____

_____

_____   _____

Chairman of the Church Planting Committee   Date

_____   _____

Church Planter   Date

Sample 6: Partnering Church/New Congregation Covenant

Responsibility of the Partnering Church

I. The partnering church agrees to associate with the new congregation for a period of at least _____ years during which time the partner church will offer support in the areas of administration, finances, leadership training, and other helps as deemed necessary by both.

II. The partnering church shall appoint or elect a Mission Development Council (MDC), or a subcommittee, of not less than three and not more than five members, whose primary responsibility shall be that of giving assistance to the new congregation.

III. The MDC should serve as a liaison group between the partnering church and its new congregation. The MDC:

    A. Shall receive all reports, information, requests, and business related to the new congregation.

    B. Shall make all recommendations relative to the new congregation to the partnering church.

IV. The partner church shall make a commitment to a prayer support ministry for its new congregation.

V. The partner church should form a core group to work with the pastor of the new congregation as leaders in its start (when feasible).

VI. The partner church will lead in the selection of the pastor for the new congregation. If the newer established congregation loses its pastor, a search committee shall be elected and composed of two members from the new congregation, two members from the sponsoring church, and the partnering church pastor or his designee.

VII. The partner church shall establish guidelines to assist the future relationships between itself and its new congregation.

    A. Covenant relationships—pastor to pastor

        1. A covenant relation between the two pastors will be established and will include a mutual understanding of the lines of authority and accountability.

        a. Goals for the new church:

            i. The new congregation will be encouraged to express its own vision and statement of purpose, define its objectives, and set goals.

            ii. Assistance may be needed from the Missions Development Council.

            iii. The partnering church should have an opportunity to review and approve the statement.

        b. Goals for the partnering church such as duration of partnering, financial support, etc.

            i. Expectations of each other

       ii. Responsibilities toward each other

      iii. A time for regular meetings to develop a mutual relationship that would allow for counseling, planning, sharing, praying, encouraging, instructing, and evaluating.

VIII. The partner church shall be responsible for the title to all real estate, buildings, property, and all financial commitments of the mission until such time the new congregation is constituted into a church.

  IX. The new congregation shall follow the policies of the partner church when:

    A. Voting to receive (or not to receive) as members all persons desiring to become a part of the new church family. (Members of the new congregation should be listed as members of the partnering church on a separate membership roll.)

    B. Observing the ordinances of the church.

      1. The pastor of the new congregation should be authorized by the partnering church to administer the ordinances.

  X. The partner church shall assist the new congregation in the administration of its finances by:

    A. Helping it to open its own checking account. It works best to have the partner church keep the books the first year. This will aid in reporting procedures and guidance in bookkeeping. The plan should be to turn the books over in the second year.

    B. Funds from all sources related to the new congregation should be kept in a separate account from that of the partner church.

    C. All checks should have two signatures. At some point before the books are turned over, a representative from the mission church should get involved in the bookkeeping, allowing for a smooth transition.

      1. The partnering church will handle the new church pastor's salary and other remuneration from the church as agreed upon and with the same care and promptness as for the partnering-church pastor.

      2. Any supplement to the new-church pastor's salary from any sources should be deposited in the treasury of the new congregation and thus become part of the funds used for this purpose.

      3. Adequate insurance and annuity, preferable through the SBC Annuity Board, should be provided for the pastor as agreed upon.

Responsibilities of the New Congregation

The mission will:

  I. Be faithful in teaching biblical doctrine.

    A. Teach, preach, and practice sound biblical doctrine.

II. Be loyal to the denomination.
   A. Establish and maintain a healthy, friendly relationship with the partner church, local association, state convention, and Southern Baptist Convention.
III. Be regular in its contributions to the association, Cooperative Program, and the three special mission offerings.
   A. The mission will be responsible for making these contributions to the appropriate entities.
   B. Contributions for these causes should not be made through the partnering church.
IV. Plan its programs and adopt a budget, which should be approved by the partnering church.
   A. The treasurer elected by the new congregation will handle the income and expenditure of all mission funds.
   B. A second person authorized by the mission will act as signatory with the treasurer on all checks.
   C. Both these financial records and procedures should be reviewed annually by the partner church and the new congregation.
V. Establish financial maturity.
   A. It will teach biblical stewardship and move church toward financial maturity and self support.
VI. Choose and train capable leaders.
   A. It will identify potential leaders and encourage them to accept leadership positions in the mission.
VII. Organize its programs and ministries.
   A. As commanded by its growth, the new congregation will organize and develop the basic functions of the church, which include Bible study, discipleship, development, mission education, stewardship, and evangelism.
   B. It will establish outreach ministries to reach unchurched people in the surrounding community and will begin ministries in neighboring communities that may develop into missions and future churches.

SIGNATURES:

_____   _____
Pastor of Partnering Church   Date

_____   _____
Pastor of New Congregation   Date

This is only a sample relationship agreement. Individual churches should make changes and additions as deemed necessary.

Sample 7: A Covenant Agreement

We, the members of _____ Church, do hereby covenant with each other before God to:

Be family; to be committed to each other; to love, accept, and forgive each other until death or God's call causes us to part.

Live in Jesus Christ and take His commands seriously.

Help one another grow toward Christian maturity by bearing one another's burdens, encouraging one another, exhorting one another, praying for one another, confessing our sins to one another, speaking the truth in love to one another, admonishing one another, building up one another, teaching one another, comforting one another, submitting to one another, serving one another, patiently bearing with one another, being hospitable to one another, greeting one another, living in peace with one another, regarding one another as more important than ourselves, caring for one another, exercising our spiritual gifts to serve one another, being kind and tenderhearted to one another, being devoted to one another, accepting one another, forgiving one another, loving one another.

We invite fellow members to pray for us, teach us, correct us, or rebuke us, if necessary, in a spirit of gentleness and humility should we stray from our Lord's commands, because the thing we desire most in life is to serve Christ. We voluntarily submit ourselves to one another and to the discipline of the church. Such discipline will always be for the loving purpose of restoration—restoration to fellowship with God and with the covenant community—and it will always be done in accordance with Matthew 18:15–22.

Bring honor to the body of Christ by maintaining a good testimony.

We enter into this covenant because we have the common purpose of obeying Jesus Christ, and because we believe that we need one another's help to do this.

As believers, and disciples of Jesus Christ, we have entered into a covenant relationship with the God of Abraham, Isaac, and Jacob—with the God who revealed Himself in Jesus. Since the blessings and promises of the covenant have been freely extended and given to us, out of wonder, love, thanksgiving, and reverence, we hereby accept and take up the covenant responsibilities that go with such a privilege. This is our reasonable service, and we should do nothing less.

God help us all! We rely on His grace and hold fast to His promise that there is now no condemnation for those who are in Christ Jesus.

Helpful "One Another" Passages of the New Testament (KJV)

- "Salt is good: but if the salt have lost its saltness, wherewith will ye season it? Have salt in yourselves, and have peace one with another" (Mark 9:50).
- "A new commandment I give unto you, That ye love one another; as I have loved you, that ye also love one another" (John 13:34).
- "By this shall all men know that ye are my disciples, if ye have love one to another" (John 13:35).
- "This is my commandment, That ye love one another, as I have loved you" (John 15:12).
- "These things I command you, that ye love one another" (John 15:17).
- "Owe no man any thing, but to love one another: for he that loveth another hath fulfilled the law" (Rom 13:8).
- "And the Lord make you to increase and abound in love one toward another, and toward all men, even as we do toward you" (1 Thess 3:12).
- "But as touching brotherly love ye need not that I write unto you: for ye yourselves are taught of God to love one another" (1 Thess 4:9).
- "Seeing ye have purified your souls in obeying the truth through the Spirit unto unfeigned love of the brethren, see that ye love one another with a pure heart fervently" (1 Pet 1:22).
- "For this is the message that ye heard from the beginning, that we should love one another" (1 John 3:11).
- "And this is his commandment, That we should believe on the name of his Son Jesus Christ, and love one another, as he gave us commandment" (1 John 3:23).
- "Beloved, let us love one another: for love is of God; and every one that loveth is born of God, and knoweth God" (1 John 4:7).
- "Beloved, if God so loved us, we ought also to love one another" (1 John 4:11).
- "No man hath seen God at any time. If we love one another, God dwelleth in us, and his love is perfected in us" (1 John 4:12).
- "And now I beseech thee, lady, not as though I wrote a new commandment unto thee, but that which we had from the beginning, that we love one another" (2 John 1:5).
- "Be kindly affectioned one to another with brotherly love; in honor preferring one another" (Rom 12:10).
- "Be of the same mind one toward another. Mind not high things, but condescend to men of low estate. Be not wise in your own conceits" (Rom 12:16).
- "Now the God of patience and consolation grant you to be likeminded one toward another according to Christ Jesus" (Rom 15:5).

- "Let us therefore follow after the things which make for peace, and things wherewith one may edify another" (Rom 14:19).
- "Wherefore comfort yourselves together, and edify one another, even as also ye do" (1 Thess 5:11).
- "Wherefore receive ye one another, as Christ also received us to the glory of God" (Rom 15:7).
- "And I myself also am persuaded of you, my brethren, that ye also are full of goodness, filled with all knowledge, able also to admonish one another" (Rom 15:14).
- "Let the word of Christ dwell in you richly in all wisdom; teaching and admonishing one another in psalms and hymns and spiritual songs, singing with grace in your hearts to the Lord" (Col 3:16).
- "Salute one another with a holy kiss. The churches of Christ salute you" (Rom 16:16).
- "All the brethren greet you. Greet ye one another with a holy kiss" (1 Cor 16:20).
- "Greet one another with a holy kiss" (2 Cor 13:12).
- "Greet ye one another with a kiss of charity. Peace be with you all that are in Christ Jesus. Amen" (1 Pet 5:14).
- "That there should be no schism in the body; but that the members should have the same care one for another" (1 Cor 12:25).
- "For, brethren, ye have been called unto liberty; only use not liberty for an occasion to the flesh, but by love serve one another" (Gal 5:13).
- "With all lowliness and meekness, with longsuffering, forbearing one another in love" (Eph 4:2).
- "And be ye kind one to another, tenderhearted, forgiving one another, even as God for Christ's sake hath forgiven you" (Eph 4:32).
- "Forbearing one another, and forgiving one another, if any man have a quarrel against any: even as Christ forgave you, so also do ye" (Col 3:13).
- "Submitting yourselves one to another in the fear of God" (Eph 5:21).
- "Likewise, ye younger, submit yourselves unto the elder. Yea, all of you be subject one to another, and be clothed with humility: for God resisteth the proud, and giveth grace to the humble" (1 Pet 5:5).
- "Wherefore comfort one another with these words" (1 Thess 4:18).
- "But exhort one another daily, while it is called Today; lest any of you be hardened through the deceitfulness of sin" (Heb 3:13).
- "Not forsaking the assembling of ourselves together, as the manner of some is; but exhorting one another: and so much the more, as ye see the day approaching" (Heb 10:25).
- "And let us consider one another to provoke unto love and to good works" (Heb 10:24).

- "Confess your faults one to another, and pray one for another, that ye may be healed. The effectual fervent prayer of a righteous man availeth much" (Jas 5:16).
- "Finally, be ye all of one mind, having compassion one of another; love as brethren, be pitiful, be courteous" (1 Pet 3:8).
- "Use hospitality one to another without grudging" (1 Pet 4:9).
- "As every man hath received the gift, even so minister the same one to another, as good stewards of the manifold grace of God" (1 Pet 4:10).
- "Let us not therefore judge one another any more: but judge this rather, that no man put a stumblingblock or an occasion to fall in his brother's way" (Rom 14:13).
- "But if ye bite and devour one another, take heed that ye be not consumed one of another" (Gal 5:15).
- "Let us not be desirous of vain glory, provoking one another, envying one another" (Gal 5:26).
- "Lie not one to another, seeing that ye have put off the old man with his deeds" (Col 3:9).
- "Speak not evil one of another, brethren. He that speaketh evil of his brother, and judgeth his brother, speaketh evil of the law, and judgeth the law: but if thou judge the law, thou art not a doer of the law, but a judge" (Jas 4:11).
- "Grudge not one against another, brethren, lest ye be condemned: behold, the judge standeth before the door" (Jas 5:9).

Appendix 3: Community Exegesis Resources

Community Exegesis Worksheet	Date_____ Area _____ Caller(s) _____ _____

1. Are you an active member of a nearby church?

___ No	___ Yes
• Why do you think most people around here attend church? _____ _____ _____ _____ _____	• May I ask which one? _____ • What are some of the things you like most about your church? _____ _____ _____ **Thank you very much for your time. God bless you!**

2. If you were looking for a church, what kind of things would you be looking for?

_____
_____
_____
_____

Below is a list of various programs a new church might develop to serve this community. Please check any that might be of interest to you and/or your family. Thank you!

SUPPORT GROUPS	ADULTS	WORSHIP	MUSIC
☐ divorce recovery	☐ What is a Christian? class	☐ Sunday, 8 a.m.	☐ contemporary
☐ unemployment	☐ home Bible studies	☐ Sunday, 10:30 a.m.	☐ traditional
☐ victimization	☐ social events	☐ Sunday evening	☐ concerts
☐ alcohol/drugs	☐ making new friends	☐ contemporary	☐ choirs
☐ singles	☐ teaching tapes	☐ traditional	
☐ weight control			
☐ other _____			

MEN	WOMEN	FAMILY	CHILDREN
☐ Bible study	☐ church during	☐ marriage enrichment	☐ high quality nursery
☐ service projects	☐ exercise	☐ parenting	☐ Sunday school classes
☐ friendship	☐ crafts	☐ financial planning	☐ children's
	☐ friendship		☐ adult worship
			☐ neighborhood
			☐ Bible clubs
			☐ Christian school
			☐ full-time preschool

YOUTH	SPORTS	OTHER
☐ junior high group	☐ Bible study	☐ _____
☐ high school group	☐ basketball	☐ _____
	☐ volleyball	
	☐ soccer	
	☐ other _____	
	☐ softball	

Last name_____ Mr._____ Mrs._____ Ms. _____
Street Address _____
City_____Zip_____Phone _____
Marital Status _____
Children: number _____ ages _____

1. How long have you lived here (in years)?
   ☐ 0–1   ☐ 2–3   ☐ 4–5   ☐ 6–10   ☐ More than 10

2. How many miles do you drive roundtrip to work?
   ☐ 0–25   ☐ 26–50   ☐ 51–100   ☐ More than 100
3. Which newspaper do you take? _____
4. How would you rate your knowledge of the Bible?
   ☐ Good   ☐ Satisfied   ☐ Would like to know more
5. Would you like to study the Bible and make friends if you could do so comfortably in a home?
   ☐ Yes   ☐ No (please skip to question 8)
6. What would be your three best times for a home Bible study?

Day	Morning	Afternoon	Evening
_____	☐	☐	☐
_____	☐	☐	☐
_____	☐	☐	☐

7. Would you be willing to host a home Bible study?
   ☐ Yes   ☐ No
8. What advice would you give us in starting a new church in this community? _____
   _____
   _____

9. Would you like to learn more about Jesus and the church?
   ☐ Yes ☐ No
10. May we keep you informed about our progress as we begin the new church?
    ☐ Yes (confirm name and address above)   ☐ No

Thank you very much for your time. God bless you!

Comments: _____
_____
_____
_____

Follow-up: _____
_____
_____
_____

Planter Core Group Community Match Worksheet

Instructions: Use this worksheet to assess the degree of match or mismatch between the church planter, leadership team, and core group and community. A classic mismatch would involve a high degree of compatibility between the church, leadership team, and core group but little in common with the community.

Group	Social Economic and Education Check all that apply	Teaching and Communication Preferences	Primary Leadership and Personality	Generation*	Music Skill Level	Church Background	Cultural Adaptability
Church Planter or Pastor	☐ Lower Income ☐ Middle ☐ Upper ☐ HS/GED ☐ Some College ☐ College Grad ☐ Post Graduate	☐ Visual ☐ Auditory ☐ Kinesthetic ☐ Experiential ☐ Oral ☐ Literary ☐ Dynamic ☐ Academic ☐ Common Sense ☐ Imaginative	☐ Dominant ☐ Influence ☐ Steadiness ☐ Compliant ☐ Extroverted ☐ Introverted ☐ Judging ☐ Perceptive	☐ The GI Generation ☐ Builder ☐ Boomer ☐ GenX ☐ Millennial ☐ Mosaic	☐ Unskilled ☐ Amateur ☐ Sophisticated ☐ Skilled	☐ Churched / Saved ☐ Unchurched ☐ Traditional ☐ Contemporary ☐ Liturgical ☐ Formal ☐ Informal ☐ Experiential ☐ World Religion ☐ Sect/Cult	☐ Rigid ☐ Low ☐ Moderate ☐ High ☐ Eclectic
Leadership Team	☐ Lower Income ☐ Middle ☐ Upper ☐ HS/GED ☐ Some College ☐ College Grad ☐ Post Graduate	☐ Visual ☐ Auditory ☐ Kinesthetic ☐ Experiential ☐ Oral ☐ Literary ☐ Dynamic ☐ Academic ☐ Common Sense ☐ Imaginative	☐ Dominant ☐ Influence ☐ Steadiness ☐ Compliant ☐ Extroverted ☐ Introverted ☐ Judging ☐ Perceptive	☐ The GI Generation ☐ Builder ☐ Boomer ☐ GenX ☐ Millennial ☐ Mosaic	☐ Unskilled ☐ Amateur ☐ Sophisticated ☐ Skilled	☐ Churched ☐ Unchurched ☐ Traditional ☐ Contemporary ☐ Liturgical ☐ Formal ☐ Informal ☐ Experiential ☐ World Religion ☐ Sect/Cult	☐ Rigid ☐ Low ☐ Moderate ☐ High ☐ Eclectic
Core Group	☐ Lower Income ☐ Middle ☐ Upper ☐ HS/GED ☐ Some College ☐ College Grad ☐ Post Graduate	☐ Visual ☐ Auditory ☐ Kinesthetic ☐ Experiential ☐ Oral ☐ Literary ☐ Dynamic ☐ Academic ☐ Common Sense ☐ Imaginative	☐ Dominant ☐ Influence ☐ Steadiness ☐ Compliant ☐ Extroverted ☐ Introverted ☐ Judging ☐ Perceptive	☐ The GI Generation ☐ Builder ☐ Boomer ☐ GenX ☐ Millennial ☐ Mosaic	☐ Unskilled ☐ Amateur ☐ Sophisticated ☐ Skilled	☐ Churched ☐ Unchurched ☐ Traditional ☐ Contemporary ☐ Liturgical ☐ Formal ☐ Informal ☐ Experiential ☐ World Religion ☐ Sect/Cult	☐ Rigid ☐ Low ☐ Moderate ☐ High ☐ Eclectic
Ministry Focus Group	☐ Lower Income ☐ Middle ☐ Upper ☐ HS/GED ☐ Some College ☐ College Grad ☐ Post Graduate	☐ Visual ☐ Auditory ☐ Kinesthetic ☐ Experiential ☐ Oral ☐ Literary ☐ Dynamic ☐ Academic ☐ Common Sense ☐ Imaginative	☐ Dominant ☐ Influence ☐ Steadiness ☐ Compliant ☐ Extroverted ☐ Introverted ☐ Judging ☐ Perceptive	☐ The GI Generation ☐ Builder ☐ Boomer ☐ GenX ☐ Millennial ☐ Mosaic	☐ Unskilled ☐ Amateur ☐ Sophisticated ☐ Skilled	☐ Churched ☐ Unchurched ☐ Traditional ☐ Contemporary ☐ Liturgical ☐ Formal ☐ Informal ☐ Experiential ☐ World Religion ☐ Sect/Cult	☐ Rigid ☐ Low ☐ Moderate ☐ High ☐ Eclectic

*Note: Designation names and dates for generational groups and bracket years vary depending on different sources consulted: For this worksheet, use the following: GI Generation (1914–1930), Builder (1930–1946), Boomer (1946–1963), Gen-X (1964–1981), Millennial (1981–1998), Mosaic (1998–)

Sample: Classic Mismatch

Group	Social Economic and Education	Teaching and Communication Preferences	Primary Leadership and Personality	Generation	Music Skill Level	Church Background	Cultural Adaptability
Church Planter or Pastor	☐ Lower Middle, College Grad	☐ Auditory, Oral	☐ Extrovert	☐ Builder	☐ Unskilled	☐ Churched, Saved, ☐ Traditional	☐ Low
Leadership Team	☐ Lower Middle, High School/ GED	☐ Auditory, Oral	☐ Extrovert	☐ Builder	☐ Amateur	☐ Churched, Saved, ☐ Traditional	☐ Low
Core Group	☐ Lower Middle, High School/ GED	☐ Auditory, Oral	☐ Steadiness ☐ Extroverted ☐ Introverted and Judging	☐ Builder	☐ Unskilled	☐ Churched ☐ Saved and Unsaved, ☐ Traditional	☐ Moderate
Ministry Focus Group	☐ Upper Middle, College Grad and Postgrad	☐ Visual, Literary	☐ All types	☐ Younger Boomer, Older GenX	☐ Sophisticated	☐ Unchurched Saved, Unchurched Unsaved, Contemporary	☐ Eclectic

Sample: Higher Degree of Match

Group	Social Economic and Education	Teaching and Communication Preferences	Primary Leadership and Personality	Generation	Music Skill Level	Church Background	Cultural Adaptability
Church Planter or Pastor	☐ Postgraduate	☐ Auditory	☐ Extrovert, Director	☐ GenX	☐ Amateur	☐ Churched, saved, Contemporary	☐ High
Leadership Team	☐ College grad.	☐ Auditory	☐ Extrovert, Influencer	☐ GenX	☐ Skilled	☐ Unchurched, saved, Contemporary	☐ High
Core Group	☐ Some College, College Grads	☐ Auditory and Kinesthetic	☐ Extroverts	☐ Younger Boomers and Mixed Xers	☐ Skilled and sophisticated	☐ Unchurched saved, Unchurched unsaved, Contemporary	☐ Moderate
Ministry Focus Group	☐ Some College, College, ☐ Postgrad	☐ Visual, Auditory	☐ Perceptive	☐ Mixed: Gen X and Younger Boomers	☐ Amateur ☐ Sophisticated	☐ Unchurched saved, Unchurched unsaved, Contemporary	☐ High

Appendix 4: Helpful Web Sites for Sponsoring Churches

Demographic Web sites

www.namb.net – free demographic studies for SBC churches.
www.demographicsnow.com – demographics
www.census.gov
www.freedemographics.com
www.ethnicharvest.org/region/regionindex.htm

Church Planting Web sites

www.churchplantingvillage.net/
www.topfive.org- Steve Sjogrens top ten resources for planters
www.churchplanting.net
www.churchplants.com
www.coachnet.org
www.PlanterDude.com
www.plantthefuture.org
www.plantachurch.com
www.regalcinemedia.com/meetingsnonprofit.asp
www.mislinks.org/church/chplant.htm
www.newchurchspecialties.org
www.cmtcmultiply.org
www.bradboydston.com/html/church_planting.html
www.easumbandy.com/resources/index.
php?action=searchresults&pl_option[1]=3
www.plantingministries.org/
www.imb.org/CPM
www.churchplantinggnw.org
www.weplantchurches.com/
www.churchplanter.com/
www.outreach.ca/
www.crmnet.org/index.html
www.churchplantingtowin.org
www.newthing.org
www.church-planting.org/
www.bradboydston.com/handbook
www.mislinks.org/chplant.htm
www.youresource.com
www.nazerenenewchurches.org
www.cpcoaches.com

Sermon Preparation Resources

www.pastors.com
www.creativepastors.com
www.ginghamsburgglobal.org
www.preachingplus.com
www.barna.org
www.sermonnotes.com
www.willowcreek.com
www.northheartland.org
www.northpoint.org
www.highbeam.com
www.twincitieschurch.com
www.bible.org
www.wiredchurches.com

Media Resources

www.thedetailsgroup.com
www.willowvideo.com
www.ministryandmedia.com
www.faithhighway.com
www.digitaljuice.com
www.harbingeronline.com
www.lumicon.org
www.textweek.com/movies/themeindex.htm
www.churchideas.com
www.e-zekiel.com
www.ultimatepowerpoint.com
www.projectorpeople.com
www.mplc.com/index2.htm
www.partingwater.com
www.logodesign.com
www.churchmedia.net

Music Resources

www.hillsong.com
www.integritymusic.com
www.encouragingmusic.com
www.willowcharts.com
www.willowcharts.com
www.worshipideas.com
www.olga.net
www.1christian.net

www.lyricsfreak.com
www.sheetmusicplus.com
www.letitsing.com
www.worship.com
www.moreworshipideas.com

Mailer Resources

www.Detailsdirect.org
www.outreach.com
www.thedetailsgroup.com
www.breakthroughchurch.com
www.faithspan.com

Bible Study Software

www.e-sword.net – free Bible study software
www.logos.com
www.quickverse.com

Other Helpful Links

www.acstecnologies.com – A church management software company for church plants and larger churches

www.injoy.com – John Maxwell's Leadership Resources

www.portablechurch.com – The premier resource for churches in portable locations

www.churchgrowthsoftware.com – A simple but efficient church management software for a Purpose Driven Church.

www.nacba.net – National Association of Christian Business Administrators: Salary surveys for churches; an invaluable tool for setting salaries in a growing church.

www.purposedriven.com – Purpose Driven Ministry Web site

www.onlinerev.com – Rev Magazine online

www.leonardsweet.com – Leonard Sweet's resources

www.friezeconsluting.com – A collection of management and administrative resources to assist churches.

www.family.org – Focus on the Family's Web site

www.churchsmart.com

General Web sites

www.crosswalk.com
www.jesusvideo.org

www.fastcompany.com
www.servantevangelism.com
www.smartleadership.com – free leadership resources
www.epicnow.org
www.evangelismtoolbox.com
www.christianitytoday.com

Audio/Video Resources

"Structure Your Church on Purpose"– Rick Warren
www.pastors.com

Creative Planning Kit

Ed Young
www.creativepastors.com

Places to Find Other Resources on the Satellite Strategy

www.ChurchPlantingVillage.net
www.leadnet.org/resources
Leadership Journal Spring 2003
davel@communitychristianchurch.org
www.newchurches.com

Appendix 5: Sample Congregational Sponsoring Readiness Survey

When do you know if your church is ready to sponsor a new work? Taking the sufficient time to train and equip your membership is a vital first step for preparation towards sponsoring a new work. How do you begin the task of preparation though? The best way to begin is by getting your leadership on board. Also begin by surveying the membership regarding its desires to plant a new church. The more your congregation affirms the sponsoring of the new work, the easier it will be to lead them effectively. Giving spiritual birth to a new church is God's plan for healthy church multiplication and reproduction. Evaluating one's local commitment and actual readiness to sponsor a new work is critical. Here are some pertinent questions you will want to consider as you conduct the survey within your church membership:

1. Do you and your people have a burden for reaching lost people?
2. Has your congregation previously shown an ongoing willingness to boldly step out in faith by sponsoring a new work?
3. Do you have a church-planting vision for either your immediate region or a particular portion of the country?
4. Is your congregation spiritually mature and able to handle birthing a new congregation?
5. Has your congregation demonstrated and practiced a generous spirit before? In what ways has this been demonstrated?
6. Are you willing to take a risk at something never tried before?
7. Does your congregation have a genuine kingdom mind-set?
8. Are you willing to invest resources (people, finances) outside the walls of your local church?

Cultivating the commitment towards church planting takes time and a continual focus on the Great Commission. Evaluating the present levels of commitment towards church planting within your membership is vital. When clarifying such commitment, it is important to identify the membership's values toward a great commission focus, compassion for lost people, commitment to develop a relevant approach to doing ministry, a solid vision for the harvest field, confidence in the power of God to accomplish the work, and a generous spirit. Members' attitudes will range from highly committed to openly hostile. Development of a working grid displaying the membership will prove most helpful.

Conducting the following local church sponsorship survey provides another successful way to determine your church's readiness.

A Local Church Sponsorship Survey[1]

As a potential sponsoring church: (Rate our readiness to sponsor)

1. Does our church have a conviction that God wants us to be a primary partner or help cluster sponsor a new church?

Yes   Somewhat   No
10   8   6   4   2   0

2. Has our church mobilized church-planting prayer intercessors that we communicate with regularly about our desire to help sponsor a new church?

Yes   Somewhat   No
10   8   6   4   2   0

3. Does our church have a strategic plan for partnering or sponsoring a new church that is updated on an ongoing basis?

Yes   Somewhat   No
10   8   6   4   2   0

4. Do we have an effective communication strategy in place to develop an increasing commitment to church planting in the hearts of all our people?

Yes   Somewhat   No
10   8   6   4   2   0

5. Have we established communication with our State Convention or local association to help us identify and assess a qualified new church planter?

Yes   Somewhat   No
10   8   6   4   2   0

6. Do we have a bold commitment to generating funds for primary partnering or helping to sponsor a new church?

Yes   Somewhat   No
10   8   6   4   2   0

7. Do we have a working relationship with a church-planting specialist from NAMB or a qualified church-planter missionary consultant to offer expertise in areas where we need development?

Yes   Somewhat   No
10   8   6   4   2   0

8. Do we have a commitment from our planter to be assessed and trained and to provide a written church-planting proposal and growth milestone plan prior to being approved and funding given?

Yes   Somewhat   No
10   8   6   4   2   0

---

[1] Adapted from the *Local Church Sponsorship Survey,* by Larry McKain. Further information on parent church surveys may be found by contacting Larry McKain, Executive Director, New Church Specialties, 6502 NW Mil-Mar Drive, Kansas City, MO 64151 or LMcKain@NewChurchSpecialties.org.

9. Do we have a commitment to provide qualified, on-going coaching for our church planter for the first 12–18 months of the new church project, or until the church is assured of achieving the church planting objectives?

	Yes	Somewhat	No		
10	8	6	4	2	0

10. Do we have a local support system for the new church that encourages the church planter and his spouse with support and love throughout the length of this commitment?

	Yes	Somewhat	No		
10	8	6	4	2	0

Total Points Possible – 100   Total Points = _____

The most valuable asset any of your members can give the church is their time. If someone were to come to me and say, "Pastor, I have four hours a week to give to our church in ministry," the last thing I'm going to do is put him or her on some committee. Rick Warren was right when he said, "Committees discuss, while ministries do. Committees argue, while ministries act. Committees maintain, while ministries minister. Committees talk and consider, while ministries serve and care. Committees discuss needs, while ministries meet needs." We must minimize maintenance in order to maximize time for ministry. Maintenance is church work: budgets, buildings, and organizational matters. Ministry is the work of the church. The more people you involve in maintenance decisions, the more you keep from ministry.

Appendix 6: Suggested Sample of Sponsored Church-Plant Time Line

First Year Budget

	Months 1–3	Months 4–6	Months 7–9	Months 10	Months 11	Months 12
Action Steps Completed	Begin praying for the new work. Launch team meeting places secured; visit and survey local churches. Research your target area.	Launch team to conference at NAMB, or Saddleback, or Woodstock. Hold first core group meeting with goal of *twelve adults*.	Housing secured for lead planter. *55 adults in core group.*	Second level of supporting team moves on site (not full plant team).	Continue to build launch team. Child care and worship team have dress rehearsal. Hosts (Greeters) meet and prepare for launch.	Follow-up on new contacts.
	Develop first edition of *new work proposal.* Cast vision for new church and work with sponsoring church. Develop your outreach brochures and connection cards. (Get them printed.)	Prayer support team raised (sponsoring church). Work on your strategy for the first four months after launch (get it done and put it aside). Keep building significant relationships weekly.	Church name chosen. Begin building your Web site and host it, if not already done.	Preview service location selected and secured. Develop your launch day checklist.	*First preview service.* Begin home Bible studies 1 & 2.	*Second preview service.*
	Ask launch team to begin to read through training books and book of Acts.	Move on-site. Lead planter moves on site.	Logo selected.	Continue to build launch team. *85 adults gathered into core group.*	Continue to build launch team.	Begin Class 101.
	Continue to build launch team commitments.	Begin to build launch team commitments.	Checking account opened.	Conduct spiritual surveys of community (5k, 10K).	Begin advertising and calling on prospects.	Continue to build launch team.
	Meet with sponsoring church to develop strategic time lines.	Class 201 developed & prepared (set it aside).	P.O. box or whatever and bulk mailing permit secured.	Sound system purchased or obtained. Projector secured.	Evaluation of preview service.	Discover people with leadership gift.

	Months 1–3	Months 4–6	Months 7–9	Months 10	Months 11	Months 12
	Develop resources for strategic plan. Begin assimilation of core group. Develop core values and prepare mission statement.	Spiritual gift discovery and deployment towards gift set. *35 adults in core group begin to meet more regularly.*	Office equipment purchased or leased. Keep building significant relationships (drawing the net).	Small group leaders training. Child care equipment gathered and team trained.	Block parties begin. (Keep drawing the net.)	Expose launch team to successful like-minded churches in the area. (Field trip "What we could become!")
Salary				$	$	$
Asst. Salary						
Support Staff				$	$	$
Office Equip				$		
Printing				$	$	$
A.V. Equip				$		$
Program Supplies	Books $		$	$	$	$
Direct Mail Advertising				$		
Facility Rental				$	$	$
Kidz Stuff					$	$
Conference		$				
Travel	$	$				
Monthly Totals	$	$	$	$	$	$

Total For First Year: $

Second Year Budget

Months 13 through 18

	Month 13	Month 14	Month 15	Month 16	Month 17	Month 18
Action Steps Completed	Launch team continues to meet and develop core group.	Hold picnic or gathering event (Block party #2).	VBS or BYBC	Launch **Celebration Service.**	Celebration service continues.	Celebration service.
	Build launch team with core group.	Launch team continues to meet and grow.	Develop follow-up materials.	Launch Kidz Stuff.	Class 101 offered.	Class 201 offered.
	Select Sunday morning service site.	Staff come on board final third level	Receive mass mailing. Begin radio blitz.	Launch follow-up ministry.	Small groups launched.	Class 301.
	Have a back-up meeting place in case it is needed.	Design mass mailing Begin news-paper ads				
	Leadership training for launch.	Leadership training	Finalize preaching schedule for first ministry year.	Develop "This is (name of church)" DVD for assimilation.	Conference to CP.	
		100 adults in core group and church ministry				
	Work with radio station to secure ad time and ad.	Begin childcare development.	Get ads ready.			
	Begin work-shop team development: ministry teams established (promise land, worship team, greeting team, parking team, follow-up team, set-up team, audio/visual team, resource table team).	Maximize follow-up possibilities. Provide promotional material on children's ministry in upcoming new church.	Finalize ministry teams and leaders: kidz stuff, greeters team, set up/tear down team, sound team, worship team, follow-up tea, small group drama team.	Leadership development continues.	Leadership development (throughout) continues. DVD or VHS	**150 plus participants in primary worship service. 85 members on church roles.**
		Banners purchased.	Send mass mailing and have ads run.	Begin evaluation ministry and celebration!	Advertise again.	
Salary	$	$	$	$	$	$

	Month 13	Month 14	Month 15	Month 16	Month 17	Month 18
Asst. Salary	$	$	$	$	$	$
Support Staff	$	$	$	$	$	$
Office Equip	$	$	$	$	$	$
Printing	$		$		$	
A.V. Equip						
Program Supplies	$	$	$	$	$	$
Direct Mail/ Advertising				$		
Kidz Stuff				$	$	$
Facility Rental	$	$	$	$	$	$
Monthly Totals		$				

Months 19 through 24

	Month 19	Month 20	Month 21	Month 22	Month 23	Month 24
Action Steps Completed	Advertise for Christmas Eve	Super Bowl party	Friend day	Big event	Easter	Kidz Stuff
	Christmas Eve Community Service	Small group leader's training	Class 401 offered	Family conference	Kidz Stuff	Class 101,201, 301, 401 offered
	Gift wrap outreach	Class 101 offered	Class 201 offered		Class 101, 201, 301, 401, offered	Small groups
	Baptism celebration	Class 301 offered			Small groups	New community
		New community launched (frequency to be determined. This would affect our facility rental budget).				**200 + participants in primary worship services. 135 + members on church roles.**
Salary	$	$	$	$	$	$
Asst. Salary	$	$	$	$	$	$
Support Staff	$	$	$	$	$	$
Office Equip	$	$	$	$	$	$
Printing	$		$		$	
A.V. Equip						

	Month 19	Month 20	Month 21	Month 22	Month 23	Month 24
Program Supplies	$	$	$	$	$	$
Direct Mail/ Advertising				$		
Kidz Stuff				$		
Facility Rental	$	$	$	$	$	$
Monthly Totals	$	$	$	$	$	$

Appendix 7: Facility Needs Worksheet

Facility Worksheet Instructions

The Facility Needs Worksheet is a tool to evaluate the benefits and liability of potential meeting places for a new church. This worksheet considers cost, parking, the ability to put up signage (either temporary or permanent), space to grow, accessibility, appearance, whether or not the site would require a complete or partial set-up and tear-down each week, the potential for liability issues (such as the inability to protect children from chemicals or lack of handicap access), and adequate children and youth space.

For each trait, place a + (plus) if the trait is positive or a – (minus) if the trait is negative. For example, in the sample below, three schools are considered by the sponsoring church. The local high school and elementary schools have good adequate parking. However, the junior high school has limited parking.

Sample

Facility Needs Worksheet Instructions: Place a + or – in the box for each trait. Room is provided to compare multiple sites.	Cost	Parking	The ability to put up signage	Proximity to target group	Space to grow	Accessibility	Appearance	Set up/tear down weekly	Liability issues	Children and youth space
Schools (Jr. High)	+	-	-	-	-	+	-	-	+	-
Schools (High school)	-	+	-	+	+	+	+	-	+	-
Schools (Elementary)	+	+	-	+	+	+	+	-	+	+

Based on this worksheet, the high school offers more benefits than liabilities. The junior high offers few benefits and several liabilities. However, the elementary school has only two liabilities. Based on the vision and strategy for the new church, this tool may help determine which facility should be pursued first.

Facility Needs Worksheet

Instructions: Place a + or – in the box for each trait. Room is provided to compare multiple sites.	Cost	Parking	Ability to put up signage	Proximity to target group	Space to grow	Accessibility	Appearance	Need to set up/tear down weekly	Liability issues	Children and youth space
Schools / Colleges										
Store Front										
Dinner or Movie Theater										
Sponsor Church										
Other Church										
House										
Apartment										
Warehouse										

Instructions: Place a + or – in the box for each trait. Room is provided to compare multiple sites.	Cost	Parking	Ability to put up signage	Proximity to target group	Space to grow	Accessibility	Appearance	Need to set up/tear down weekly	Liability issues	Children and youth space
Business/Office										
Hotels										
Community Center										
Portable Building										
Clubs or Lodges										
Restaurants										
Other										

Appendix 8: Sample Launch and Constitution Services

Sample Launch Service

Hymn

Scripture Reading

Welcome and Recognition of Visitors

Introductions

Missions Development Council Statement

(CMD Council gives reasons a church is needed in the community.)

Partnering-Church Affirmation

(The partnering-church pastor affirms the new church, assuring members of the partnering church's support.)

Presentation of Mission Congregation

(Presiding person presents people involved in the mission congregation and announces locations and times of mission's regular meetings.)

Hymn

Special Music

Message

Invitation

(Invite people to become members of the new mission.)

Reception and Fellowship

Sample Motion to Constitute

"*Whereas*, We believe there is a need for a new Baptist church in this community, and *Whereas*, After prayer, we believe we have found God's divine guidance, and *Whereas*, We have consulted with fellow Christians and neighboring churches, and *Whereas*, We have called a council to consider this matter, and the council has recommended we proceed with the constitution of the new church, *Resolved*, That we enter into the organization of a Baptist church."

318

Sample Constitution Service

Hymn

Scripture Reading

Prayer

Reading of the Mission Congregation's History

Welcome and Guest Recognition

Statement of Meeting's Purpose

Recommendation to Constitute

(The partnering church recommends that the mission congregation constitute.)

Vote to Constitute

(Members of the new church vote. The church is born at this point.)

Adoption of Church Covenant

Adoption of Articles of Faith, Constitution, and Bylaws

Vote to Affiliate

(Vote is unnecessary if the constitution states that the church is affiliated with the local association, state convention, and Southern Baptist Convention.)

Recognition of Charter Members

Election of Officers

(A nominating committee should present names of moderator, clerk, pastor, teachers, and other officers.)

Partnering-Church Vote

(Partner votes to recognize the new congregation as a constituted church.)

Special Music

Message or Charge to New Church

Invitation for New Members

Offering

Benediction

Right Hand of Fellowship to Members of the Newly Constituted Church

Fellowship Time

General Index

Scripture Index